EUROPEAN POLITICS

An Introduction

Jan-Erik Lane and Svante O. Ersson

SAGE Publications
London • Thousand Oaks • New Delhi

SAGE Publications Ltd
6 Bonhill Street
London EC2A 4PU

SAGE Publications Inc
2455 Teller Road
Thousand Oaks, California 91320

SAGE Publications India Pvt Ltd
32, M-Block Market
Greater Kailash – I
New Delhi 110 048

British Library Cataloguing in Publication data

A catalogue record for this book is available from the British Library

ISBN 0 7619 5286 1
ISBN 0 7619 5287 X (pbk)

Library of Congress catalog record available

Typeset by Photoprint, Torquay, Devon
Printed in Great Britain by The Cromwell Press Ltd, Broughton Gifford, Melksham, Wiltshire

EUROPEAN POLITICS

We dedicate this book to the two scholars from whom we over the years learnt the most in the conduct of comparative politics: Arend Lijphart (University of California at San Diego) and Giovanni Sartori (Columbia University)

Contents

Preface

Is is possible to speak of European politics today given the developmental trends initiated in 1989? We believe so, at least when we decided to take up the task of writing a textbook that would surpass the distinctions between Western, Northern, Southern and Eastern Europe. At the same time, we were aware of the fact that such an approach rested on a hypothesis about convergence that must be regarded as a very contested one. Where one scholar sees similarities others observe differences. And how is one to add it all up, noting similarities in certain aspects of society and differences in others?

In order to stay open-ended about the possibility of a European politics, we placed the convergence hypothesis at the centre of attention. In the social sciences there is an implicit model about social change that the convergence theme is attached to. Focusing on convergence implies not only trying to assess the extent of convergence in various aspects – economic, social, political – but also entails the search for some kind of model of convergence, which would identify conditions for macro changes. The convergence model would contain a few ideas about why and how processes of convergence take place and under what circumstances. There are in the European context a number of forces that fuel convergence, economic conditions such as growing trade and economic integration, social conditions that promote urbanization and third sector expansion as well as institutional conditions such as the democratization wave in the former Communist countries. What we wish to enquire into is how far these macro conditions have brought about increasing similarities in the politics of the European states. It is impossible not to include and underline the convergence implications of the making of the European Union.

However, the convergence trends will not eradicate the many differences in politics between the countries that we have included in this study. The key question is whether the differences between Western and Eastern Europe that used to be so conspicuous are now abating, meaning that we can concentrate on the similarities and differences among all European countries without any division into North, South, West and East. We have included 31 countries in our analysis of convergence, drawing the line between inside Europe and outside Europe along the borders to Russia, Belo-Russia, the Ukraine and Turkey. And the analysis of similarities and differences has been done by classifying the countries into five sets, three West European categories and two East European ones – tentatively.

We approach European politics in terms of a simple convergence framework, comprising only two elements: (1) Factors that hinder or are conducive to convergence, discussed in Chapters 1–4; (2) Convergence in political institutions, behaviour and culture, enquired into in Chapters 5–9.

Into each chapter we have entered information about the politics and society in at most 31 countries for a clearly specified time period: 1990–5. Since the purpose has been to write a small compact volume, a concentration on certain themes has been a necessity. Thus, among the political outcomes we look at certain key behavioural patterns such as the party systems, the formation of governments as well as the structure of public policies. It may well be premature to assses now how far convergence has occurred in Europe, but the question is no doubt a relevant one although our answer may need to be revised in a not too distant future, as for example the presentation of political culture should be done more thoroughly as more information becomes available.

The book was finalized at the Mannheimer Zentrum für Europäische Sozialforschung, where Franz Pappi offered a most stimulating environment for comparative research on Europe, given its huge data bases. Various chapters were discussed at seminars, at which a number of suggestions as to improvements were made.

We have used data from the *World Values Survey 1990–1* (Inglehart, 1993), the *Polity II: Political Structures and Regime Change* (Gurr, 1990), the *Central and Eastern Euro-Barometers* (Reif and Cunningham, 1992–5), and the *Eftabarometer* (EOS Gallup Europe, 1992). These datasets have kindly been made available to us via the Swedish Social Science Data Service (SSD) in Göteborg. We are solely responsible for the interpretation of these data.

Jan-Erik Lane and Svante Ersson
Mannheim, February 1996

Introductory Chapter:
Convergence versus Divergence

European politics takes on a new meaning following the fall of the Berlin wall. It is no longer adequate to talk about Western Europe contra Eastern Europe, as if they were totally different societies harbouring entirely different political systems. What is emerging in the 1990s is one Europe that covers several parts: the Scandinavian countries, Finland and Iceland in Northern Europe; the United Kingdom, Ireland, the BeNeLux countries and France in Western Europe; Portugal, Spain, Italy and Greece in Southern Europe; Germany, Austria and Switzerland in Central Europe; as well as a number of countries in Eastern Europe such as the Baltic countries (Estonia, Latvia and Lithuania), Poland, the Czech Republic, Slovakia, Romania, Hungary, the former Yugoslavia and Bulgaria. The aim of this book is to analyse the politics of all these European countries from one specific angle, namely that of convergence. We will devote much time to documenting similarities and differences between these countries in Northern, Western, Southern, Central and Eastern Europe.

The convergence theme is relevant from several perspectives. First there is the socio-economic one, as one may ask to what extent the catch-up development in the former Communist states is successful. In trying to establish a kind of market regime the former Communist countries copy Western Europe, but does this model work out in practice with the hopes of delivering more affluence to its populations? Second there is the political perspective, as system transition involves not only the insertion of Western economic institutions but also Western political institutions in the form of democracy. How far can the new party systems in East Europe be compared with the party systems in West Europe? Third one may speak of the cultural perspective by looking at the extent to which political attitudes and social belief-systems tend to become more similar between the countries in Europe.

Our basic question is whether political behaviour and political institutions tend to converge to one kind of political regime in all European countries: party government, or representative democracy based on political parties. Answering this question one may start from an analysis of the actual differences among European states as of today in terms of historical legacies, social structure, economic life and output, although politics is never a reflection of the environment. One may then proceed to consult studies about West European politics (Smith, 1989; Pelassy, 1992;

Keating, 1993; Mény, 1993; Guchet, 1994; Allum, 1995) as well as about East European politics (Lovenduski and Woodall, 1987; Deppe et al., 1991; Banac, 1992; Rothschild, 1993; White et al., 1993; Roskin, 1994) in order to assess the extent of similarities and differences. A number of general European enquiries are also helpful (Immerfall, 1994; Steiner, 1994; Gallagher et al., 1995; Hayward and Page, 1995; Therborn, 1995).

One may argue that divergence has been the prevailing angle from which various scholars have interpreted European politics from a macro theoretical perspective. Speaking of divergence versus convergence it is willingly admitted that it is preferable to examine data about key political phenomena at more than one point of time, but we are mainly concerned with looking at similarities and differences between the countries during the period 1990–5.

The European Scene

To us an analysis of European politics should at least cover the major states from the Atlantic Ocean to the borders of the former Soviet Union (Archer and Giner, 1971; Giner and Archer, 1978). Admitting that the concepts of Central, Western, Northern, Southern and Eastern Europe may be interpreted in various ways we mainly include states that have a population in excess of 100,000 inhabitants. Thus, we have 33 cases or units of analysis for 1995. Our approach is state centred – that is, we focus on the states in Europe as they have actually existed in this century. Put simply, the frequent and often drastic changes in what have been recognized as states in Europe testify to the basic observation that European politics is characterized by instability, war and conflict.

We have not included a number of small states in Europe such as Lichtenstein, Andorra, San Marino, Monaco and the Vatican State. Access to data has also forced us to concentrate upon a smaller set than the 33 states listed in Table I.1. It should be pointed out that the situation with regard to the Bosnian state is not entirely clear, involving both a federation between Muslim Bosnians and Croatians as well as an attempt to find a new state solution after the civil war ended in 1995.

One may note, looking at the number of states from one decade to another, that only 14 of these countries have been independent and recognized as states during the entire century. Bypassing the period of Nazi-German occupation these states are: Belgium, Bulgaria, Denmark, France, Greece, Italy, Luxembourg, the Netherlands, Portugal, Romania, Spain, Sweden, Switzerland and the United Kingdom. The overall development of European statehood between 1900 and 1995 has meant almost a doubling of the number of states. A first large increase resulted from the Versailles treaty in 1919. Then the number of states actually shrank up until 1940 when the Soviet Union annexed the Baltic States and Austria became connected with Nazi-Germany through the Anschluss of 1938. From 1950 to 1990 the number of states is fixed (26), but the fall of the

Table I.1 *European states in the twentieth century*

	1900	1910	1920	1930	1950	1960	1970	1980	1990	1995
Albania			•	•	•	•	•	•	•	•
Austria-Hungary	•	•								
Austria			•	•	•	•	•	•	•	•
Belgium	•	•	•	•	•	•	•	•	•	•
Bosnia										•
Bulgaria	•	•	•	•	•	•	•	•	•	•
Croatia										•
Czechoslovakia			•	•	•	•	•	•	•	
Czech Republic										•
Denmark	•	•	•	•	•	•	•	•	•	•
Estonia			•	•						•
Finland			•	•	•	•	•	•	•	•
France	•	•	•	•	•	•	•	•	•	•
Germany	•	•	•	•						
Germany DR					•	•	•	•	•	
Germany FR					•	•	•	•	•	•
Greece	•	•	•	•	•	•	•	•	•	•
Hungary			•	•	•	•	•	•	•	•
Iceland					•	•	•	•	•	•
Ireland				•	•	•	•	•	•	•
Italy	•	•	•	•	•	•	•	•	•	•
Latvia			•	•						•
Lithuania			•	•						•
Luxembourg	•	•	•	•	•	•	•	•	•	•
Macedonia										•
Montenegro	•	•								
Netherlands	•	•	•	•	•	•	•	•	•	•
Norway		•	•	•	•	•	•	•	•	•
Poland			•	•	•	•	•	•	•	•
Portugal	•	•	•	•	•	•	•	•	•	•
Romania	•	•	•	•	•	•	•	•	•	
Serbia	•	•								
Slovakia										•
Slovenia										•
Spain	•	•	•	•	•	•	•	•	•	•
Sweden	•	•	•	•	•	•	•	•	•	•
Switzerland	•	•	•	•	•	•	•	•	•	•
UK	•	•	•	•	•	•	•	•	•	•
Yugoslavia			•	•	•	•	•	•	•	•
Number	18	19	26	27	26	26	26	26	26	33

Sources: Russett et al. (1968), Banks (1971), *Fischer Welt Almanach* (1995).

Soviet Empire in 1991 and the collapse of Yugoslavia in 1991–2 resulted in the foundation of several new states.

What is the logic of politics in these European states? Shall we focus upon a few salient differences between these states formulated by means of divergence models, or can one go about finding out whether there are mechanisms operating within these states that are conducive to conver-

gence with regard to political institutions and political behaviour? Let us
see where research stands today.

Macro Interpretations of European Politics

One key question when enquiring into European politics on the basis of the
design of a research strategy for the purpose of mapping similarities and
differences in the political life of European countries is whether one may
identify a couple of fundamental model(s) behind the wide range of
country façade. The extensive regime transition processes after the
collapse of Communism involve institutional changes that implement
democratic politics and a market economy. Is it possible to find more
specific patterns of variations that the states in Europe tend to adhere to or
to practise?

In the literature on European politics the prevailing mode of interpretation has been that of divergence. A number of well-known models claim
that what is interesting when one compares politics in various European
countries is to note how they differ on many crucial dimensions.

With regard to state institutions there is for instance the federal model,
launched by Daniel Elazar among others, which argues that whether a
state has a unitary or federal format is of great importance. Implicit in this
theory is a radical distinction between two types of states (Elazar, 1987),
but is such a sharp separation really possible to apply to existing states in
Europe? Another divergence model makes a similar clear-cut distinction,
this time between presidential and parliamentary executives, as for
instance with Juan Linz, who argues that the latter performs better than
the former (Linz, 1994). Yet, can European presidentialism and parliamentarism be analysed in such a model?

In relation to party systems there is the Giovanni Sartori model, which
argues that the combination of fractionalization and polarization distinguishes the party system of one country from another. Understanding
how different the party systems can be in various countries involves not
only separating the two-party systems from the multi-party systems, but
also assessing the extent to which there is large or small ideological
distance between the parties (Sartori, 1976). The occurrence of polarized
pluralism in a country entails an entirely different kind of political life than
merely a high level of fractionalization in the party system.

Model dualism also characterized the famous Duverger analysis of the
consequences of election systems for the formation of party systems and
government durability. Already in 1951 Duverger stated his idea of a sharp
distinction between plurality systems and proportional systems, predicting
that the former enhanced twopartism resulting in durable single majority
governments and the latter multipartism which lead to unstable coalition
governments (Duverger, 1964).

Turning from the input side of the state to the output side, there is the
Gosta Esping-Andersen model of the public sector variation. It states that

divergence is the most typical feature in the examination of the public sector in various West European countries. The structure of the public sector in a country reflects the way its welfare regime has been framed and implemented. And there are three fundamentally different welfare regimes in Western Europe (Esping-Andersen, 1990). Yet, it may be worthwhile examining the public sector in all European countries in order to see whether the most recent reform endeavours have brought about more similarities between West and East European countries.

The most comprehensive divergence model is that of Arend Lijphart. Lijphart's general model claims that there are two basically different political systems in Europe, the Westminster type and the Consensus type (Lijphart, 1984). Lijphart listed eight ideal-type characteristics of the two models covering not only federalism versus unitarism as well as executive–legislature–judiciary relationships but also the election and party systems. What is the relevance for the entire Europe of today of the sharp distinction introduced by Lijphart in relation to the analysis of West European politics? Is it true that today the countries in Europe either tend towards the Westminster model or the Consensus model?

Lijphart was well aware of the fact that his two ideal-types in the terminology of Max Weber did not correspond to reality, which was more complex. He asked: 'How do our twenty-two democratic regimes cluster on the two underlying dimensions of the majoritarian-consensual contrast?' (Lijphart, 1984: 215). His answer is the following empirical classification, if selecting only West European countries (Lijphart, 1984: 216–18):

- *Majoritarian*: the United Kingdom, Ireland, Luxembourg, Sweden, Norway.
- *Majoritarian-Federal*: Germany, Austria.
- *Consensual-Unitary*: Denmark, Finland, Iceland.
- *Consensual*: Switzerland, Belgium, the Netherlands, Italy, France.

Thus, in reality Lijphart's divergence perspective comprises four models. Besides the distinction between the majoritarian and consensual processes of politics, which cover relationships between the executive, the legislature and the judiciary in addition to a main outline of the party system, there is the classical separation between unitary and federal state institutions. How well do these four categories, combining *Konkurrenzdemokratie* versus *Konkordanzdemokratie* (Schmidt, 1995) with Unitarism and Federalism, fit European realities in the 1990s, when the Communist Model is irrelevant meaning that we must include Eastern Europe among the sets of European democracies? And how do they mix in the new democracies in Southern Europe (Lijphart et al., 1988)?

The divergence models have no doubt pinned down a number of interesting country differences, but what needs to be researched today is whether these models may at the same time have underestimated the extent to which country politics in Europe exhibits numerous similarities.

The main divergence models were launched in relation to the variation in politics within Western Europe, as the differences between West and East hardly needed to be underlined since the East European countries practised an entirely different framework for politics and economics. However, what remains of the relevance and validity of the divergence models today when the Iron Curtain has been removed? Let us focus upon the similarities instead and see where that may lead us.

To us, the starting-point is that the politics of European countries have a number of communalities: (1) parliamentarism; (2) a multi-party system; (3) frequent coalition governments; and (4) a welfare state of some sort. Actually, arriving at such a European model would be conducive to internal coherence and set Europe aside from the other continents. We wish to pursue the analysis of these similarities a few steps further: to what extent are there basic similarities in key political features among states in Western, Central, Eastern, Northern and Southern Europe? Which are the mechanisms involved? The drive towards coherence depends not only upon the transition processes in the former Communist states but also reflects processes of change in other parts of Europe.

It may be noted that an earlier model about European convergence from the 1960s did not pass the test; namely, the idea that liberal market economies and Communist states would grow more and more alike as a function of rising affluence (Tinbergen, 1961; Galbraith, 1967). The Communist welfare state faltered because the planned economies in Eastern Europe failed. The outcome of the Cold War was just the opposite; namely, huge differences in living conditions between Western and Eastern Europe that were perhaps larger in 1990 than ever during the interwar period (Janos, 1994). The countries in Eastern Europe have now turned to a different system model, copying the capitalist democracies in the West in the hope of reducing these vast differences in quality of life. The engine in this system transformation is *constitutional* or *institutional policies*, or the reshaping of political and economic institutions by fiat. However important rules are for social life, we must remember that the critical question is: Are the overall differences in terms of actual behaviour or outcomes between the countries in Europe decreasing over time when one looks at economics and politics?

At the same time one has to pay attention to how the similarities and differences among the countries in Western Europe develop. The new democracies in Southern Europe are also attempting to catch up. How successful have they been since 1975? No doubt their state institutions and their economies have grown to be more like those of other West European states, but how similar is their politics to the countries in Northern, Western and Central Europe (Haller and Schachner-Blazizek, 1994)?

In the literature one may find an emphasis on factors that are conducive to growing similarities. On the one hand, there is literature dealing with the social consequences of technology development and diffusion (Kaelble, 1987: 140–1). Industrialization at various stages make for more uniform ways of life, breaking down historical or cultural legacies. On the other hand, a body of writing focuses upon the logic of democratic politics which is expressed in games played in similar ways by different players from various countries (Overbye, 1994: 155–7).

Here, one would wish to underline strongly the process of institutional integration in Europe, both economically and politically, chiefly in the form of the establishment of the European Union. Most former Communist countries are already associated with the EU, and it is expected that this process of extending the territory of the EU will continue. However, the possible entrance of several Eastern European states into the EU will depend upon how the economies and the political systems of these countries develop in the coming years. The more stable the East European countries are in supporting a democratic market regime, the more likely is it that they all will become members of the Union. Thus, EU harmonization and increasing regime similarities between the countries in Europe are two processes that sustain each other.

The convergence framework appears to us to be the approriate one for the assessment of the probability that the European states will become more alike in several major political aspects, such as the state format, the party system, the pattern of government formation and public policies. What, more specifically, is involved in choosing the convergence concept as the foundation for the analysis of a mass of information about society and state in Europe?

The Convergence Approach

Convergence is social change but not all kinds of social change equal convergence. The concept of convergence enters macro social theory, modelling how large social systems, such as societies or economies or polities, change and develop over time (Kerr, 1983; Sztompka, 1993; Chirot, 1994; Langlois et al., 1994). One may find convergence ideas in the major schools of sociology such as Marxism and modernization theory. Basically, 'convergence' stands for increasing similarities.

The literature on convergence is fairly extensive. There are available a couple of good overviews of the various scholarly contributions in this field (Bennett, 1991; Coughlin, 1992; Kalberg, 1993). Assessments of the convergence concept as employed in macro sociological literature have been conducted by Alex Inkeles (Inkeles, 1981). He points at a number of important distinctions between various types of convergence and divergence. And Inkeles also makes it clear that it is vital to specify what elements of the social system one is referring to when discussing convergence (Inkeles, 1981). Corresponding to these distinctions are a number of pitfalls in convergence analysis, some of which are discussed below.

- *Subsystem*: two or more social systems or societies may converge in certain respects but not in others meaning that it is vital that one makes clear what subsystem one is referring to such as the polity, the economy, the family or the social structure. Various subsystems of the most general social system, that is the society, may be identified and there is no given order in which the importance of these various subsystems may be decided. It is possible that convergence takes place with regard to one of them but not in relation to the other. The problem of how one adds or subtracts convergence in one subsystem from divergence in another subsystem has not been resolved. It is extremely dangerous to make generalizations about convergence, if one does not explicitly specify the subsystem one is dealing with.
- *Time*: two social systems or subsystems may converge during one time period but start to diverge during another period of time. It is essential to specify the time frame for convergence. Perhaps convergence is inherently a time bound phenomenon meaning that convergence always takes place between two different points of time. Or one may speak of 'convergence' in two different senses, one thick and one thin. In the *weak* interpretation of the convergence concept, two societies are converging when they are similar in certain respects. According to the strong interpretation, two societies converge if and only if the similarities between two societies increase from one point in time to another point of time. The first concept of convergence only requires that two societies or subsystems are rather similar whereas the second concept of convergence demands much more, namely that two societies or subsystems develop from dissimilarities towards similarities over time. Correspondingly, one may speak of a static and dynamic version of the convergence concept.
- *Goal*: convergence may be general or specific depending upon whether it refers only to growing similarities or if there is a specific goal towards which convergence tends to take place. Two well-known convergence theories, Marxism and the modernization theory, argued not only that societies tend to converge but also that they move towards a common end state, although that goal state differed in these two convergence models. The question of finality and intentionality is a difficult one in the convergence approach. Not only is the nature of the convergence process disputed, some claiming that societies tend towards some specific end state whereas others deny this seeing more of random walks or circularity in developmental trends. The degree of control or governance in convergence is another contested question, which is certainly relevant in a European context: Is convergence driven by major social forces which no one may control or is convergence something that may be accomplished or at least promoted by taking actions in the form of institutional redesign? Maybe institutional policies such as the making of an economic or political constitution are crucial? The approach of the EU to European integration is no doubt founded on such a belief in intended convergence.

- *Causal mechanism*: stating that two social systems are converging in some respects is like taking merely a first step, because one would also wish to know if behind the convergence of two systems there is some mechanism that explains why there are increasing similarities between the systems. The question of the mechanism behind convergence has been much discussed in the literature. Both Marxism and modernization theory underline the crucial role that economic factors play, although, again, the interpretation of the nature of these economic factors is different. The theory of the post-industrial society may be regarded as harbouring a convergence model, predicting major consequences from the fact that many societies are moving from industrialization to another stage, a society based on an economy orientated towards service production.

Our enquiry into the European countries is basically about the thin concept of convergence. This means that we are first and foremost interested in measuring the extent of similarities between the countries in Europe with regard to a few subsystems or societal sectors, as things now stand after the demolition of the Iron Curtain in 1989. We certainly make no assumption about an inner logic of convergence which would drive societies towards a common end state. Our objective is only to enquire into if and how the societies of the countries in Europe are becoming increasingly similar, as well as to examine whether the factors that are conducive towards convergence operate more strongly in the early 1990s than just after the Second World War. In our approach to European politics we use chiefly the *thin* or the *static* concept of convergence.

Our Framework of Analysis

When applying the convergence concept to reality there is the philosophical difficulty of specifying what is to count as a similarity or a difference. When are two social systems similar? It is always possible to find some differences between any social societies or political systems. One can only tell whether certain aspects of society or specific subsystems are similar or different.

When modelling convergence one has to decide from the outset what the focus of convergence is, that is, which properties one wishes to assess concerning convergence. After that decision has been taken the conduct of research on convergence involves three basic steps: (1) selecting the cases, that is, which countries or country sets are to be compared with regard to convergence; (2) assessing the extent to which convergence is actually taking place; and (3) identifying the forces that are conducive to or hinder convergence.

There are two sides of the coin when studying convergence: the cases to be studied and the properties with which one will measure similarities and differences. One may emphasize either the importance of a detailed understanding of the cases or one may underline the modelling of relationships between properties. Striking a balance between the weight to be given to empirical matters on the one hand and conceptual matters on the other hand we include all European countries but concentrate upon a few dimensions in a country's politics. Thus, we study: (1) the nature of the state; (2) the party system; (3) government formation; and (4) the public sector. The amount of similarities and differences in these important political dimensions must count heavily in an assessment of political convergence.

Democracy in the European context is first and foremost party government. The stability and vitality of democracy in Eastern Europe is connected with how party government operates in the former Communist countries. And the institutions of party government imply two things: on the one hand that electoral politics will focus upon the political parties forming a party system, and on the other hand that government formation is to a considerable extent controlled by the parties, making various kinds of coalitions. Who wins elections in Europe and who forms governments? The European state is an example of big government. This means a large number of public employees as well as big budgets, covering lots of public programmes carrying expenditures.

Although the path to an extensive state has been very different in the West having a market economy compared with the East and its planned economies, both the state in Western Europe and the state in Eastern Europe face the problem of how to mix the public and the private sectors. Is there any convergence in relation to the relative size of the public sectors between countries all over Europe, for instance with regard to the provision of welfare services such as education and health care or in terms of transfer payments (i.e. income redistribution)? The welfare state has been firmly entrenched in almost all European countries. There used to exist a so-called Communist welfare state, but the dismantling of the command economy in Eastern Europe has led to a sharp reduction in its commitments. At the same time the welfare state in Western Europe has matured, stabilizing at a high level of commitments in terms of allocative and redistributive tasks after several decades of public sector growth.

In addition, we include information about attitudes and belief-systems in order to map similarities and differences in political culture. The case for convergence in European politics would be a strong one if there were not only numerous similarities between the country institutions but also with regard to culture. Thus, the spread of democratic politics to Southern and Eastern Europe would result in political stability, only if there is also a civic culture that supports a democratic regime, that is, trust in the politics of party government. In the study of political culture there is a set of models which describe processes of macro change, which – it is argued – characterize all societies in their post-industrial stage, the post-materialism theme or more generally post-modernity theory (Klingemann and Fuchs, 1995; Kaase and Newton, 1995).

To sum up, we arrive at the following list of properties that we single out as of special interest in relation to European politics in the early 1990s:

1 *State institutions*: state format, the executive, the legislature and the judiciary.
2 *The party system*: fractionalization, polarization and volatility.
3 *Government formation*: coalition behaviour.
4 *The public sector*: the welfare state.
5 *Political culture*: post-modernization.

It seems to us that any talk about political convergence in Europe would have to be based upon an assessment about how similar or different the countries in Europe – North, South, West and East – are with regard to the five sets of properties listed above. In the thin sense, political convergence would imply numerous similarities in political institutions and behaviour. How can we explain them?

Among the conditions that promote convergence in politics one would include socio-economic forces. Convergence will be driven not only by unintended developmental trends in the economy and the social structure but also by the conscious adoption of similar legal institutions. The EU integration process with its emphasis on harmonization of legal institutions plays a major role here, although it has thus far only been in operation in Western Europe, or more specifically in 12 countries. Although we emphasize the implications of economic integration in Europe, we also remind ourselves about the autonomy of politics. There are, one must underline, forces that work against convergence. To cover these forces we employ the concept of historical legacies, although it is far from a specific notion. Historical traditions sustain ways of life in general as well as specific sets of institutions.

We suggest that a number of factors either promote convergence or hinder it. Factors 2 and 3 below would enhance convergence – we believe – whereas factor 1 below reduces convergence. We single out the following factors that are relevant when accounting for country similarities and differences in key political aspects:

1 *Historical legacies*: state formation, economic modernization, and ethnic and religious cleavages.
2 *Socio-economic factors*: affluence, economic growth, social structure and social cohesion.
3 *Institutional factors*: European integration.

Measuring political convergence by focusing upon present-day similarities in institutions and behaviour makes heavy demands upon access to information. There is still little information available, in particular concerning Southeastern and Eastern Europe. And not all the information is comparable. It has not been possible to include all the states from Table

I.1. Thus, Slovenia, Croatia and the FR Yugoslavia, that is, Serbia and Montenegro, from Tito's Yugoslavia have been included but Bosnia and the FYROM had to be excluded.

Finally, when it comes to our case, Europe, we have grouped the countries in Europe in a special way, which relates to on the one hand the Iron Curtain, that is, the distinction between Western and Eastern Europe, and on the other hand to the seminal convergence process in Europe stemming from European integration, namely, the EC and the EU institutions. Thus, the classification of countries follows the process of European integration starting in 1957 and going up to the transformation of the EC into the EU in 1993. We have the following categories:

CORE EC: BeNeLux countries, France, Germany and Italy.
OTHER EC: Denmark, the United Kingdom, Ireland, Greece, Portugal and Spain.
OUTSIDE EC: Austria, Finland, Sweden, Norway, Iceland and Switzerland.
CORE EAST: Poland, the Czech Republic, Slovakia, Hungary, Romania and Bulgaria.
EAST PERIPHERY: Estonia, Latvia, Lithuania, Slovenia, Croatia, FRY and Albania.

Fundamentally, the classification recognizes the great differences between Western and Eastern Europe in terms of affluence. As a matter of fact, the classification starts from one of the most influential divergence models in the social sciences, the modernization approach. What must be researched is whether these differences also make politics different in the West as compared with the East. We remain open to the argument about the autonomy of politics in relation to economics, but first we pin down how extensive the economic differences are between West and East European countries in the early 1990s.

The classification is also based upon the evolution of European integration in terms of the EC institutions and the enlargement of the EC to cover more and more states in Europe. In 1957, the Treaty of Rome was signed by a group of states that may be designated the core in continental Europe. In 1973, 1981 and 1986 the EC institutions were extended to cover other states (George, 1991; Nugent, 1994). Several states in Western Europe were, however, not integrated into the EC framework, as Sweden, Finland and Austria entered the new EU as late as 1995 with Switzerland, Norway and Iceland declining EU membership. Looking back one would wish to know whether EC membership has been attended by convergence among its member states.

When the EU is looking east reflecting upon the possibility of permitting new states to enter its institutions, then it seems as if there is a two-step procedure involved; the first possible enlargement covering a few core Eastern states such as those that have association status today – Poland, Hungary and the Czech and Slovak Republics, Romania and Bulgaria – and the second possible extension including the remaining states. There has been talk about Turkey entering, but this seems to us unlikely, as Europe does end at the Bosporus, as it were. Looking forward one may expect the EU to invite new member states among the countries that are most similar to its already included members.

A considerable part of the explicit and intended efforts at political convergence have been channelled through the EU framework in the post-Second World War period. By grouping the states in Europe with regard to their relationships to the EU one may test the hypothesis that explicit and intended convergence has been of importance. The contrary hypothesis would be that convergence is driven by latent forces, meaning that socio-economic development matters more than institutional integration. What are the political consequences of the differences in economic development between West and East European countries? The country information is organized around certain statistical parameters, as we attempt to give a quantitative perspective on European politics. Thus, we focus on the mean, the maximum and the minimum scores for each of our groups. The statistical apparatus has been kept at a minimum, but there are a few appendices containing correlation measures.

Conclusion

Social system convergence must start from one point and move towards some other point. That is the essence of the convergence notion. It could concern any kind of social system such as a society, or a subsystem like the polity or the economy. Convergence could be continuous or discrete, depending on whether the process is smooth or involves jumps or leaps. Convergence must occur in terms of certain properties and one needs to be aware of the possibility that two systems converge in certain respects but diverge on other properties. Convergence may be either intended or unintended, recognized or unrecognized, explicit or implicit, manifest or latent. The concept of convergence involves both the notion of similarities and the idea of a development over time. We deal more with the former than the latter.

Assessing basically the extent of similarity we first deal with the fundamental state institutions, which is why we analyse the constitutional fabric of European states. Second, the running of the state requires politicians, who in a European context act through political parties. Third, we focus on the recruitment of governments, where typical of the European context is the coalition government. Fourth, measuring the amount of similarities in country politics one must look at public policies, that is, the public sector. Finally, we enquire into political beliefs and values in order to find out whether institutions and behaviour are backed by a common European political culture.

The extent to which convergence takes place in Europe must be influenced besides onlingering historical legacies by the overall development of the European economy as well as that of the national economies in

Europe. We look at the differences in the economies of these countries in a broad sense including not only affluence and economic growth, but also inflation and unemployment. In addition, we examine the social correlates of economic development by looking at various types of data about social structure as well as social cohesion. Finally, the development of the EU (EC) must be looked into, both in terms of increasing the depth of the collaboration among already accepted member states and with regard to extending the EU to include all countries in Europe.

One may take the analysis of political and economic convergence one step further by including information about political culture. To what extent is there emerging in Europe a core set of political attitudes or belief-systems that scholars have different names for? One might be tempted to connect post-materialist values in particular (Inglehart, 1990) or modernity in general (Bourdieu, 1990) with socio-economic development. However, one must constantly remind oneself that convergence in one social system does not automatically translate into changes in another social system. The autonomy of politics in relation to the economy or the social structure is a profound insight in both Anglo-Saxon and Continental political analysis.

One could look upon Marxist analysis and the modernization approach as the two main convergence models. There are some interesting similarities and differences between the two frameworks. They were similar in being concerned with overall convergence at the macro level, they were finalistic in assuming a direction in the convergence processes and they were economistic, underlining economic change as the main causal mechanism. The differences between the two refer to the identification of the end state as well as with the interpretation of the pattern of convergence, Marxism adhering to a dialectic pattern of change whereas modernization theory was more evolutionary. Whereas the Marxist paradigm foundered on the erroneous prediction of the coming of a socialist economy that would be superior to a capitalist economy, modernization theory never really managed to clarify what the expression 'modern society' refers to. Thus, in a sense both these major convergence models failed due to the strong assumption about finality. However, we have borrowed from these two convergence approaches their emphasis on economic structure when grouping the 31 European countries discussed into five sets of countries, classifying them on the basis of affluence on the one hand and on the basis of their formal ties with the European Community on the other hand.

Is it possible to take a few steps towards an alternative convergence model explaining the similarities in European politics? We end our enquiry into the politics of Western and Eastern Europe by suggesting a tentative model of party governments, which may make sense of our findings. J.H. Goldthorpe argued in the early 1980s that convergence was decreasing among modern Western societies stating:

> In sum, what may be maintained is that over recent decades Western capitalist societies have moved in divergent directions in their responses to economic

problems and further that, in consequence, they now face different sets of political choices in which 'real ideological alternatives' are in fact inherent. (Goldthorpe, 1984: 340)

This observation may certainly have been adequate in relation to the whole set of advanced capitalist societies, but does it hold in relation to the new European realities in the early 1990s? Let us start examining this question systematically by first focusing on the economy and the social structure, then political life in democratic institutions and finally political culture. We deal though initially with historical legacies, as country differences in Europe today may reflect their various political histories in the form of inherited patterns of cleavages conducive to conflictual behaviour.

1

Historical Legacies

Political convergence in Europe will not only reflect the forces that promote increasing similarities, but of equal importance is how different the countries were earlier, at the starting-point, so to speak. In a longitudinal perspective on politics what happened in the past plays a major role in shaping the present and the future. One may describe the historical forces that operate through time as 'onlingering legacies'. Most probably, the stronger the historical legacies are entrenched the more the starting-point would limit what is attainable over a period of time. The purpose of this chapter is to discuss and measure this rather vague concept of historical legacies, if feasible.

When analysing historical legacies one may investigate the literature on macro social structures and their development over time. We focus here on the so-called modernization theme in sociological thought. The various modernization theories predict that country politics will be heavily influenced by how the transition from a traditional to a modern society takes place as well as when the transition period is initiated, the starting-point of modernity as it were.

Historical legacies are made up of patterns of conflict and cooperation between and among the major groups in a society. Cleavages are key elements in historical traditions as they enter the cultural patterns that structure the relationship between individuals and social groups. Thus, below we look at historical legacies by means of the modernization approach and the cleavage model.

Tradition and Country Identity

A historical legacy involves both a set of behaviour patterns and a set of belief-systems. Such country specific patterns in terms of social structure or culture make the country distinct as well as more or less special. Methodologically speaking, is it possible to identify a few concepts with which one could analyse country traditions or historical legacies comparatively? Or are country traditions so special that they defy comparison implying that the historical legacy of a country can only be understood in its own context?

The fact that one country has a different legacy from another country does not negate that country traditions can be analysed by means of general concepts. In the social sciences one makes a distinction between a nomothetical and an idiographic approach which is relevant in this connection (Przeworski and Teune, 1970). The nomothetical framework underlines the employment of systematic factors that range over more than one country for use in the conduct of comparative analysis. The idiographic approach, on the other hand, calls for an interpretation of each single country, based on its own specific presuppositions. We follow here the methodology for the conduct of comparative enquiry, which stresses the effort to employ abstract concepts and systematic indicators (Lijphart, 1971, 1975; Collier, 1991; Sartori, 1991). However specific a country tradition may turn out to be, it remains the case that only a comparative analysis can reveal with some degree of certainty what the differences are in various country legacies and their import for present-day politics.

Now, modernization models imply that each country has a configuration of traditional practices which come under strain as the profound process of industrialization and urbanization gets under way. The modernization process affects social structure, the economy as well as politics. What differs from one country to another is the length of time of social transformation as well as how disruptive the process is.

The modernization framework is basically a longitudinal one, as it considers time as crucial. Each country is on a developmental path from traditional to modern society. The main direction of change is the same for any society wherever it is placed on the earth, as there exists a natural sequence of developmental stages behind the appearances. Yet, countries may differ cross-sectionally in terms of how developed they are at one point in time, as for instance at the present time.

The modernization approach was launched in the 1950s and received much attention in the 1960s (Levy, 1952; Sutton, 1963; Deutsch, 1963). It has received renewed interest in the early 1990s following a relatively long period of decline (Lipset et al., 1993; Lipset, 1994).

One specific type of modernization model focuses on the occurrence of a critical event at one point in time for a country, for example, when it became independent or received a so-called modernized leadership. The model entails that the longer the time span since the introduction of a modern state in the country, the more likely it is that the country will be a developed one. This factor is referred to by the word 'institutionalization' and it may be measured by indicators such as the year of independence, or the year of political modernization or the starting-point of economic modernization (Black, 1966). Is there a variation with regard to the occurrence of these critical time points among European countries?

Turning now to the cleavage models, one may argue that they are closely connected with the modernization approach, because they also look on a country as having more or less fixed structural characteristics such as ethnicity, religion and class. The process of modernization may only change these fundamental cleavages in the social structure very slowly.

Cleavages may be manifest or latent. Their political relevance would be beyond doubt when political conflict is channelled along cleavage lines.

However, the cleavage models also entail that latent cleavages play a behind-the-scenes role. Cleavages may be activated to and fro and they will dominate in a country if the cleavage pattern expresses mutually reinforcing cleavages instead of cross-cutting ones.

Countries tend to vary considerably in relation to the occurrence of cleavages, latent or manifest. Thus, a few countries have mainly ethnic cleavages, while other countries are characterized by religious cleavages and still others by class cleavages. Cleavage patterns tend to prevail over long time periods and they are conducive to the emergence of traditions. One may enquire into whether class will be more relevant than ethnicity and religion in the modern society or that class conflicts will attenuate over time, as was sometimes stated in the modernization approach.

In the literature on cleavages a few measurement indicators have been devised that may be employed for comparative research. On the one hand, there are the ethnic and religious fragmentation indices. On the other hand, one may employ indicators that identify the adherence to a certain creed such as Catholicism or Protestantism. What do these cleavage indicators tell us about ethnic and religious traditions in Europe?

Cleavages

Some kinds of cleavages tend to occur in any society. One would be amazed not to find urban–rural, core–hinterland, gender and rich–poor cleavages in any country. It is true though that these standard cleavages may characterize various countries differently. But if one searches for special configurations of cleavages that may be truly distinctive for a country, then ethnic and religious cleavages would come to the fore. Here, we may expect to find country traditions that are really distinct.

First, we distinguish between two indicators on ethnic and religious structure, one measuring the extent of fragmentation or the probability that two randomly sampled persons will belong to different groups in a country (Rae and Taylor, 1970: 32), and the other measuring the percentage of the population adhering to one dominant ethnic or religious grouping. Second, we look more carefully into the diversity of religious creed, mapping the strength of Catholicism, Protestantism, orthodox Christianity and Islam. Let us take a look at data about ethnic and religious structure in the early decades of this century (Table 1.1).

The finding in Table 1.1 is that both ethnic and religious cleavages were slightly more pronounced in Eastern Europe than in Western Europe. In particular the scores for the position of the major group within the ethnic and religious structures are lower in Eastern than in Western Europe. There were though strong ethnic and religious cleavages in some of the countries in the set of what is now CORE EC countries as well as in Spain.

The modernization models predicted that religious and ethnic cleavages would decrease in relevance as countries move along their developmental path towards an industrialized and urbanized society. Does this hold up for

Europe? One may test the validity of the modernization perspective for Europe by looking at whether these kinds of cleavages still exist and attempt to estimate their relevance to present-day politics. Table 1.2 has the information about the occurrence of cleavages today.

The data do not support the implications of modernization models about an overall decline in the occurrence of ethnic and religious cleavages. The country pattern is the same around 1990 as in the early decades of the twentieth century, but one must note that there is considerable variation within the country sets as was the case around 1900. Interestingly, the two sets with the highest scores for both ethnic and religious fragmentation are on the one hand the set of EAST PERIPHERY countries and the set of CORE EC countries on the other hand.

Today heavy ethnic fragmentation is to be found in: Switzerland, Latvia, Belgium, Estonia, Luxembourg, Yugoslavia, Croatia, Spain and Lithuania. To the ethnically homogeneous societies one counts the following: Portugal, Poland, Denmark, Norway, the United Kingdom and Austria – in both cases following the order of the ranking of the countries on the ethnic fragmentation index. One may observe that Poland has become more homogeneous over time whereas Luxembourg has developed in the other direction.

There can be little doubt about the relevance of ethnic cleavages in the countries that score high on the index of fragmentation regarding ethnicity. Here we have not only the multicultural societies of Switzerland and Spain but also the bipolarity in Belgium between Walloons and the Flemish as well as in the Baltic countries with sizeable Russian minorities. Ethnic tensions have hardly decreased in the Balkans during the twentieth century. Generally speaking, ethnic identification has become more conspicuous since the Second World War, partly as a result of the large migration into Western Europe and between West European countries (Stephens, 1976; Minority Rights Group, 1993).

One can raise the sensitive question of whether nationalism in ethnically divided societies takes on a different form in Eastern Europe compared with Western Europe. In the civil war in former Yugoslavia it was as if centuries of conflict and hatred had been buried in the collective consciousness of the different ethnic groups, only to explode into meaningless atrocities. Could something similar happen elsewhere in Eastern Europe? And is nationalism in Western Europe contained and channelled into civilized forms of conflict? There is hardly any data available which would allow us to answer these questions, but one may wish to point out that the nationality problems in Spain and the UK often find violent outlets, still unresolved. Yet, it cannot be doubted that ethnic nationalism could be a source of future conflict in Eastern Europe, especially if borders of Eastern Europe to the former USSR are questioned or if Russia and the Ukraine become more unstable.

Religiously fragmented countries lie where the great world religions met and religious wars were fought. They include today: the Netherlands,

Table 1.1 *Ethnic and religious structure, 1900–20*

Country set	Ethnic fragmentation	Major ethnic group	Religious fragmentation	Major religious group
CORE EC	.19 (6)	86.7 (6)	.19 (6)	84.5 (6)
OTHER EC	.13 (6)	91.8 (6)	.11 (6)	93.8 (6)
OUTSIDE EC	.13 (6)	92.3 (6)	.12 (6)	91.0 (6)
CORE EAST	.42 (6)	73.2 (6)	.32 (6)	80.0 (6)
EAST PERIPHERY	.28 (7)	83.6 (7)	.35 (7)	77.4 (7)
All	.23 (31)	85.5 (31)	.22 (31)	85.1 (31)

Note: Ethnic structure refers to the 1920s whereas religious structure refers to around 1900.

Sources: Ethnicity: Tesnière (1928), Shoup (1981); Religion: Flere (1991), Barrett (1982), Leff (1988).

Table 1.2 *Ethnic and religious structure around 1990*

Country set	Ethnic fragmentation	Major ethnic group	Religious fragmentation	Major religious group
CORE EC	.27 (6)	83.2 (6)	.38 (6)	69.8 (6)
OTHER EC	.11 (6)	94.0 (6)	.17 (6)	90.3 (6)
OUTSIDE EC	.19 (6)	88.8 (6)	.28 (6)	81.2 (6)
CORE EAST	.21 (6)	88.0 (6)	.35 (6)	75.0 (6)
EAST PERIPHERY	.34 (7)	76.9 (7)	.40 (7)	74.3 (7)
All	.23 (31)	85.9 (31)	.32 (31)	78.0 (31)

Source: The data on ethnic and religious structure is based on EB (1994).

Germany, Switzerland, Albania, the Czech Republic, Hungary, Slovakia and Yugoslavia. Into the set of homogeneous countries from a religious point of view enter the following: Greece, Spain, Portugal, Luxembourg, Slovenia, Ireland, Iceland and Belgium. But whereas the ethnic fragmentation index taps much of the political relevance of ethnicity, the index on religious fragmentation does not. Religion may be a strong force in society not only in religiously divided countries like the Netherlands, Switzerland and Slovakia but also in religiously homogeneous countries. One must look at the denomination in addition to fragmentation.

Which are the main denominations and how strong are they? Table 1.3 illustrates how religious creed has fared in Europe in this century. Here there is support for the prediction from the modernization models that secularization spreading over time will lower the relevance of religious cleavages. The percentages of the population that are recorded as 'Other' have increased sharply, particularly within the CORE EAST and the CORE EC countries. The increase in the number of non-believers clearly indicates secularization. Actually, the increase in the religious fragmentation

Table 1.3   *Religious denominations, 1900–90*

Country set	Catholic		Protestant		Orthodox		Muslim		Jew	Other	
	1900	1990	1900	1990	1900	1990	1900	1990	1900	1900	1990
CORE EC	80	73	19	13	0	0	0	2	5	7	15
OTHER EC	50	51	33	24	14	16	2	1	5	3	8
OUTSIDE EC	22	24	76	70	1	0	0	0	5	3	7
CORE EAST	52	45	9	7	32	29	3	2	5	2	19
EAST PERIPHERY	44	42	22	21	20	18	11	13	1	2	6
All (31)	49	47	32	27	13	12	4	3	1	1	11

Sources: See Tables 1.1, 1.2 and Central Intelligence Agency (1994).

index over the century depends to a large extent on the growth in the number of non-believers.

Of the major world religions Protestantism especially has been on the retreat all over Europe. There is also a decline in the relative strength of Catholicism, whereas the considerable minority of Jewish groups around 1900 in Poland, Hungary, Latvia, Slovakia, Romania and Austria were almost completely wiped out during the Holocaust.

Today the basic pattern in Europe is that the CORE EC countries adhere more to Catholicism than Protestantism whereas the opposite holds true of the OUTSIDE EC countries in Western Europe. The OTHER EC countries tend to be mixed comprising substantial Catholic and Protestant groups. The CORE EAST and the EAST PERIPHERY countries are either mainly Catholic or Orthodox.

The countries with the largest Catholic populations are Italy, Spain, Luxembourg, Portugal, Slovenia, Poland, Ireland and France. A large portion of the population adheres to Protestantism in Iceland, Sweden, Denmark, Finland, Norway and Estonia. Orthodox populations are to be found in large numbers in Greece, Bulgaria, Romania and Yugoslavia, whereas substantial Muslim groups exist in Albania, Yugoslavia and Bulgaria. In religiously homogeneous societies Catholicism, whether Roman or Orthodox, has a much stronger bind on politics than Protestantism, as one may see when comparing Southern with Northern Europe, partly due to the fact that secularization has been stronger in Protestant countries (O'Brien and Palmer, 1993).

There are onlingering ethnic and religious traditions or legacies in Europe but they have little to do with the East–West separation. Several of the main features of the country pattern of ethnic and religious cleavages were already in place around 1900. Ethnicity has grown in relevance, especially in divided societies. But the force of religion has been reduced as a result of secularization, a tendency which applies to both religiously homogeneous and heterogeneous societies.

What, then, of the starting-point of modernization? Surely, there must be consistent differences between Eastern and Western Europe here? Yet,

Table 1.4   *State institutionalization*

Country set	Year of independence	Introduction of modernized leadership
CORE EC	1695 (6)	1797 (6)
OTHER EC	1374 (6)	1803 (6)
OUTSIDE EC	1669 (6)	1833 (6)
CORE EAST	1934 (6)	1860 (6)
EAST PERIPHERY	1969 (7)	1875 (7)
All	1736 (31)	1835 (31)

Sources: Black (1966), EB (1994).

measuring the occurrence of modernization in Europe one may distinguish conceptually between state institutionalization, economic modernization and political modernization or democratization.

State Institutionalization

When considering the starting-point of the modernization processes one may focus upon the institutionalization of the state. Country politics could have a distinct flavour reflecting for how long there has been a modern state in place. And surely it must imply a difference if political independence has been recently won or whether it has been taken for granted for centuries. The indicators that tap state institutionalization include rough estimates of the year of independence and the year of the introduction of a so-called modernized leadership, which concept stands for the initiation of the introduction of institutions and policies that one connects with the modern legal-rational state.

Table 1.4 shows data for indicators on state institutionalization in the form of averages for two critical starting-points for country politics in time. The EC countries have on an average had a longer history of state institutionalization than the other countries. At the same time as one notes the very early dates of independence for one set of countries, the OTHER EC set, one may question the meaningfulness of some data about the occurrence of the year of independence. Thus, the following questionable or arbitrary years are stated as independence dates: 800 for Denmark, 836 for Sweden, 843 for France, 1066 for the United Kingdom, 1140 for Portugal, 1492 for Spain and 1499 for Switzerland. One can interpret critical events in the history of a country differently, depending on what one means by 'state independence'. But it is true that several of the now existing states in Eastern Europe reached recognition much later than most West European ones.

The scores on the starting-point of modernized leadership are more informative. And one sees that the West European countries had modernized leadership from around 1800 whereas in Eastern Europe it was from around 1870. Often the introduction of modernized leadership was connected with the life of some major political figure or the occurrence of a major event, such as abolishing the remnants of feudalism or traditional authority putting a modern state with a formal bureaucracy into place. For some countries it may be tied to a specific point in time when a new constitution was enacted, carrying so-called modern political institutions. One must take care to note that the date of political modernization is not the same as the year of democratization, which comes much later.

One notes the early occurrence of a modernized leadership in the following countries: the United Kingdom, France, Belgium, the Netherlands, Luxembourg and Switzerland. Early state institutionalization may certainly have resulted in different country traditions, as the pace of putting a modern state in place varies from one country to another. As a matter of fact the length of time of state institutionalization constitutes a striking historical legacy that distinguishes Western Europe from Eastern Europe. But what about economic modernization?

Economic Modernization

It was typical of the modernization framework that it was believed that political development went hand in hand with economic development. Black states: 'the available information regarding comparative levels of development of societies tends to show that the other aspects of modernization are reasonably correlated with the political' (1966: 90). However, one may remain alert to the possibility that economic modernization is delayed in relation to political modernization. It is conceivable that these two processes may occur more or less separately in time, which in itself could impact upon politics in a country. When did the European economies start to take-off, according to the Rostow analysis of the process of industrialization (Rostow, 1960)? The take-off year is another crucial starting-point.

Economic modernization was initiated much earlier in some European countries. It then spread from the core to the peripheral countries. Table 1.5 gives information about the time frame for the process of industrialization, first the year of initiation of economic modernization and then two indicators that can be used to measure how far economic modernization had progressed after the First World War, namely GNP per capita and agricultural employment as a percentage of all employment during the interwar period.

Economic modernization was well under way in the EC countries before the end of the nineteenth century, whereas for Eastern Europe the starting-point occurred generally during or after the First World War. Yet, also in Northern and Southern Europe the industrialization-urbanization process began later than in Central Europe which lagged behind the United Kingdom as the first country to embark upon the industrialization process.

Compare the initiation years for the United Kingdom (1825), France

Table 1.5   *Economic modernization*

Country set	Year of economic modernization	GNP 1925 ($) per capita	Agricultural employment 1930 (%)
CORE EC	1858 (6)	821 (6)	26 (6)
OTHER EC	1892 (6)	596 (6)	39 (6)
OUTSIDE EC	1902 (6)	776 (5)	33 (5)
CORE EAST	1918 (6)	346 (5)	58 (5)
EAST PERIPHERY	1918 (7)	407 (4)	67 (5)
All	1898 (31)	605 (26)	44 (27)

Sources: Moore (1945), Kirk (1946), Black (1966) and Bairoch (1976).

(1848), Belgium (1848), the Netherlands (1848) and Germany (1871) with those of Sweden (1905), Norway (1905), Finland (1919) as well as those of Spain (1909), Portugal (1910) and Greece (1918). Rostow (1960: 38) actually places the critical year of take-off for the economy somewhat earlier: the United Kingdom = 1783, France = 1830, Belgium = 1833, Germany = 1850 and Sweden = 1868. Again, there is a certain amount of arbitrariness about these time points called 'take-offs', but they indicate the basic pattern of how industrialization spread, from the centre to the periphery in Europe.

   Looking at the indicators on economic activity during the interwar years we see that two sets, CORE EC and OUTSIDE EC, were more advanced economically than OTHER EC, EAST PERIPHERY and CORE EAST. Basically, the GNP per capita data for 1925 refer to the separation between the more affluent countries in Northern and Western Europe and the less affluent countries in Southern and Eastern Europe (Good, 1994; Maddison, 1995). One very informative indicator on economic modernization is the relative size of the agricultural workforce. On this indicator there is a clear West–East divide in the 1930 data.

   Economic modernization was initiated after the introduction of modernized leadership in Europe. The time lag is about 50 years in most countries, which is evidence for the hypothesis that industrialization needs an institutional base provided by the modern state. One interesting exception is Germany with almost the same starting-points in time for modernized leadership and economic modernization. The differences in economic activity between the European countries were quite substantial in the interwar years, reflecting the variation with regard to the time point for the beginning of industrialization. Now, if the modern state preceded the modern economy in Europe, how about the relationship in time between economic modernization and the coming of democracy?

Democratization

In approaching the concept of democratization in terms of the institutionalization of civil and political rights one looks at the historical development

Table 1.6 *Introduction of democracy and democracy indicators for the interwar period*

Country set	Male suffrage	Female suffrage	Democracy index 1920–4	Democracy index 1920–39
CORE EC	1898 (6)	1932 (6)	8.4 (6)	7.8 (6)
OTHER EC	1917 (6)	1936 (6)	8.0 (6)	7.5 (6)
OUTSIDE EC	1897 (6)	1924 (6)	9.8 (6)	9.2 (6)
CORE EAST	1916 (6)	1932 (6)	5.8 (6)	4.7 (5)
EAST PERIPHERY	1927 (7)	1937 (7)	7.1 (5)	4.5 (5)
All	1912 (31)	1933 (31)	7.9 (28)	6.9 (28)

Sources: Suffrage: Sternberger and Vogel (1969); Gerlich (1973); Hewitt (1977); Therborn (1977); Nohlen (1978); UN (1991); Janova and Sineau (1992); Democracy index: Gurr (1990).

of human rights. For some countries in Europe institutional change took an evolutionary path, such as in Scandinavia, whereas for others the developments in rights involved dramatic changes as well as reversals as in the Baltic countries and Poland.

The extent of democracy can be measured by means of indices that take into account a number of aspects of a democratic regime. One such indicator is the year of introduction of universal suffrage for men and women. Another is the Gurr index of democracy, which may be employed for mapping the extent of democracy during the interwar years (Table 1.6). The democracy index focuses upon the protection of a variety of human rights including the right to vote in fair and free elections (Jaggers and Gurr, 1995).

There are a number of points to be emphasized in relation to Table 1.6. First, male suffrage was introduced much earlier than female suffrage in all country sets. If universal suffrage is the indicator on political modernization, then the Eastern countries are little different from the Western, as all were late with the recognition of female suffrage. Focusing only upon male suffrage the CORE EC and OUTSIDE EC country sets preceded the other country sets by an average of 20 years.

Male suffrage was first introduced in the following countries: France (1848), Switzerland (1848), Germany (1867), Greece (1877), Norway (1898) and Finland (1906). Looking at the year of introduction of female suffrage the timing in the different countries is the following, listing the first comers as: Finland (1906), Norway (1913), Iceland (1915), Poland (1918), the Netherlands (1919) and Ireland (1922). Not until 1971 was female suffrage recognized in Switzerland, always considered as an example of stable democracy.

Second, the data on the occurrence of democracy between the First and Second World War indicate clearly that Eastern Europe did have experience of this type of regime in both CORE EAST and EAST PERIPHERY. During the interwar years democracy was stronger institutionalized in Western Europe than in Eastern Europe, where authoritarian regimes made a come-back in one country after the other. But the same defeat of democracy took place also in countries in Western Europe, namely, Germany, Italy, Spain and Portugal.

Actually, the authoritarian wave got much of its momentum from events in Western Europe, as in Italy when Mussolini marched on Rome in 1922, or in Spain where Primo de Rivera established a military government in 1923, as well as in Greece with the Pangalos' takeover in 1925 and Portugal in 1926 (Comes da Costa). When Germany and Austria went authoritarian with the *Machtübernahme* by Hitler and Dolfuss, respectively, then democracy was indeed a fragile regime in Western Europe. All the East European countries fell to authoritarian regimes in the interwar period, beginning with Hungary in 1919 (Horthy), then Bulgaria in 1923 and Albania in 1924 (King Zogu), Poland in 1926 (Pilsudski), Lithuania in 1926 (Smetona) and Yugoslavia in 1929 (King Alexander). With the establish-ment of Nazi-Germany the fascist pressure increased and an authoritarian regime was introduced in Estonia in 1934 (Päts), Latvia in 1934 (Ulmanis) and Romania in 1938 (King Carol II). With the dissolution of Czecho-slovakia in 1938 and Franco's victory in 1939 in the Spanish civil war authoritarianism reached its peak all over Europe (Rothschild, 1974; Lee, 1987; Kitchen, 1988; Luebbert, 1991; Karvonen, 1993a).

The key finding here is that Western Europe hardly has an entirely different democratic legacy from Eastern Europe. There was not only universal suffrage in Eastern Europe around 1920 but also other demo-cratic institutions. And these institutions did not survive the onslaught of fascism whether in the East or the West.

When we move to measure the occurrence of democracy after the Second World War as in Table 1.7, then there is an altogether different picture just a couple of years after the armistice. Note the rather high democracy scores for the country sets CORE EAST – 6.0 – and EAST PERIPHERY – 5.0 – in 1945, where CORE EC had 8.0, as several countries in Eastern Europe had a short experience with democracy before the introduction of Com-munist rule in the late 1940s. But one must again recall that a few countries in Western Europe had dictatorships for several years after 1945, such as Portugal, Spain and Greece, which shows up in the rather low index scores for the country set OTHER EC.

The East European countries were step by step transfromed in so-called Peoples' Democracies modelled on the Soviet type of politico-economic regime with the exception of Tito's Yugoslavia which pressed for its own kind of system. Thus, left-wing authoritarian constitutions were enacted as follows: Romania in 1945, Bulgaria in 1947, Hungary and DDR in 1949 as well as Poland in 1952. The most spectacular event in the Communist transformation was the Prague coup in 1948 (Seton Watson, 1950; Zinner, 1963; Bloomfield, 1979; Kaplan, 1981; Myant, 1981; Rageau, 1981; Fowkes, 1993).

The conclusion is that one cannot simply say that Eastern Europe has an

Table 1.7   *Democracy indicators after the Second World War*

Country set	Democracy index 1945	Democracy index 1950
CORE EC	8.0 (5)	10.0 (6)
OTHER EC	6.8 (6)	6.4 (6)
OUTSIDE EC	9.2 (6)	10.0 (6)
CORE EAST	6.0 (6)	2.0 (5)
EAST PERIPHERY	5.0 (2)	2.0 (2)
All	7.3 (24)	6.9 (25)

Source: The democracy index is based on Gurr (1990).

authoritarian legacy whereas Western Europe has none. One of the fundamental questions in the research on political convergence in Europe – its sources and obstacles – concerns the impact of the long authoritarian experience for the countries in Eastern Europe. However, there is a parallel question about the political systems in Southern Europe (Kurth and Petras, 1993). If there are difficulties in consolidating democracy in CORE EAST and EAST PERIPHERY due to the Communist experience, then perhaps the present problems in Italy and Spain also to some extent reflect a historical legacy of undemocratic institutions?

Culture

Historical traditions are often said to express deep seated belief-systems or culture. The concept of culture is a vague one referring to various ways of life. As manifestations of different cultures one may point to recurrent behaviour patterns or onlingering attitudes, be these fundamental beliefs or values. Country cultures may surface in the educational system or in the family system. We focus on the latter.

The interaction in family systems may be based on individualistic values or be orientated towards collectivistic ones. Todd (1983) has introduced a scheme that classifies the different family systems in various countries. Since the basic pattern of family interaction does not fluctuate over time, Todd's scale may be employed for measuring country traditions. Actually, it may be regarded as an indicator on culture in accordance with Wildavsky's culture concepts, where the institutionalization of individualism is a key aspect (Thompson et al., 1990). Family systems may be either egalitarian or non-egalitarian, depending on how the inheritance is distributed as well as hierarchical or non-hierarchical, reflecting whether parents tend to exercise authority over their grown-up children.

Table 1.8 recasts the Todd scores ranking the various family systems in European countries according to the distinction between individualism and collectivism, where the first is characterized by inequality in inheritance and equality in interaction whereas the latter is based upon inequality in

Table 1.8   *Individualism–collectivism*

Country set	Individualism	Mix	Collectivism
CORE EC	1	5	0
OTHER EC	2	4	0
OUTSIDE EC	0	5	1
CORE EAST	0	3	3
EAST PERIPHERY	0	1	6
All	3	18	10

Source: Based on Todd (1983).

interaction and equality in inheritance. There exist mixed forms of family systems in Europe.

In a *pure* individualist family system the emphasis is on inequality with regard to inheritance and lenience, and reciprocities in the authority structure. In a *pure* collectivistic family pattern obedience is underlined as well as equality in inheritance. The finding in Table 1.8 is that there exist clear country differences in the basic orientation of the family system. The West–East difference is marked, but there is also a North–South division. Countries that score high on the indicator on liberal family traditions include the West European countries such as Denmark, the Netherlands and the United Kingdom whereas the East European ones score low: Albania, Bulgaria, Estonia, Hungary, Latvia, Lithuania and Yugoslavia as well as Finland. Interestingly, one may note that most countries in the set OUTSIDE EC have mixed systems, combining lenience in the authority structure with more of equality in inheritance.

Configuration of Legacies

We have identfied a few historical traditions above: length of time since the initiation of state institutionalization, the experience of democracy, the starting-point for economic modernization as well as ethnic and religious fragmentation. If a country scores high or low on one of them, is it then also the case that it tends to score low or high on the others? Appendix 1.1 contains information about the extent to which various kinds of historical legacies tend to go together.

Political and economic modernization are connected with early state independence. And early political and economic modernization resulted in the democratization of the political system in the early twentieth century. This pattern separates Western Europe from Eastern Europe and constitutes the major difference between the West and the East in terms of path dependence with regard to time and the evolution of chief events such as the formation of states as well as the modernization of the economy and the polity.

Interestingly, a liberal family structure is typical of the countries with early political and economic modernization. This means that a few countries in Western Europe that set up states early founded on individualistic values had an edge in terms of modernization over the other European countries in terms of both economic and political development, especially in relation to those countries which have experienced collectivist values.

But how extensive are the consequences of early modernization? The transition to a democratic regime, meaning the introduction of male or female suffrage, does not depend on modernization, because most countries in Europe accepted democratic institutions at roughly the same time, that is, around the First World War, although several of them abandoned democracy during the interwar years or after the Second World War. Moreover, the modernization models imply not only a West–East difference but also a general core–periphery separation where some countries in both Northern and Southern Europe were late-comers.

At the same time it is true that in European politics historical legacies vary from one country to another. Historical traditions do not form a monolithic whole implying that countries with one kind of legacy also have all the other kinds. Instead, historical legacies such as religious or ethnic cleavages occur independently of each other. Thus, countries with an ethnic legacy and those with a religious legacy are not the very same ones. The cleavage model does not entail any separation between Western and Eastern Europe.

Conclusion

There can be no doubt that historical legacies have an impact on European integration today. Different country traditions set limits to convergence in Europe. But what needs to be discussed is how large a force traditions and legacies is today. An important source of country traditions in politics is the cleavage structure, which tends to remain fairly stable over time. Ethnic and religious fragmentation is high in several countries, both in the West and the East.

There is a special East European legacy that is distinctive of the countries behind the collapsed Iron Curtain, namely late state institutionalization and modernization. Modern states as well as economic modernization in the form of industrialization were introduced earlier in Western Europe than in Eastern Europe. Although many countries had experience of democratic rule introducing universal suffrage for both men and women at almost the same time, it is a fact that the tradition of democracy varies between Western Europe and Eastern Europe.

Yet, the basic difference is Communism and not authoritarian rule, because several West European countries have had much experience of fascism in the twentieth century. It is impossible to bypass the experience of harsh authoritarian rule in Eastern Europe after 1945, which meant that the 1989 initiated system transition had to result in political instability

Table 1.9   *Political violence and protest, 1930s*

Country set	Strikes	Violence	Protest	Riots	Government instability
CORE EC (5)	.22	.24	.34	1.4	.94
INSIDE EC (5)	.30	.24	.35	1.2	.58
OUTSIDE EC (5)	.08	.08	.11	.3	.23
EAST (10)	.03	.21	.33	.5	.35
Mean	.14	.20	.30	.8	.50

Source: Banks (1994).

when new democracies were introduced in the East (Barany and Volgyes, 1995).

We end here by remembering that many West European countries have not always been politically stable. Table 1.9 has a few indicators on the occurrence of political violence and protest at a critical point of time, namely, around 1930, when democracies in Western Europe had to fight for their existence and were not always successful.

On all the various indicators on political stability the countries in the EAST set scored lower than the countries in the Western sets around 1930. The scores on government instability and the occurrence of riots are particularly high for the countries that later on went on to constitute the European Community. In politics changes, not only minor changes but even major systemic ones, can occur during the short life of the average person.

How much of the past exists in today's politics? One may wish to give historical legacies a major role when interpreting what is happening at the moment. In such a longitudinal perspective the past constrains the future. The opposite position is to underline the forces that operate momentarily, such as economic and social conditions. In a cross-sectional approach one could attempt to understand the variation in European politics not by invoking the past but by focusing on, for example, the present differences in economic and social structure. Let us try that perspective in the following two chapters.

Appendix 1.1 *Relationships between indicators on country traditions (Pearsons' correlations)*

	Modernization	
	Political	Economic
State independence	.59	.51
Male suffrage	.22	.39
Female suffrage	.03	−.13
Democratic Experience 1920–39	−.50	−.50
Ethnic fragmentation 1990	.06	−.11
Religious fragmentation 1990	−.12	−.24
Protestantic Creed 1990	−.20	−.08
Collectivist family	−.66	−.64

Note: Modernization is measured by the year of introduction of modernized leadership (political) and the starting-point of industrialization (economic), low scores meaning early modernization. Correlation Coefficient shows the degree to which two variables are related. Correlation coefficients range from −1.0 to +1.0. If there is a perfect negative correlation (−1.0) between A and B, whenever A is high, B is low, and vice versa. If there is a perfect positive correlation (+1.0) between A and B, whenever one is high or low, so is the other. A correlation coefficient of 0 means that there is no relationship between the variables. Pearson's Correlation Coefficient, or Pearson's *r*, shows the degree of linear relationship between two variables that have been measured on interval or ratio scales, such as the relationship between height in inches and weight in pounds.

Sources: Tables 1.1–1.7.

2

The Economy

It is well-known that the economies of the European countries differ in terms of aggregate output. The level of affluence measured by various indicators displays divergence, mainly between Western and Eastern Europe, but also along a North–South division. These differences between country economies are no doubt quite considerable. The first purpose of this chapter is to identify these large differences in affluence set against the background of the country variation in key macroeconomic aggregates. Yet, economic development may bring about convergence in affluence among countries or regions within a country, if they interact with each other on a regular basis.

The convergence model of economic growth implies that more affluent regions will grow at a less rapid pace than the less affluent regions (Barro, 1991; Barro and Sala-i-Martin, 1992). Evidence for the convergence model has been found in a negative relation between levels of affluence and long-term growth rates for the states in the United States. But what about Europe (Neven and Gouyette, 1994)? Thus, the second purpose in this chapter is to examine the relevance of the convergence model of economic growth in relation to Europe as a whole.

Economic growth theory entails the implication that the levels of affluence should in the long run be equalized between regions or countries, given free movement of capital and labour between them. However, the conditions for economic convergence may not be fulfilled, as for instance when Western Europe adhered to one kind of economic system and Eastern Europe to another economic regime with little interaction between the two. What is taking place in the early 1990s with regard to convergence in affluence, given the trend towards convergence on economic institutions and the pick up in trade between Western and Eastern Europe?

We end this chapter by looking at a few measures of economic outcomes which may be employed to obtain a picture of how vast the economic differences are between Western Europe and the former command economies. The institutional transformation following the 1989 upheavals was attended by a sharp reduction in economic output in Eastern Europe, which raises the issue of whether the use of the so-called shock therapy could have worked out differently (Sachs, 1993; Åslund, 1995; Gowan, 1995).

Affluence

One may wish to distinguish between various indicators on how rich or poor a country is. Table 2.1 presents one standard indicator on country

Table 2.1   *Affluence as real GDP per capita, 1950–85*

Country set	RGDPC50	RGDPC60	RGDPC70	RGDPC85
CORE EC (6)	3320	4684	6845	9567
OTHER EC (6)	2307	3055	4604	6564
OUTSIDE EC (6)	3556	4934	6975	9955
CORE EAST (5)	1975	2930	4092	5498
EAST PERIPHERY (1)	1101	1778	2885	5063
All (24)	2753	3851	5579	7877

Source: Summers and Heston, 1988.

affluence, the real GDP per capita indicator from 1950 to 1985. It takes currency fluctuations and inflation into account but bypasses information about the income distribution as well as the actual quality of life that real purchasing power may buy. The basic problem, however, is to estimate total output in a reliable way for the former Communist countries. The Summers and Heston series that we employ is hardly less reliable than other series in the literature (Alton, 1989; Lancieri, 1993; Schmiedling, 1993).

Was there economic convergence between 1950 and 1985, that is, up until the collapse of the command economies? Well, the picture is somewhat mixed. On the one hand, the differences between the country sets increased with two sets of countries doing exceptionally well, namely the CORE EC and OUTSIDE EC. Although affluence has increased in the other sets of countries, the pace did not quite match that of these countries, although one country in EAST PERIPHERY, namely, former Yugoslavia, also did very well. On the other hand, one may observe that the East European economies first competed well with the West European ones, but then later ran into profound difficulties. The differences between Northern Europe and Southern Europe remain large.

Let us use the gross national per capita income measure for looking at more recent developments (Table 2.2). Here a different picture emerges, which displays the immense differences between, on the one hand, the countries in CORE EC and in OUTSIDE EC, and on the other hand the countries in Eastern Europe with the OTHER EC countries somewhere in between. The severe economic decline for the command economies is apparent in the data stated according to this indicator. Clearly economic divergence along the West–East separation took place after 1980 and was reinforced by the economic system transition after 1989, although the pre-1989 figures for Eastern Europe have been questioned as they could be too high. In any case, one may ask whether the reduction in output in the early 1990s was a result of the reforms that did away with the command economies or whether they simply followed the collapse from within of these economies.

Let us use yet another indicator, which attempts to take actual purchasing power into account (Table 2.3). The country differences are very well captured by the classification according to EC relationships. CORE EC and

Table 2.2   *Gross national product per capita, 1985–94*

Country set	GNPC85		GNPC89		GNPC92		GNPC94	
CORE EC	10 100	(6)	18 400	(6)	23 700	(6)	25 510	(6)
OTHER EC	5 720	(6)	10 450	(6)	14 100	(6)	15 085	(6)
OUTSIDE EC	12 400	(6)	22 370	(6)	26 200	(6)	25 947	(6)
CORE EAST	2 350	(5)	2 500	(5)	1 950	(6)	2 357	(6)
EAST PERIPHERY	2 040	(1)	2 950	(1)	3 150	(4)	2 748	(6)
All	7 635	(24)	13 450	(24)	14 585	(28)	14 329	(30)

Sources: GNPC85: World Bank (1987); GNPC89, GNPC92: World Bank (1994); GNPC94: World Bank (1996).

Table 2.3   *Purchasing power parities, 1991–94*

Country set	PPP91		PPP92		PPP94	
CORE EC	18 400	(6)	19 200	(6)	21 323	(6)
OTHER EC	12 600	(6)	13 100	(6)	15 226	(6)
OUTSIDE EC	17 950	(6)	18 200	(6)	19 813	(6)
CORE EAST	5 100	(6)	5 200	(6)	5 568	(6)
EAST PERIPHERY	6 135	(5)	4 100	(4)	4 205	(2)
All	12 724	(24)	12 527	(28)	14 615	(26)

Sources: PPP91: UNDP (1994); PPP92: OECD (1994c), World Bank (1994); PPP94: World Bank (1996).

OUTSIDE EC have a much higher level of affluence than the other three country sets, and at the same time there is a clear gulf between the two East European sets, CORE EAST and EAST PERIPHERY, and the remaining West European set, OTHER EC. Here we have an example of sharp divergence between the countries in Europe, the consequences of which for the differences in social structure will be examined in Chapter 3.

When one focuses upon purchasing power parities, then the distances between the country sets shrink considerably, but they remain wide with regard to the distinction between Western Europe and Eastern Europe. Purchasing power is not that low in the EAST CORE and it is only slightly higher than in EAST PERIPHERY. The set of OTHER EC countries are at a rather high level although not comparable with that of CORE EC and OUTSIDE EC. By measuring affluence by means of puchasing power parities one arrives at the following ranking of the richest countries for 1994: Luxembourg, Switzerland, Germany, France, Norway, Denmark, Austria and Belgium. And at the opposite end of the scale we had in the same year: Romania, Lithuania, Bulgaria, Poland, Latvia, Hungary, Slovakia and Estonia.

The pattern of affluence is transparently one of economic divergence, but what is the direction of change in the European economy? Let us now look at economic growth, the key question here being whether despite the

Table 2.4 *Economic growth in the 1990s (percentages)*

Country set	GNPC65–80, per capita	GNPC80–92, per capita	Real GDP growth			
			1991	1992	1993	1994
CORE EC	3.2 (5)	2.2 (6)	2.3	1.4	−.6	2.6 (6)
OTHER EC	3.4 (6)	2.5 (6)	1.5	1.4	.6	3.2 (6)
OUTSIDE EC	2.9 (5)	1.8 (6)	−.5	−.7	−.4	3.2 (6)
CORE EAST	5.1 (1)	.1 (4)	−12.3	−6.0	−1.0	3.2 (6)
EAST PERIPHERY	–	−1.0 (3)	−13.5	−20.3	−4.5	3.9 (6)
All	3.3 (17)	1.4 (25)	−4.5	−4.8	−1.2	3.2 (30)

Sources: GNPC65–80: UNDP (1994); GNPC80–92: World Bank (1994); Real GDP 1991–4: EBRD (1994, 1995), OECD (1994e, 1995c).

evidence of profound economic divergence in Europe along the EC distinctions there are any signs of economic convergence.

Economic Growth

Since we have already established that the distance in overall affluence between Western and Eastern Europe increased sharply at the end of the time period of the command economies it would be most interesting to focus on recent economic growth data. Such information would provide us with a clue to whether we may expect the economic differences to widen still further or if there is a process of convergence taking place, once the economic systems in Eastern Europe have been transformed. It may well be the case that things have to become worse before they become better in Eastern Europe.

Table 2.4 provides the most recently available information about economic growth in Europe. Can we detect any trend towards a pick up in the economies of Eastern Europe? As a matter of fact, there are in the growth figures for 1994 measuring the rate of change in real gross domestic product, signs of a turnaround in Eastern Europe. However, the late 1980s and early 1990s were dismal for both COR EAST and EAST PERIPHERY. It may be noted that CORE EC has had a slightly better growth performance than OUTSIDE EC during the latest recession.

When we look at the 1994 figures for economic growth, then we have evidence of economic convergence, because the top growth countries include some in Eastern Europe: Albania, Estonia, Ireland, Slovenia, Norway, Poland and the Slovak Republic as well as Denmark. However, the convergence trend is not a strong one as among the low growth countries we find also East European countries: Croatia, Greece, Bulgaria, Portugal, Lithuania, Latvia, Hungary, Spain, Switzerland and Sweden.

It does seem to be a warranted conclusion that the economies in Eastern Europe have gone through a harsh period of transformation in dismantling the planned economy in favour of a market economy. Most of them will

Table 2.5　*Economic growth rates and levels of affluence (Pearsons'
correlation)*

	GNPC65–80		GNPC80–92		GNPC85–93	
	E	WE	E	WE	E	WE
RGDPC50	−.79	−.82	.28	−.12	.14	−.47
RGDPC60	−.77	−.79	.26	−.21	.12	−.54
RGDPC70	−.72	−.71	.29	−.29	.18	−.57
RGDPC80	−.57	−.52	.33	−.27	.21	−.60
N	(17)	(16)	(22)	(18)	(23)	(18)

Sources: Tables 2.1, 2.4 and World Bank (1995a).

from now on pick up and begin to close part of the large gap between
themselves and the economies in Western Europe (Winiecki, 1994),
especially if they get their economic institutions correct.

If economic convergence works as the affluence-growth model predicts,
then national income should start expanding at a rapid pace in Eastern
Europe. The most recent evidence suggests that this is also taking place in
countries such as Estonia, Poland, Slovenia, the Slovak and Czech
Republics as well as Romania.

We test the convergence model for two sets of countries, Western
Europe (WE) and the whole of Europe (E), by computing a statistic for the
relationship between various measures of economic growth onto measures
of the level of affluence (Table 2.5). There are methodological difficulties
involved in the test of the convergence model, because factors other than
affluence impact on economic growth rates (Quah, 1993).

The chief finding here is that economic convergence has clearly taken
place in Western Europe since the end of the Second World War. The high
negative correlation between level of affluence and long-term average
economic growth rate in Western Europe implies the so-called catch-up
effect. The poor countries in Southern Europe have been able to close the
gap to the rich countries in Central and Northern Europe considerably.

But another finding in Table 2.5 is that it is too soon to tell how things
will go in Europe as a whole. There is a sign of a negative relationship
between level of affluence and economic growth for the entire Europe only
in the growth numbers for the first half of the 1990s ($r = -.29$). One may
ask whether convergence in affluence will be enhanced by the ongoing
process of institutional innovation in Eastern Europe. Let us examine this
problem some more.

Institutional Convergence

It is true that in certain respects it is premature to talk about economic
convergence in Europe, as the transition from one economic system to

another in the former Communist countries did involve a considerable loss of economic output. But there are two basic questions involved in the convergence theme. Besides the question of differences in economic affluence, there is the problem of economic institutions, or how quickly the East European countries are transforming their planned economies into a market economy. Various countries use different policies in order to introduce and enforce the institutions of the market economy, including the choice of privatization strategies to sell off the many state enterprises.

The outcomes of the reform strategies vary from one country to another in Eastern Europe. It seems as if the countries with high growth rates have come far in introducing so-called capitalist institutions whereas the process of institutional reform has been very slow in the Southern parts of Eastern Europe and perhaps also in Latvia and Lithuania in the North. Table 2.6 gives an overview of how far the institutional reforms of the economies in Eastern Europe have progressed. Besides bringing down the overall size of the public sector generally, different privatization strategies have been employed in various East European countries. On the one hand, the institutions of the market economy have been introduced, though with differing success and transparency. Here we find the protection of property rights and the introduction of financial markets, including a stock exchange. On the other hand, state enterprises have been hived off to the private sector using alternative strategies from floatation of shares over the sell out of entire companies to the distribution of shares to ordinary citizens. Land has been privatized and the weight of collectivist forms of agriculture has been reduced.

Although all the former Communist countries now have constitutional protection of private property rights, the vitality of private sector institutions differs considerably. The institutions of the market economy have been most successfully implemented in the former East Germany due to the highly energetic integration of the GDR into the FRG. The so-called *Treuhand* was given the responsibility for dismantling the public enterprises in the new *Länder* of the extended Germany, which it executed in a short time period of five years at no doubt staggering costs.

Comparing the 1994 data with the 1995 data in Table 2.6 the trend for Eastern Europe is crystal clear: marketization. In Albania, Romania and Bulgaria the institutions of the market economy have not yet emerged as strongly as one might have expected. In addition only a few big firms have been privatized, mainly to Western multinationals. The stock exchanges are not operating well and there are problems with the convertability of the currency. However, in the Czech Republic the private sector is clearly larger than the public sector, which also applies to Estonia, Poland, Hungary and the Slovak Republic. In some East European countries private ownership of land remains a problem to be sorted out. The dismantling of collective ownership or state ownership of land has become messy due to the numerous claims from people who used to own land

Table 2.6 *Institutional reforms of the economy*

	Private sector share of GDP (percentages)		Index of strength of market institutions	
	1994	1995	1994	1995
Albania	50	60	15	17
Bulgaria	40	45	15	16
Croatia	40	45	19	19
Czech Republic	65	70	21	21
Estonia	55	65	20	21
Hungary	55	60	20	21
Latvia	55	60	17	18
Lithuania	50	55	18	19
Poland	55	60	20	20
Romania	35	40	16	17
Slovakia	55	60	20	20
Slovenia	30	45	19	20

Note: The ranking of the place of market institutions in the economy is based on six dimensions: large-scale privatization, small-scale privatization, enterprise restructuring, price liberalization and competition, trade and foreign exchange system, and banking reform. Each country is ranked on each dimension from 1 to 4, where all West European countries have been given a total of 24.

Sources: EBRD (1994, 1995).

before the advent of communism. Thus, collective land ownership remains in place in, for example, Bulgaria, Albania and Lithuania.

However, one should not belittle the strength of civil society in Eastern Europe. Table 2.7 shows that despite the domination of the planned economy in Eastern Europe over many decades, the amount of private ownership of housing around 1990 was extensive indicating a certain amount of independence of civil society from government. The institutional transformation in Eastern Europe appears in the scales measuring economic freedom in the 1980s and the 1990s.

The resurrection of society at the expense of the state in Eastern Europe is a piecemeal process as no country tried a shock procedure of introducing market institutions overnight, as it were. Civil society with its economic institutions protecting private property and minimizing transaction costs by means of stock exchanges listing and evaluating joint stock companies for private shareholders may suffer setbacks when the process of change generates too much strain. The sharp rise in unemployment has provided the former Communist parties with ample opportunities to warn of the negative consequences of introducing capitalist institutions too quickly. Now, the probability of a convergence process between the East European and West European economies depends not insignificantly upon the speed with which they are integrated into the West European economies through increased trade. Let us look at the recent increase in trade between Western and Eastern Europe.

Table 2.7 *Economic freedom*

Country set	Private ownership in housing 1990	Economic freedom	
		1980s	1993–95
CORE EC	54.4 (6)	1.2 (6)	6.8 (5)
INSIDE EC	64.3 (6)	1.7 (6)	6.5 (6)
OUTSIDE EC	60.0 (6)	1.0 (6)	6.5 (6)
CORE EAST	70.8 (4)	4.8 (6)	4.2 (6)
EAST PERIPHERY	79.2 (2)	4.1 (7)	– (0)
All	63.0 (24)	2.5 (31)	6.0 (23)

Sources: The scores on economic freedom in the 1980s where low scores stand for high economic freedom are taken from Wright (1982) whereas the scores on economic freedom in the 1990s, scaled the other way around, are from Gwartney et al. (1996); private ownership in the housing sector estimated by the proportion of dwellings that are owner occupied stems from EB (1994); see also ECE (1995a).

Table 2.8 *Openness of the economy*

Country set	Impex 1990	Impex 1993
CORE EC	99.3 (6)	87.2 (6)
INSIDE EC	67.2 (6)	64.8 (6)
OUTSIDE EC	68.8 (6)	68.2 (6)
CORE EAST	56.0 (3)	71.8 (6)
EAST PERIPHERY	57.5 (2)	102.5 (4)
All	78.7 (23)	77.2 (28)

Sources: Impex 1990: EB (1994); Impex 1993: OECD (1995b), *Europa World Yearbook* (1995).

Trade Patterns: Increasing Interaction

The high level of affluence in Western Europe is based on the orientation of these economies towards extensive trade. The West European economies are without exception open economies, meaning that exports and imports account for a considerable portion of the GDP. This is true in particular of the small West European economies. The extent of openness is measured by the Impex indicator: exports plus imports as a share of GDP. Table 2.8 shows data on the variation in openness of the economies in Europe.

The Impex indicator maps dependency on trade. The countries that score very highly on the extent of openness in the economy include the small rich countries: Luxembourg, Belgium, Ireland, the Netherlands, Austria and Norway. The countries with a more closed economy are the large ones such as Italy, Spain, Poland, France, Germany and the United Kingdom. However, the main characteristic of the European economies,

Table 2.9   *Patterns of trade (percentages)*

Country set	Trade outside Europe				Trade with Western Europe		Trade with Eastern Europe	
	1990		1992		1990	1992	1990	1992
CORE EC	25	(6)	25	(6)	73	73	2	2
INSIDE EC	27	(6)	26	(6)	72	73	2	1
OUTSIDE EC	26	(6)	24	(6)	72	73	3	3
CORE EAST	48	(5)	27	(2)	37	65	14	7
EAST PERIPHERY	37	(1)	47	(2)	53	35	10	18
All	31	(24)	27	(22)	64	68	5	4

Source: UN (1993a).

also those of Eastern Europe, is a fairly large extent of openness in the economy. The main developmental trend is that openness is up sharply for the East European countries as they are dismantling their connections according to the COMECON framework.

One may take one more step and look at how trade is conducted. Which countries trade with which countries? Table 2.9 contains a few indicators that describe how the European countries trade with themselves and the world outside of Europe. We include data from two time points in the early 1990s in order to see if we can detect any trend, however small in the pattern of trade, which is measured in terms of percentage shares of the trade with various parts of the globe.

Already in the early 1990s it is possible to detect that changes have taken place in the trading patterns. What we are referring to is the East European countries (CORE EAST and EAST PERIPHERY) where trade with mainly Russia is decreasing rapidly but trade with Western Europe is increasing quickly. It appears that there is extensive intra trade within Western Europe, or about 73 per cent of the traded goods and services in West European countries come from these very same countries. Considering these numbers there is little wonder about the force behind European economic integration in terms of the creation of the Common Market. Eastern Europe will certainly add to the already huge internal trade within Europe, especially the CORE EC countries.

Economic Stability

The fate of the process of institutional reform in Eastern Europe hinges upon the development of economic stability in these countries. What matters to each and every one is the standard of living, which has more flavour than what the simple GDP or GNP scores can convey. Let us begin with unemployment and inflation.

One may employ the distinction between the short-run and the long-run perspective when one analyses the overall state of the economy. Actually,

Table 2.10   *Unemployment 1990–4*

Country set	1990		1992		1994	
CORE EC	7.5	(6)	8.0	(6)	9.4	(6)
OTHER EC	9.5	(6)	11.5	(6)	12.7	(6)
OUTSIDE EC	2.5	(6)	5.5	(6)	7.6	(6)
CORE EAST	2.5	(5)	10.5	(6)	11.4	(6)
EAST PERIPHERY	4.0	(4)	10.0	(6)	9.9	(6)
All	5.4	(27)	9.1	(30)	10.2	(30)

Sources: EBRD (1994, 1995); OECD (1994e, 1995d).

macroeconomic aggregates can vary extensively from one year to another, which is why it makes sense to average out extreme values for one year or two. The long-run perspective looks at average scores, for instance with regard to economic growth rates. But it holds true that sharp short-term fluctuations may have significant political repercussions, especially in sensitive aggregates such as unemployment and inflation. Table 2.10 presents information about the increase in unemployment.

That unemployment has become a major characteristic feature of Europe in the 1990s is apparent from Table 2.10. In 1994 the average unemployment figures for all the country sets with the exception of OUTSIDE EC lie around 10 per cent of the workforce. One may establish that the economies in Europe differ much less on unemployment than on total output. It should be pointed out that unemployment statistics have to be handled with caution, because the figures tend not to be strictly reliable, due to the fact that definitions of 'employment' and 'economically active' vary between countries.

The 1990 unemployment scores reflect the entirely different approach to employment in the former command economies, where employment was a citizen right. The transition to a market economy has been attended by sharp increases in unemployment, as it is now no longer possible to have redundancies in the labour force in the new firms meaning much unemployment especially in countries where the transition process is sluggish. However, since unemployment has shot up also in Western Europe the country differences between Western and Eastern Europe are less pronounced now than before. Unemployment is very high or above 12 per cent in the following countries: Spain, Albania, Finland, Poland, the Slovak Republic, Slovenia, Ireland, Croatia, Bulgaria and Belgium as well as France and Denmark. And it is much lower, or beneath 6 per cent, in the following countries: Estonia, Luxembourg, Lithuania, Austria, Switzerland, Norway, the Czech Republic and Iceland.

And what about inflation? Table 2.11 gives average and yearly data for inflation (INF). We have already seen that unemployment has increased considerably during the recent depression. The data indicate divergence, but hyperinflation in Eastern Europe is on the decline.

Inflation has clearly been reduced all over Europe in the 1990s. But

Table 2.11   *Inflation*

Country set	INF85–93	INF91	INF92	INF93	INF94
CORE EC (6)	3.4	3.9	3.4	3.2	2.7
OTHER EC (6)	7.8	8.1	6.6	5.0	4.6
OUTSIDE EC (6)	6.0	5.5	3.2	3.4	1.7
CORE EAST (6)	39.5	127.3	61.0	72.5	42.7
EAST PERIPHERY (6)	52.6*	235.2	725.7	243.8	24.0
All (30)	19.6	76.0	160.0	65.6	15.1

Note: * = 4 cases.

Sources: INF85–93: World Bank (1995a); INF 1991–4: EBRD (1994, 1995), OECD (1994e, 1995c).

Table 2.12   *Current deficits and state debt as a percentage of GDP*

Country set	Central government deficit		Total state debt, 1991
	1991	1993	
CORE EC	−4.4 (5)	−4.8 (5)	80.7 (5)
OTHER EC	−5.9 (6)	−5.2 (6)	68.2 (5)
OUTSIDE EC	−0.8 (4)	−10.5 (3)	41.3 (4)
CORE EAST	−4.2 (5)	−5.0 (3)	–
EAST PERIPHERY	−7.3 (2)	−0.7 (2)	–
All	−4.4 (22)	−5.4 (19)	65.0 (14)

Sources: Deficit: UNDP (1994: 206), World Bank (1995b: 181); Debt: UNDP (1994: 198).

hyperinflation has occurred in several East European countries, reflecting the frequent use of seigniorage (governments paying by printing money) in these countries. Inflation has been particularly bad in the following countries: Poland, Lithuania, Latvia, Estonia, Romania and Bulgaria. The economies with low inflation include: the Netherlands, Ireland, France, Belgium, Austria, Denmark and Germany. Yet, the pattern is not one of divergence over time as several West European countries also have substantial rates of inflation such as Iceland, Greece, Portugal, Italy and Spain around 1990–1. At the same time one must observe that inflation tends to stabilize in the former command economies. In 1994 only Bulgaria had an inflation rate above 100 per cent, but it remains true that inflation is a divergence aspect of the European economies.

Inflation in Western Europe has been highly subdued during the recession in the early 1990s, characterized by deflationary pressures in several markets. But the recession in the early 1990s involved that deficit spending by governments increased thus augmenting the accumulated state debt (Table 2.12).

Deficit spending is certainly not confined to Eastern Europe. A number of countries had high yearly deficits in the early 1990s including Greece,

Table 2.13 *Human development index 1970–95*

Country set	HDI70		HDI85		HDI90		HDI94		HDI95	
CORE EC	.85	(6)	.98	(5)	.97	(5)	.91	(6)	.92	(6)
OTHER EC	.81	(6)	.96	(6)	.95	(6)	.89	(6)	.91	(6)
OUTSIDE EC	.86	(6)	.99	(6)	.98	(5)	.92	(6)	.93	(6)
CORE EAST	.82	(5)	.93	(5)	.91	(5)	.82	(5)	.83	(6)
EAST PERIPHERY	.76	(1)	.92	(1)	.85	(2)	.83	(4)	.81	(4)
All	.83	(24)	.96	(23)	.94	(23)	.88	(27)	.88	(28)

Sources: HDI 1970–95: UNDP (1990, 1991, 1992, 1994, 1995).

Albania, Italy, Bulgaria and Poland; but those countries with a low or high yearly deficit one year are not always the same as those with a low or a high deficit the following year. A huge state debt was to be found in Belgium, Italy, Ireland, Greece and the Netherlands. Although data are missing it is well known that some East European countries are heavily burdened by an accumulated state debt, such as Hungary. Sweden is an example of how large deficits may be turned into a huge state debt in a relatively short period of time.

One may wish to broaden the analysis of economic outcomes further by taking into account indicators on quality of life including social correlates of economic development such as life expectancy and illiteracy. Or one may enquire into how national income is divided in the population.

Quality of Life: Human Development Index and Income Distribution

Much effort has been devoted to complementing the economic indicators on well-being by somehow integrating measures of the social correlates of poverty and affluence, respectively. One widely used indicator is the broad human development index, which takes three conditions into account, namely life expectancy, educational attainment and real GDP per capita (PPP in US dollars).

Table 2.13 illustrates how the level of human development has increased steadily in Western Europe since the Second World War, which involved massive destruction all over Europe, but also that Eastern Europe suffered a decline in the aftermath of the system transition in 1989–90.

The interesting finding in Table 2.13 is not that there are systematic differences between the country sets, where the East European sets show lower human development scores than the West European sets. But what amazes one is that the differences are so small when it comes to measuring quality of life by an index that takes several aspects of well-being into account including total output per capita. Although the scores for CORE EAST and EAST PERIPHERY are probably somewhat too low due to the few cases for which there is reliable data, it is still the case that the differences are not great. Countries in OUTSIDE EC tend to score somewhat higher than those in

Table 2.14   *Income inequality in the 1990s*

	Income of lowest 20%	Income of highest 10%	Income of highest 20%	Ratio
CORE EC	7.0 (5)	23.7 (5)	39.2 (4)	5.7 (5)
OTHER EC	5.5 (5)	25.8 (5)	39.8 (3)	7.0 (3)
OUTSIDE EC	4.2 (6)	25.9 (6)	39.0 (4)	6.3 (4)
CORE EAST	10.0 (4)	21.7 (4)	36.6 (3)	3.5 (3)
EAST PERIPHERY	5.3 (1)	27.4 (1)	–	–
All	6.3 (21)	24.6 (21)	38.7 (15)	5.7 (15)

Sources: Lowest 20% and highest 10% share of income: EB (1994), Highest 20%: World Bank (1995b: 220–21); Ratio of income of highest 20% households to lowest 20% households between 1980 and 1992: UNDP (1995: 197).

CORE EC and a little higher than those in OTHER EC. On the whole, the human development index scores very high for Europe which partly explains its attraction for migration waves from other continents.

Finally, Table 2.14 renders information about the distribution of income. Actually, in the literature on the measurement of affluence and standard of living the lack of information about how the national income is distributed has been considered a major omission. High GDP scores or significant GDP growth figures may not mean much for the quality of life of the average citizen, if the fruits of high economic output are not shared among all.

Income equality may be enhanced by two different factors, affluence and public policy. One the one hand, redistributive policies of various kinds may accomplish more income equality, if they work as intended. On the other hand, income equality is predicted to rise when the overall level of affluence goes up. All over Europe the poorest 20 per cent of the population receive about 5–6 per cent of the national income whereas the richest 10 per cent take about 25 per cent. The fact that income inequality is roughly the same in Europe reflects two different conditions enhancing equality, namely, affluence in the West and redistributive policies in the East.

Yet, one may note that despite redistributional ambitions in the West income inequalities remain large, even within OUTSIDE EC where the Nordic countries are harboured with their policy orientation towards promoting equality of incomes. At the same time one must take into account that the fall in total output after 1989 has meant not only less for the average citizen in Eastern Europe but also increasing income inequalities (Atkinson and Micklewright, 1992).

Although income distribution data are not available for all European countries, Table 2.14 indicates that income inequality is slightly higher among countries within OTHER EC, that is, countries that are neither rich nor poor nor have experienced the substantial welfare state ambitions to redistribute life opportunities. The overall picture is that income equality is most even in the CORE EAST countries and least equal in Southern Europe, the United Kingdom and Switzerland. In the Swiss case the explanation is simply that redistributive ambitions never received a prominent place in public policy whereas in the United Kingdom it may partly be explained by the rise of the New Right to government power (Atkinson et al., 1995).

Conclusion

Economic divergence is the most conspicuous feature of the European economies. The country differences may be summarized by a simple grouping of the countries along the classification of European countries introduced in the Introductory chapter. CORE EC and OUTSIDE EC countries are very affluent, OTHER EC countries are affluent whereas CORE EAST and EAST PERIPHERY countries are poor, by European standards that is. It should be emphasized that the differences between the country sets in economic affluence are so pronounced that it will be vital in the coming chapters to examine what the consequences are for society in general and politics in particular.

Economic integration in Europe proceeds along two lines, one concerns economic institutions and the other relates to trade. One visible aspect of the first is the integration of the financial markets in Europe, including their extension to cover the East European countries. With regard to the second aspect, there is the ever-growing reciprocity between the economies in Europe as manifested by the explosion in intra-regional and between-region trade in goods and services as well as in the mobility of labour. The internationalization of the country economies of all European states with a sharp increase in trade between almost all the countries on the European continent is a profound process enhancing convergence.

Today there are institutional processes resulting in the creating of common institutions and the harmonization of regulations for economic activity. They are driven by the EU on the one hand, and by the profound system transitions taking place in the former Communist countries on the other hand. The introduction and implementation of the institutions of the market economy in Eastern Europe has met with varying success in different countries. In Estonia, Poland, the Czech Republic and Hungary the so-called capitalist institutions safeguarding extensive private property rights, allocating capital to joint stock companies by means of stock exchanges and providing for currency convertability are in place. In Bulgaria, Romania and Lithuania several of the large enterprises remain state companies and collective ownership of land is still a reality.

We predict that the European economies will grow more alike on macroeconomic aggregates as these two major integrative forces work themselves out in full scale. Thus, we will see more economic convergence around the year 2000. The process of increasing similarities between the European economies includes not only total output but also unemployment, inflation and deficit spending and state debts. It must be admitted though that the evidence for the start of a convergence process in terms of total output or affluence is not clear-cut. Economic divergence remains a highly characteristic feature of the European economies.

Now what are the social implications of economic structure? The structure of society has an open texture meaning that one dimension does not mirror another, at least not completely. Can we draw the conclusion from the evidence in this chapter about sharp economic differences between the country sets that also social structure when unpacked into its various aspects varies tremendously between the country sets? Chapter 3 is devoted to this question.

3

Social Structures

Chapter 2 outlined the profile of the economies of the countries in Europe. The purpose in this chapter is to begin looking at the consequences of the vast economic differences between European countries by examining the social attributes of economic structure. In Chapters 5 to 9 we enquire into whether also political differences between the European countries reflect the substantial divergence between the economies of these countries.

Let us start by asking the following question: What traces of the evolution of a post-industrial society can we find in data about the social structure of the European countries? According to Emile Durkheim societies develop towards an increasingly refined division of labour which puts pressure on social cohesion (Durkheim, 1964, 1970). To him, writing at the turn of the century, the reduction in agrarian employment and the profound urbanization process was attended by anomie, or the lack of integration in terms of a shared system of values. Is this model still of relevance when we come to the post-industrial society in Europe evolving after the Second World War (Bell, 1976a)?

First, structural characteristics are examined concerning population structure and the labour force. Second, we deal with how advanced the social structure is by examining data about access to information of various kinds. How different are the country sets in terms of access to modern information technology? Third, we examine those aspects of social structure that one refers to as social cohesion. The legacy of Communism must loom large over Eastern Europe, but did it involve an entirely different social structure accompanied by a different type of social cohesion? Are there perhaps signs of anomie or alienation in both Western and Eastern Europe? Finally, we look at gender-related developments, as the post-industrial society combines a high level of affluence with a strong commitment to equality.

Demographic Structure

Looking at the overall size of the population in the countries of Europe we observe that the size of the country populations differ tremendously among the European countries, from tiny Iceland with 250 000 inhabitants to giant Germany with 82 million people. Interestingly, there are systematic differences between the sets of countries that we operate with (Table 3.1).

As the data confirm, the populations in Europe have been growing

Table 3.1   *Size of population 1950–94 (thousands)*

Country set	1950		1970		1994	
	Average	CV	Average	CV	Average	CV
CORE EC (6)	29 300	.92	34 200	.90	37 200	.88
OTHER EC (6)	16 900	1.11	19 200	1.10	21 100	1.07
OUTSIDE EC (6)	4 350	.59	5 000	.57	5 600	.56
CORE EAST (6)	11 700	.66	14 400	.72	16 000	.79
EAST PERIPHERY (7)	2 800	.78	3 400	.76	4 100	.75
All (31)	12 700	1.34	14 900	1.31	16 400	1.29

Note: The coefficient of variation (CV) measures the amount of variation within a set: the higher the CV, the larger the variation within a set.

Sources: EB (1994, 1995).

Table 3.2   *Population growth 1950–93 (percentages)*

Country set	1950–60	1960–70	1970–80	1980–90	1990–93
CORE EC (6)	.8	.9	.5	.3	.6
OTHER EC (6)	.5	.6	.8	.2	.2
OUTSIDE EC (6)	1.1	1.0	.4	.5	.7
CORE EAST (6)	1.2	.8	.6	.3	− .3
EAST PERIPHERY (7)	1.3	1.4	1.0	.8	.1
All (31)	1.0	.9	.7	.5	.3

Source: EB (1994).

slowly since the end of the Second World War. The average country population is up from some 12.7 million people in 1950 to roughly 16.4 million today – an increase of almost 30 per cent over a period of 50 years, that is, less than 1 per cent a year. The finding here though is that the country variations have decreased. The small countries are to be found in the OUTSIDE EC set and the EAST PERIPHERY set whereas the other sets comprise much larger populations. One must recognize that the countries within the country sets are far from similar, as the CV scores indicate.

The large countries in Europe include besides Germany, the United Kingdom, France, Italy, Spain, Poland and Romania in descending order, according to the 1994 data. The small countries comprise Iceland, Luxembourg, Estonia, Slovenia, Latvia, Albania and Ireland.

The two sets of East European countries have moved closer to the three sets of West European countries in terms of the size of the country population, but will this trend be maintained? Table 3.2 offers a few clues about what to expect in the decade to come.

From Table 3.2 it appears that the most recent trends are quite the opposite to those overall trends for the entire period since 1945. Popula-

Table 3.3 *Age distribution 1960–92 (percentages)*

Country set	1960		1970		1980		1992	
	<14	>65	<14	>65	<14	>65	<14	>65
CORE EC (6)	25	11	24	12	21	13	18	15 (6)
OTHER EC (6)	27	10	27	11	25	12	20	15 (6)
OUTSIDE EC (6)	27	10	25	12	22	13	19	15 (6)
CORE EAST (5)	28	8	24	10	24	11	22	12 (6)
EAST PERIPHERY (2)	35	6	35	6	31	7	23	12 (7)
All (25)	27	9	26	11	23	12	20	14 (31)

Sources: 1960–70: World Bank (1980); 1980: World Bank (1984); 1992: ILO (1993b), UN (1994), EB (1995), UNDP (1995).

tion growth is higher in Western Europe than in Eastern Europe, reflecting partly the heavy immigration to the former countries as a result of the system crisis in the latter countries, and partly reflecting a demographic crisis with decreasing birth rates as, for instance, in former East Germany (Eberstadt, 1994).

In the foreseeable future there will no longer be higher rates of population increase in Eastern Europe than in Western Europe. Recently, population growth has been most rapid in Albania, Iceland, Austria, Luxembourg and the Netherlands and slowest in Bulgaria, Latvia, Estonia, Romania and Hungary.

At the same time as one observes that population growth is low in Europe today, it remains the case that the population has grown by some 30 per cent since 1950, partly due also to immigration. There is a real absolute increase in the number of people in all the five country sets, which one must remember when looking at relative figures on employment or political participation.

Now, one salient aspect of the demographic structure is the age distribution. Table 3.3 gives data about the relative sizes of certain cohorts such as the young (< 14 years) and the elderly (> 65 years). Countries with the largest component of elderly include Sweden, Norway, the United Kingdom, Denmark, Austria, Germany and Switzerland, whereas the lowest component of elderly is to be found in Yugoslavia, Poland, Iceland, Slovenia, Lithuania and Romania. At the moment there is thus an East–West difference here in that whereas the group of elderly is almost as large as the group of youngsters in Western Europe, it is only half that size in Eastern Europe.

The main developmental trend in Table 3.3 is the same for the various country sets. It is characteristic of the CORE EC set and the OUTSIDE EC set, namely, the richest countries in Europe, that they tend to have a larger proportion of elderly and a smaller proportion of youngsters than the other sets, particularly the East European countries. But the overall trend in the population structure is that the differences between the country sets

Table 3.4   *Labour force participation*

Country set	1970		1980		1990	
	Average	CV	Average	CV	Average	CV
CORE EC (6)	40.7	.06	42.0	.05	45.3	.07
INSIDE EC (6)	41.3	.11	42.7	.17	45.0	.16
OUTSIDE EC (6)	44.8	.10	48.7	.07	50.7	.05
CORE EAST (6)	52.2	.04	50.7	.03	48.5	.05
EAST PERIPHERY (7)	46.7	.07	48.6	.09	49.3	.07
All (31)	45.2	.12	46.6	.11	47.8	.09

Sources: Marer et al. (1992), OECD (1992), ILO (1993b), EB (1994).

decline as the relative size of the young cohort declines everywhere and the relative size of the elderly cohort also increases in Eastern Europe.

Occupational Structure

Another relevant aspect of social structure is sectoral employment. Besides agriculture and industry one must today include the service sector when describing the fundamentals of the occupational structure in general – that is, how the labour force is distributed over different kinds of employment. We expect to find considerable differences between the country sets in occupational structure, but what is the overall development? Let us begin by looking at labour force participation – that is, the proportion of the population employed or actively seeking work (Table 3.4).

Clear differences used to exist between the country sets with regard to labour force participation, as the participation rate was consistently higher in Eastern than in Western Europe.

Looking at the distribution in the 1970 data, the following countries had the highest rates of labour force participation: Romania, Hungary, Poland, Czechoslovakia, Latvia, Switzerland and Sweden. The lowest rates were to be found among the Netherlands, Ireland, Spain, Belgium, Iceland and Italy.

However, in the early 1990s little is left of these differences. Convergence is enhanced as a result of considerably higher participation rates in Western Europe and lower rates in Eastern Europe. One may surmise that the increases in Western Europe reflect the major changes involved with the entrance of women into the labour force while at the same time the participation rate is somewhat lower in the East. In 1990 the following countries had the highest participation rates: Latvia, Sweden, Switzerland, Finland, Lithuania, Bulgaria and Czechoslovakia. The lowest rates were to be found in Ireland, Greece, Spain, Belgium, France, Italy and Hungary. At the same time the low CV scores indicate that the countries within the five sets tend to be rather similar.

Let us proceed with the analysis of the occupational structure by looking

Table 3.5   *Female workforce participation/labour force*

Country set	1970		1980		1990		1993	
	Average	CV	Average	CV	Average	CV	Average	CV
CORE EC (6)	30.3	.16	34.5	.12	39.5	.08	40.3	.09
INSIDE EC (6)	29.3	.21	35.0	.20	39.3	.14	40.0	.14
OUTSIDE EC (6)	36.7	.14	39.8	.15	43.3	.09	43.5	.09
CORE EAST (6)	43.8	.04	45.2	.02	45.7	.03	46.3	.03
EAST PERIPHERY (7)	43.6	.16	44.1	.14	45.4	.10	46.7	.08
All (31)	37.0	.22	39.9	.17	42.7	.11	43.5	.11

Note: Missing values in some cases have been replaced by estimated scores.

Sources: OECD (1983, 1995a), World Bank (1984), Marer et al. (1992), ILO (1993b, 1994, 1995), EB (1995).

at the participation of women in the workforce, meaning the women who either are employed or actively seek work as a percentage of the total labour force (Table 3.5). Here, the finding is that of another kind of convergence, namely that the West European countries are growing more like the East European ones, which already in 1970 had an extensive female workforce. Even today the level of female participation in employment is larger in the CORE EAST and EAST PERIPHERY sets than in the sets of West European countries, scoring above 40 per cent. Again the low CV scores inform us how similar countries are within the country sets.

In 1990 the highest rates of female participation occur in Estonia, Latvia, Lithuania, Sweden, the Czech Republic, Finland and Slovakia. The lowest rates are displayed by Catholic countries such as Ireland, Luxembourg, Spain, Italy but also Orthodox Greece and heterogeneous Switzerland.

The above convergence in the labour force derives from women's emancipation in Western Europe. In the last decades women have increasingly entered the labour market in the capitalist countries. This is evident when looking at another measure on female participation, relating the female workforce to all women (Table 3.6). The percentage of women who work or seek work seems to have stabilized at around 40 per cent in Europe, somewhat lower in the EC countries and somewhat higher in Eastern Europe.

One would wish to include data about other aspects of employment such as the size of the labour force in agriculture and industry as well as the relative portion of those in third sector employment, but the inherited structure of the planned economies in Eastern Europe makes it difficult to make comparisons. Here we start with data about the size of the labour force that is active in agriculture (Table 3.7), which information presents few problems of validity and reliability.

The obvious trend evident from Table 3.7 is a sharp reduction everywhere in the number of people employed in agriculture. On average the relative size of the population in agriculture has been cut by half in only 20

Table 3.6   *Female workforce participation/all women*

Country set	1970		1980		1990		1993	
	Average	CV	Average	CV	Average	CV	Average	CV
CORE EC (6)	24.0	.21	28.3	.15	35.0	.07	35.5	.11
INSIDE EC (6)	24.3	.32	29.5	.36	35.5	.30	36.0	.28
OUTSIDE EC (6)	31.8	.19	37.7	.18	43.3	.12	42.3	.09
CORE EAST (6)	44.5	.06	44.3	.05	45.8	.04	42.8	.12
EAST PERIPHERY (7)	41.1	.22	42.7	.20	43.6	.16	43.6	.14
All (31)	33.4	.32	36.7	.26	40.7	.18	40.2	.17

Sources: See Table 3.5.

Table 3.7   *Agrarian employment (percentages)*

Country set	1970		1980		1990		1993	
	Average	CV	Average	CV	Average	CV	Average	CV
CORE EC (6)	10.5	.54	7.0	.58	4.9	.49	4.3	.44
INSIDE EC (6)	23.3	.58	17.5	.62	12.8	.64	10.2	.66
OUTSIDE EC (6)	14.4	.39	9.7	.34	7.0	.35	6.9	.56
CORE EAST (6)	30.3	.42	20.6	.35	19.7	.33	18.7	.60
EAST PERIPHERY (7)	35.9	.44	25.1	.56	23.1	.65	17.6	.37
All (31)	23.3	.64	16.3	.68	13.9	.78	11.7	.73

Sources: Vienna (1991, 1995), Marer et al. (1992, 1993), OECD (1992, 1995a), ILO (1993b, 1994, 1995), EB (1994), ECE (1995b).

years. Yet, despite convergence the differences between the country sets remain pronounced, where especially the CORE EC and the OUTSIDE EC sets are distinct with a tiny portion of the population in agriculture. The relative size of the population employed in agriculture is substantially larger in the OTHER EC, CORE EAST and EAST PERIPHERY sets, but it is clearly on the retreat in all countries in Europe. And what about employment in industry (Table 3.8)?

Industrial employment proper declines in all the West European sets, a prediction that the theory of the post-industrial society entails. At the same time industrial employment is more extensive in Eastern Europe than in Western Europe but total output is much larger in the latter than in the former. The only possible interpretation is that labour productivity is substantially higher in countries where third sector employment looms large. It seems that all countries converge on the tendency that higher levels of industrial output may be accomplished by fewer people employed in industry.

Table 3.9 gives data about the levels of service employment which

Table 3.8   *Employment in industry (percentages)*

Country set	1970		1980		1990		1993	
	Average	CV	Average	CV	Average	CV	Average	CV
CORE EC (6)	42.3	.09	37.0	.11	31.2	.15	29.7	.17
INSIDE EC (6)	34.3	.20	33.9	.10	30.2	.10	28.1	.10
OUTSIDE EC (6)	39.2	.11	35.1	.11	31.1	.14	28.0	.14
CORE EAST (6)	40.7	.18	44.9	.09	42.0	.10	36.8	.13
EAST PERIPHERY (7)	35.1	.21	38.5	.18	37.1	.20	35.8	.21
All (31)	38.2	.17	37.9	.15	34.4	.19	31.8	.20

Sources: See Table 3.7.

Table 3.9   *Service employment (percentages)*

Country set	1970		1980		1990		1993	
	Average	CV	Average	CV	Average	CV	Average	CV
CORE EC (6)	47.2	.12	56.1	.11	64.0	.08	66.0	.09
OTHER EC (6)	42.4	.18	48.6	.22	57.1	.16	61.8	.13
OUTSIDE EC (6)	46.4	.09	55.3	.10	61.9	.08	65.1	.10
CORE EAST (6)	29.1	.19	34.6	.13	38.3	.15	44.6	.22
EAST PERIPHERY (7)	29.0	.36	36.4	.25	39.8	.21	46.6	.17
All (31)	38.5	.28	45.9	.25	51.8	.25	56.5	.21

Sources: See Table 3.7.

confirm the above interpretation. This concept stands for both the public sector workforce and such categories in the private sector as personnel in the financial sectors, the hotel and the travel businesses. In the so-called advanced countries in Western Europe, namely the CORE EC and OUTSIDE EC sets, third sector employment is almost twice as large as in the CORE EAST and EAST PERIPHERY sets. At the same time service employment is rising in all country sets.

The highest levels of service employment are to be found in Northern Europe: the Netherlands, Belgium, the United Kingdom, Norway, Sweden and Denmark. On the other hand, East European countries display the lowest rates such as Albania, Bulgaria, Poland, Lithuania and Slovakia. Third sector employment is of roughly the same size in CORE EC and OUTSIDE EC countries, or around 65 per cent of total employment, and these countries have the most advanced economies in Europe. The transformation of employment in Europe has been dramatic during the last decades involving a rise in overall service employment from less than 40 per cent to almost 60 per cent, while at the same time the labour force has grown substantially due to population increase and the emancipation of women.

Table 3.10   *Newspapers, radio and television per capita, around 1990*

Country set	Newspapers	Radio	Television
CORE EC	28.5 (6)	2.1 (6)	2.8 (6)
OTHER EC	19.7 (6)	2.4 (6)	3.5 (6)
OUTSIDE EC	50.2 (5)	1.6 (6)	2.9 (6)
CORE EAST	33.0 (4)	4.1 (6)	3.7 (6)
EAST PERIPHERY	4.0 (1)	5.3 (7)	5.1 (7)
All	17.5 (22)	3.2 (31)	3.6 (31)

Note: The indicator on newspapers measures how large a proportion of the population reads one daily paper (UNDP, 1994), the indicator on access to radio measures the number of persons per radio (EB, 1994) and the indicator on access to television is scored in the same way (EB, 1994).

European Post-industrialism: The Information and Media Society

The available information about the latent aspects of social structure in Europe indicates convergence. Although there remain considerable country differences – West versus East but also North versus South – with regard to the relative size of agricultural employment, it is true that all countries in Europe have been affected by the emergence of a post-industrial society: low population growth rates, high female workforce participation, a sharp reduction in agrarian employment as well as a clear advance in service employment. And what about the important aspects of the post-industrial society that are linked with information technologies? What are the main country differences?

The post-industrial society is often said to be connected with a culture called 'modernity'. One of the characteristics of modernity is the major role that information plays in the day-to-day lives of people. Access to information is channelled through various mass media and the availability of information technologies for people differ from one country to another. Here we focus upon three aspects: the spread of newspapers, radios and televisions, the use of telephones, modern information technology and the size of research and deveopment (R&D) resources.

Table 3.10 comprises data on how widely spread a few standard communication media are in the population of a country. There are clear differences between Western Europe and Eastern Europe in terms of access to the media. This is true in particular of the more advanced information technologies such as radio and television. When it comes to reading newspapers regularly there is also a North–South division, as people in Northern Europe read newspapers much more regularly than people in Southern Europe.

Table 3.11 takes a look at the use of telephones, which is one of the key mechanisms of communication in the information society.

As is the case with newspapers, radio and television, the country set with

Table 3.11 *Telephones, around 1990–2*

Country set	Number of telephones per 100	Number of lines per 1000
CORE EC	59.2 (6)	448.5 (6)
OTHER EC	47.2 (6)	374.0 (6)
OUTSIDE EC	67.2 (6)	537.7 (6)
CORE EAST	21.6 (5)	94.7 (3)
EAST PERIPHERY	17.3 (4)	–
All	45.1 (27)	402.1 (21)

Sources: Number of telephones: UNDP (1994); number of lines: World Bank (1994).

Table 3.12 *Users of Internet per 1000 inhabitants*

Country set	January 1995
CORE EC (5)	2.5
OTHER EC (3)	3.2
OUTSIDE EC (5)	8.3
CORE EAST (2)	.7
EAST PERIPHERY (0)	–
All (15)	4.3

Source: *The Economist*, 1–7 July 1995.

the best access to the use of the telephone technology is OUTSIDE EC, which comprises the rich Nordic countries and the affluent Central European countries of Austria and Switzerland. Table 3.11 confirms the impression from Table 3.10 that the information society is the affluent society. This observation is further corroborated by the fact that OTHER EC scores consistently lower than CORE EC, the former comprising the less affluent countries in Southern Europe. Table 3.12 presents data about the use of one high-tech information system, the Internet.

Not surprisingly, the use of such a sophisticated information technology as the Internet is most widespread in the very rich countries in Europe. At the moment Northern Europe has more Internet users than Central Europe, which in turn precede Southern and Eastern Europe. But these numbers may have changed in a year's time due to the rapid spread of high-tech information systems, especially in the countries that can afford them.

One may wish to include data about the occurrence of innovations in society indicating its overall level of advancement. Thus, Table 3.13 covers expenditures on research and development (R&D) as a percentage of GDP as well as the number of patent applications and patents granted per capita. Is the picture of country differences the same with regard to these aspects?

One must be aware of the fact that there are measurement problems in the data in Table 3.13, because various countries employ different ways of measuring the items. However, allowing for such irregularities, which help

Table 3.13   *Costs for research and development, number of patents and patent applications, around 1990*

	R&D/GDP	Patent applications	Patents granted
CORE EC	2.0 (5)	164.6 (6)	34.8 (6)
OTHER EC	1.1 (6)	23.5 (6)	2.8 (6)
OUTSIDE EC	1.9 (5)	40.2 (6)	11.6 (6)
CORE EAST	2.4 (5)	5.5 (5)	2.2 (5)
EAST PERIPHERY	–	–	–
All	1.8 (21)	60.7 (23)	13.3 (23)

Sources: Resources for R&D as a percentage of GDP: UNDP (1994); number of patent applications per capita: UN (1993b); patents granted per capita: UN (1993b).

explain the enormous differences in the scores, a somewhat mixed picture emerges. The small differences in R&D effort may be explained by the simple fact that the GDP is much higher in Western Europe than in Eastern Europe. What is probably more telling is the large differences in the number of patent applications and patents granted. Here, there is a wide gulf between the West and the East, but among the Western sets of countries CORE EC has the lead by a wide margin. The low figure for number of patents granted in OTHER EC is worth looking at more closely.

Again it should be pointed out that it is problematic to compare country data on patent applications and patents accepted, because the definition of a patent may differ from one country to another. However, patents do have a dynamic importance for social change so that one wishes to indicate their occurrence in various countries somehow. First we may establish that there is a high correlation between the two measures meaning that in countries with many applications also several patents get accepted. Thrift gives rise to ingenuity. Second we note that the countries with the highest scores on both indicators are those with the highest per capita income.

Whereas the data about the main trends in the occupational structure of European societies confirmed the prediction about the coming of a post-industrial society, the information above concerning various aspects of how advanced the countries are in terms of technology indicate considerable differences among the country sets. What we are talking about here is the level of modernity, where there is divergence between the country sets. Most modern is OUTSIDE EC, although the difference to CORE EC is not large. There is a vast gulf between these two sets and the East European sets with OTHER EC somewhere in between the least advanced and the most advanced post-modern societies. And now, what about the manifest aspects of social structure, that is, social cohesion?

Social Cohesion

Durkheim argued that the blessings of modernity involved a social cost for the individuals (Durkheim, 1964). Higher levels of income stemming from

Table 3.14   *Social cohesion: homicide and suicide*

Country set	Intentional homicide per 100 000	Suicide per 100 000	
		Men	Women
CORE EC	1.7 (6)	21.8 (6)	8.3 (6)
OTHER EC	1.7 (6)	14.7 (6)	5.3 (6)
OUTSIDE EC	1.8 (6)	28.0 (6)	9.2 (6)
CORE EAST	2.8 (4)	33.3 (4)	10.8 (4)
EAST PERIPHERY	–	30.0 (3)	7.3 (3)
All	1.9 (22)	24.4 (25)	4.2 (25)

Sources: Intentional homicide per 100 000, 1985–90: UNDP (1994); number of suicides by men and women per 100 000, 1989–93: UNDP (1995: 198).

an ever-increasing division of labour and complex economy could reduce social cohesion and enhance loneliness or apathy. Are there any traces of lack of social cohesion in the European societies as their social structures move towards a post-industrial stage? Let us look at manifest aspects of social structure.

Durkheim introduced the concepts of mechanic and organic solidarity in order to state the consequences of the social transformation from the traditional to modern society. And more specifically he interpreted the occurrence of high suicide rates as expressions of the strains on individuals involved in the transformation. Suicide would be less frequent in societies characterized by strong group cohesion as for example when Catholicism is strongly institutionalized in the family system (Durkheim, 1970).

One may search more generally for signs about the extent of social cohesion in European countries by focusing upon data about both suicide and homicide on the one hand, and divorce rates and (il)legitimate children on the other hand. We divide the indicators on social cohesion into two groups, one tapping the occurrence of violence and the other the break-up of the traditional family. Finally, we also look at information about the number of refugees and people granted political asylum, because a large influx of foreigners does add to social heterogeneity with possible consequences for social cohesion.

Table 3.14 renders information about one kind of expression of a lack of social cohesion, namely the occurrence of homicide and suicide, where one must allow for the fact that concepts and measures may vary from one country to another.

The finding in Table 3.14 is that the occurrence of suicide really differs from one country to another. It is much less frequent in the following countries: Greece, Italy, the Netherlands, the United Kingdom, Spain, Romania and Ireland – almost all countries with considerable Catholic populations. And it is much more frequent in these countries: Hungary, Finland, Austria, Switzerland, Belgium, Czechoslovakia and Denmark.

Table 3.15   *Social cohesion: divorces and legitimate children*

Country set	Divorce	Legitimate children
CORE EC	30.2 (6)	86.9 (6)
OTHER EC	21.5 (6)	80.7 (6)
OUTSIDE EC	39.8 (6)	66.5 (6)
CORE EAST	25.2 (5)	90.9 (5)
EAST PERIPHERY	34.8 (4)	81.8 (3)
All	30.1 (27)	81.0 (26)

Sources: Divorces as a percentage of marriages contracted, 1987–91: UNDP (1994); legitimate children as a percentage of all children: UNDP (1994).

The difference between CORE EC and OTHER EC on the one hand and CORE EAST and EAST PERIPHERY on the other hand is striking, but there is a similar difference in relation to OUTSIDE EC. The suicide rate among men is everywhere sharply higher than that of women.

The occurrence of homicide is a different matter, as it taps how a society protects itself against crime. The crime rates tend to be higher in Eastern Europe than in Western Europe. The highest levels of homicide are to be found in: Finland, Bulgaria, Hungary, Italy, Poland, Belgium and Portugal whereas the lowest levels are displayed by Iceland, Switzerland, Germany, Greece, Ireland, the Netherlands and Czechoslovakia.

Another expression of decreasing social cohesion are the changes in family behaviour. Table 3.15 presents data about the frequency of divorce as well as the number of legitimate children.

There is one set of countries that is different when it comes to the status of traditional family values, namely OUTSIDE EC. Among the countries with traditional Protestantism as the major religion – such as Finland, Denmark, Sweden, Norway and the United Kingdom – there is a higher divorce rate than among the Catholic countries of Ireland, Italy, Spain, Portugal and Poland. A similar observation may be made in relation to the number of children born outside of marriage, although on this aspect of modernity not only Sweden, Denmark and Norway display high rates but also Iceland, Estonia, France and the United Kingdom. Finally, let us look at the occurrence of Aids, a phenomenon that indicates modernity at the same time as it constitutes a danger to the collectivity (Table 3.16).

One may speculate about whether the huge differences in the occurrence of Aids between the Western country sets and the Eastern country sets are real or not. If real, then Aids would be highly correlated with affluence, which makes sense if one sees a high level of affluence as the basis for a new way of life involving a different pattern of contacts between individuals. Yet, the data for what they are worth indicate clearly that the occurrence of Aids is increasing all over Europe.

Table 3.16   *Aids cases, per 100 000*

Country set	1986–90	1992	1993
CORE EC	10.5 (6)	3.8 (6)	5.3 (6)
OTHER EC	8.7 (6)	3.5 (6)	4.9 (6)
OUTSIDE EC	8.1 (5)	2.2 (5)	3.3 (6)
CORE EAST	1.1 (5)	.7 (3)	.4 (6)
EAST PERIPHERY	.7 (1)	–	.1 (3)
All	7.0 (23)	2.8 (21)	3.1 (27)

Sources: Aids cases, 1986–90: Towers (1992: 209); Aids cases, 1992: UNDP (1994: 191); Aids cases, 1993: UNDP (1995: 199).

Table 3.17   *Number of refugees and asylum seekers in the early 1990s*

Country set	Refugees	Asylum seekers
CORE EC	3.1 (6)	7.7 (6)
OTHER EC	1.1 (5)	3.8 (5)
OUTSIDE EC	4.9 (5)	16.8 (5)
CORE EAST	.4 (5)	1.5 (4)
EAST PERIPHERY	37.0 (3)	– (0)
All	6.7 (24)	7.7 (20)

Sources: The number of refugees in 1993 per 1000 people: USCR (1994); number of asylum applications 1983–1992 per 1000: UNDP (1994).

Foreign Population

In the analysis of social cohesion in Europe today one may focus upon the number of foreigners in the population. Since the Second World War there have been many movements of people across borders for different reasons. Migrant labour constitutes a growing group in several countries. However, it is difficult to estimate its size as countries have different naturalization procedures. Here, we focus first on the number of refugees and asylum seekers (Table 3.17).

The East–West division appears in the data about the number of refugees and asylum seekers. The number of people in Europe who have had to leave their home country has shot up dramatically as a result of the civil war in former Yugoslavia. Several of these have gone to Western Europe, in particular to Germany, Austria and Sweden, which shows up partly in the number of asylum seekers. But there have also taken place large population movements within the former Yugoslavia between various parts of the area of that country.

Several countries in Europe have considerable numbers of immigrants. The pressure from migration has been upon countries with a dynamic economy that can provide jobs. On the other hand, countries that have a weak economy have had to give up labour to the leading European

Table 3.18   *Size of foreign populations (percentage of total population)*

Country set	1991
CORE EC (6)	9.9
OTHER EC (6)	2.0
OUTSIDE EC (5)	6.7
CORE EAST (4)	1.0
EAST PERIPHERY (0)	–
All	5.2

Source: Salt et al. (1994).

economies. The labour exporting countries are Ireland, Portugal, Spain and Greece. One may expect that labour will leave the former Communist countries to seek employment opportunities in Western Europe, especially if the European Union is enlarged. It should be pointed out that immigrants to Western Europe come from all over the world, in particular the Middle East and North Africa. Table 3.18 gives estimates of the size of the foreign population in countries where it has reached a sizeable portion.

It is the rich countries in Europe which have attracted large foreign populations. Since the politics of immigration is an issue with increasing relevance in European politics (Baldwin-Edwards and Schain, 1994), it may be interesting to list the countries with a considerable foreign population. One must remember that the size of the foreign population depends not only on the actual immigration of people but also on the naturalization policy conducted by the specific country. Some countries such as the Nordic countries give away citizenship after a limited number of years whereas a country like Switzerland in principle has no naturalization mechanism besides marriage to a Swiss citizen. One must thus distinguish between foreign population and population with a foreign extraction.

A sizeable foreign population is to be found in the following countries: Luxembourg with 29 per cent, Switzerland with 17 per cent, Belgium with 9 per cent, Germany with 8 per cent, Austria with 7 per cent, France and Sweden with 6 per cent, the Netherlands with 5 per cent, Norway with 4 per cent, Denmark and the United Kingdom as well as Hungary with 3 per cent whereas Greece has 2 per cent, Italy and Portugal and Spain 1 per cent.

In relation to Eastern Europe one interesting question is to estimate the number of emigrants over the period of Communist rule. Using one recent source (Fassman and Münz, 1994) we arrive at the following total numbers of people leaving the country between 1950 and 1992 as a percentage of the entire population in 1993: former GDR with 32 per cent (in 1989), Albania and former Yugoslavia 10 per cent, Bulgaria 7 per cent, Poland and Romania 5 per cent, and former Czechoslovakia and Hungary 2 per cent. Thus, the population losses were immense in the former East Germany but rather modest in the other Communist countries.

There is a special situation in the Baltic states where the Russians constitute a sizeable portion of the population in the early 1990s: Estonia with 29 per cent, Latvia with 33 per cent and Lithuania with 9 per cent. The newly independent Baltic states have been hesitant in granting citizenship in general to these Russians, most of whom moved to or are decendants from people who moved to these states after they were annexed to the Soviet Union. The figures for the Russian population before the annexation were, around 1935, in percentages: Estonia with 8.2, Latvia having 10.6 and Lithuania with 2.3 (Kirch et al., 1993).

Gender and Modernization

The forces of modernity may be seen operating all over Europe. They involve a number of characteristics connected with the post-industrial society such as: a high level of service employment, considerable female workforce participation, access to advanced information technologies, as predicted by Daniel Bell (1976a). The findings in this chapter also support an extension of the Durkheim analysis of the connection between social structure and social cohesion to the coming of a post-industrial society all over Europe, because it involves pressure upon traditional family values.

It seems as if the Nordic countries are on the extreme with regard to both latent and manifest aspects of post-industrial modernization. In these Protestant countries not only agricultural and industrial employment are low but the number of divorces and children born outside of marriage are much higher than in several Catholic countries. Here also the suicide rates tend to be high, but so are they in Eastern Europe where the crime rates go much higher than in Western Europe. One may regard gender as one of the most characteristic aspects of the post-industrial society. Surely, gender-related development has come furthest in Northern Europe?

The introduction of new technology, the shortening of work hours and the supply of mass higher education has been accompanied by women's emancipation, involving both social and political changes. Table 3.19 contains a few indicators that measure how far gender equality has proceeded in various parts of Europe.

If gender advancement is the measure of modernization, then the OUTSIDE EC countries are the most 'modern' ones, if indeed words such as 'modernity' can be given an unambiguous and one-dimensional interpretation. CORE EC countries would be somewhat more advanced than OTHER EC countries, which in their turn would be more modern than CORE EAST whereas the EAST PERIPHERY countries would be least advanced.

Conclusion

Extending the Durkheim model to the post-industrial society, characterized by a low level of employment in agriculture, a medium level of employment in industry and a high level of service employment, one may

Table 3.19　*Gender in the 1990s*

Country set	Gender development		Share of:		
	Index I	Index II	Parliament seats	–	Ministers
CORE EC	.85　(5)	.53　(5)	16.3　(6)		14.3　(6)
OTHER EC	.84　(6)	.48　(6)	13.7　(6)		13.8　(6)
OUTSIDE EC	.90　(5)	.67　(5)	28.8　(6)		25.3　(6)
CORE EAST	.85　(4)	.44　(4)	11.3　(6)		2.0　(6)
EAST PERIPHERY	.81　(3)	–　(0)	9.8　(4)		3.8　(4)
All	.85　(23)	.53　(20)	16.4　(28)		12.4　(28)

Sources: Gender-related development, Index (I): UNDP (1995: 76–7); gender empowerment measure, Index (II): UNDP (1995: 84–5); women's share of seats in Parliament and of ministers: UNDP (1995: 60–1).

enquire into whether so-called latent and manifest aspects of social structure go together. Could it be the case that the post-industrial society features not only a certain configuration of employment but also other attributes of the social structure such as access to information and a low level of social cohesion? The European post-industrial society could have several traits of modernity such as large service sector employment and less firm institutionalization of traditional family values.

Appendix 3.1 presents a few correlations between social structure attributes from which a picture of the post-modern society in Europe may be drawn. A large service sector is typical of a modern society. At the same time modern societies are ageing societies with fewer young relatively speaking. And in modern societies the occurrence of divorce and illegitimate children is widespread. Moreover, the foreign population tends to be substantial. Finally, access to modern technology in communications is becoming each and everyone's property.

Yet, the analysis has not only revealed convergence on the coming of a post-industrial society but also divergence on several aspects of modernity. The major country differences in modernity do not though entirely coincide with the West–East division. On the contrary, the former Communist countries were ahead with regard to gender advancement. Just as relevant is the North–South division, as the countries in Southern Europe score lower on many measures of modernity than the countries in the North. Industrial employment is much more extensive in Eastern Europe than in Western Europe and at the same time industrial output is so much higher in the latter than the former.

At the same time it is undeniable that West European societies are ahead of East European ones with regard to access to information technologies. The information society is a reality especially in CORE EC and OUTSIDE EC. The mass media are much more widely spread among the population in the West than in the East, but this also applies when comparing the North and the South in Europe.

Dieter Fuchs and Hans-Dieter Klingemann state, in *Citizens and the State* (1995), about the evolution of West-European societies over the past decades:

> Economic transformation into post-industrial society can be characterized primarily by the expansion of the service sector. Cultural transformation can be described in terms of a change in values in favour of postmaterialist value priorities. (Fuchs and Klingemann, 1995: 419–20)

As we have seen in this chapter the same economic transformation is also taking place in Eastern Europe. In Chapter 9 we will probe into the question whether political culture is similar or different all over Europe, especially with regard to political values which processes of post-modernization have an impact on.

Now, we turn the focus towards politics and enquire into whether the vast economic differences described in Chapter 2, which spill over into social structure differences, are accompanied by similar differences in political institutions and political behaviour. Chapters 5 to 8 are devoted to this task. First, however, we will examine one major force towards convergence in Europe, namely European integration. This is mainly an institutional process though, which interacts with the economic forces.

Appendix 3.1   *Correlations between social structure indicators*

	Level of service employment 1993
Age <14 (1992)	−.55
Population growth (1990–3)	.23
Female workforce participation (1993)	−.30
Telephones (1991)	−.50
Television (1992)	−.63
Patents granted	.21
Internet	.51
Homicide	−.32
Suicide	.15
Divorce	.45
Legitimate children	−.44
Asylum seekers	.43
Gender development I	.48

Sources: The indicators have been taken from Tables 3.1–3.18 above.

4

European Integration

Among the forces that enhance convergence between European countries one may include the formal organizations that work not only for economic, political and military cooperation but also for the implementation of general rules of human conduct and interaction between individuals and their government. The purpose of this chapter is to discuss institutional convergence in Europe from a wide angle, starting with the field of human rights and then taking economic and political cooperation in order to finish discussing military cooperation. Military cooperation has taken on an entirely different meaning after the dismantling of the Communist regimes and the dissolution of the Warsaw Pact.

The amount of convergence resulting from the activities of the Council of Europe and the EU (EC) depends on the one hand how their institutions are transplanted into so-called municipal law, that is into the legal order of each member state, and on the other hand how these rules of conduct are implemented. As long as they remain only paper rules, they will not have an impact on behaviour.

Let us begin with the work of the Council of Europe. After all it came first and it has the largest coverage in terms of member states. Its orientation is more specific than that of the European Union, as it has tended to focus on human rights although its mandate is larger. Yet, institutional convergence in Europe includes much more than the spread of fundamental civil and political rights, which in any case would have been implemented in the European context as more and more countries adopt a democratic regime. The European Union represents the most ambitious attempt thus far to introduce by fiat institutional convergence in a number of fields: markets, social policies and foreign policy. What needs to be assessed is the extent to which the EU has been successsful in not only devising a huge set of formal rules but also in achieving convergence in behaviour.

Council of Europe

The Council of Europe is chiefly known for its activities in the field of human rights. But its scope of action includes much more than what its Commission and Court on human rights do. Actually, the Council has had hopes of becoming the main institution for general interstate collaboration in Europe, a kind of semi-federal framework as it were. These hopes have been dashed by the evolution of other European intergovernmental bodies, which will be discussed below. Yet, the two organs of the Council, the Committee of Ministers and the Consultative Assembly, have been active in enhancing convergence between the member states of the Council in a number of fields.

The idea of a sort of confederal or even federal framework for the peoples of Europe was launched during the interwar years. In 1923 Count Coudenhove-Kalergi published a book with the title *Pan-Europa* calling for a European Federation. In 1929 Aristide Briand suggested a federal link between the European peoples in the *Memorandum on European Federal Union*. These ideas, supported by movements at the time, were soon out of step with realities in Europe of the 1930s. However, one may observe that John Maynard Keynes as early as 1920 in his *The Economic Consequences of the War* argued that the only way to peace and prosperity for Europe lay in the foundation of intergovernmental bodies for co-operation in collaboration with the United States, which would open up opportunities for the peaceful reconstruction of the powers that lost the war.

European cooperation along the lines suggested by Keynes including loans to the defeated nations became a real option after the Second World War. In 1946 Winston Churchill in a speech at Zurich set the tone: 'We must build a kind of United States of Europe'. And the Marshall Plan provided American credits for the rebuilding of war-torn Europe. In that atmosphere a Congress of Europe was called at The Hague in 1948, which after deliberations on an economic and political union resulted in a Statute of the Council of Europe, signed in 1949 in London. At that time it was hoped that the Council of Europe would be the beginning of a federal state in Europe, but these hopes had to be scaled down as other institutions began to emerge in the 1950s.

European cooperation was fuelled by the American assitance under the Marshall Plan. On 5 June 1947 Secretary of State George C. Marshall outlined the idea of a European self-help programme to be financed by the United States. The European Recovery Programme distributed 12 billion dollars' worth of economic aid over a period of four years, partly as direct grants and partly as loans. The stated purpose was to restore industrial and agricultural production, establish financial stability and expand trade. The Marshall Plan was coordinated through the Organization for European Economic Cooperation (OEEC) and the outcome was a sharp and sustained rise in economic growth in the 16 countries that were included in the recovery programme, benefiting significantly the West European chemical, engineering and steel industries.

In 1961 the OEEC was replaced by the OECD, the Organization for Economic Cooperation and Development, located in Paris. It covers some 26 countries mainly from the rich world, and it monitors economic development in order to promote economic growth, employment and financial stability. Its information system concerning the member countries is an excellent source concerning economic data in a wide sense, which is employed for a large number of publications published each year. Convergence in Europe has no doubt been stimulated by the tremendous increase in and accessibility of data about several European countries, particularly those in Western Europe. The OECD statistics have made country comparisons much more reliable and easier to accomplish. Yet, information by itself does not bring about convergence, but the enactment of common institutions may.

Institutions

The institutions of the Council of Europe are basically twofold. First, there is the Committee of Ministers and the Consultative Assembly for the general work of the Council, served by a single Secretariat. Second, there are the special institutions handling the implementation of the human rights convention, namely, the European Commission of Human Rights and the European Court of Human Rights. The Council's organs were located to Strasbourg in the region of Alsace-Lorraine (which has been a constant source of conflict between France and Germany). The Council of Europe in 1996 covers 39 countries, which have applied for and received membership status, meaning that they accept the intergovernmental conventions that guide the work of the Council. In the 1990s a number of former Communist countries have entered the Council.

The main work of the Council of Europe is orientated towards the protection of human rights by the implementation of the European Convention on Human Rights from 1950. The Convention is a most important document in the codification process of human rights. It is actually comparable in both scope and impact with the 1948 United Nations Human Rights Declaration. The European Commission of Human Rights surveys the status of civil and political rights in the member states and organizes various activities that promote the implementation of such rights. The European Court of Human Rights is a judicial institution which rules on cases submitted to it from persons in the various member states. The verdicts of the Court are recommendations to member states to take proper action, which they normally also do. The activities of the Comission and the Court are reported on in the *Yearbook on the European Convention on Human Rights* (Dordrecht: Martinus Nijhoff).

The work of the Council in the field of human rights has been heavy involving the ruling on a large number of court cases. No doubt these activities have been conducive to the implementation of a similar concept of civil and political rights all over Europe. It is thus of utmost importance that all the East European countries that are included in this study now are members of the Council, having accepted both the Convention on Human Rights and the activities of the Court. This means that around the year 2000 there will be in place a shared understanding of what human rights involve in all the European countries, including citizenship, due process rights and democratic rights.

It may be mentioned that the Council has step by step increased the scope of the activity of its Court by adding a number of protocols to its Convention. These protocols add further rights to the set of human rights. Thus, the 1952 addition covered economic rights, such as the right to compensation in the case of expropriation (First Protocol). And in 1983 a rule against the death penalty was agreed upon (Sixth Protocol). In 1984 a number of rules concerning the status of alien residents were introduced (Seventh Protocol).

There is an implementation problem in relation to the human rights activities of the Council, as not all countries accept the conventions or the court rulings within their own territory all the time. However, some countries have moved to a formal recognition of the conventions and protocols of the Council by entering them into their own municipal law or legal orders. Despite controversy over certain rules and a few court rulings one may state that the main trend is that European countries increasingly define and implement human rights in the same way.

The overall purpose of the Council is rendered in Article One of the Statute of the Council which states that the aim of the organization is to 'bring European States into closer association' by means of 'agreements and common action'. More specifically, the goal:

> is to achieve a greater degree of unity between its Members for the purpose of safeguarding and realizing the ideals and principles which are their common heritage and facilitating their economic and social progress.

The Statute of the Council also specifies how greater unity is to be accomplished, namely by:

> agreements and common action in economic, social, cultural, scientific, legal and administrative matters and in the maintenance and further realization of human rights and fundamental freedoms.

The Council of Europe was explicitly devised as an intergovernmental mechanism, whose decisions and declarations were recommendations and not binding on the member states. The Committee of Ministers is the main decision-making body of the Council whereas the Consulative Assembly, being a deliberative organ, consists of more than 200 members of the national parliaments. The work of the two bodies of the Council that deal with the ordinary activities outside of the judicial framework have become more and more institutionalized, at the present consisting of permanent representation and numerous standing committees.

The Council of Europe has adopted some 150 conventions since it began its work. The Assembly has adopted about 160 opinions, 500 orders, 1000 resolutions and 1200 recommendations. The name of some of the new conventions indicate how broadly defined the activities of the Council tend to be: Recognition and Enforcement of Decisions concerning Custody of Children (1980), Compensation of Victims and Sentenced Persons (1983),

Insider Trading (1989), Laundering, Search, Seizure and Confiscation of Proceeds from Crime (1990).

Despite the fact that a number of well-known European statesmen (Adenauer, Churchill, de Gasperi, Schuman, Spaak) at one time favoured the Council of Europe as the framework for a future European federalism, the organization became successful mainly in the specific area of human rights. There it has launched and upheld a most effective intergovernmental system for the protection of civil and political rights, constituting a model copied elsewhere, as in the American Convention on Human Rights (1969).

Outside of the judicial area the Council of Europe has offered many opportunities for regular contacts between the democratic countries in Europe. It has also engaged in making new institutions or the harmonization of old ones within international law, criminal law, civil and commercial law as well as within legal cooperation and data protection. Yet, the main bodies for economic and political cooperation within Europe have been set up outside of the Council. The same observation applies to military cooperation, which was, however, never tabled for the Council of Europe. It is now time to look at other organizations for economic, political and military cooperation among the European states.

The European Union

The most influential mechanism for bringing about institutional convergence in Western Europe has been the European Community (EC), which transformed itself into the European Union (EU) in 1993. It comprises a set of institutions that are supranational, delivering a body of law that stands in between international law and municipal law. Let us first look at the emergence of the European Community.

At the suggestion of Robert Schuman, French Foreign Minister, the European Coal and Steel Community (ECSC) was formed in 1951 by the following six member states: the BeNeLux countries, France, Germany and Italy. The treaty involved all coal and steel production in the member states being put under a joint High Authority, which would supervise the production in such a way that it would foster peace and reduce the historical animosity between France and Germany.

The same countries continued their search for institutionalized forms of collaboration by setting up the European Economic Community (EEC) and the European Atomic Energy Community (Euratom) by an agreement in 1957, which meant that from 1958 and onwards there were three communities operating in Western Europe, much along plans outlined by Frenchman Jean Monnet whose Action Committee for the United States of Europe energized the drive for 'relance européenne'.

In 1965 the three communities were brought together into one community, the European Community. It has been enlarged by the entrance of several countries. Thus, the United Kingdom, Ireland and Denmark became members in 1973, Greece entered in 1981 and Spain and Portugal joined in 1986. In 1995 Austria, Sweden and Finland became members, whereas Norway, Iceland and Switzerland have decided to stay outside of the European Union. The possibility to extend the Union eastward has been discussed much in the early 1990s, but Poland, Hungary, the Czech and Slovak Republics, as well as Romania and Bulgaria, have thus far only been able to reach association or so-called Europe Agreements with the EU.

In relation to the Union as important as the enlargement in space is the deepening of the integration in increasing numbers of areas. The activities of the European Community have grown substantially since 1965, both with regard to scope and range. Thus, more and more areas of social life have become increasingly regulated by Community decisions, but it is an open question whether policy implementation works effectively within the Union.

As the situation exists now, the constitution of the European Union consists of the Treaty of Rome as well as the revisions made over time in, for instance, the Single European Act of 1987 and the Maastricht Treaty of 1992. Now, the three pillars of the Union are as follows: (1) the EC framework; (2) foreign policy cooperation; and (3) cooperation within police. European monetary cooperation is under way with the introduction of a monetary institute in 1995 and the planning of a single European currency from 1999 – the EURO – as well as one central bank for the entire Economic Monetary Union (EMU) area. Since 1989 there has been a European Investment Bank.

The *Acquis Communautaire* is the general phrase for all of the principles of the Union governing the Community bodies as well as the member states including objectives and opinions besides proper EU law (Toth, 1991: 9). It includes conventions as well as the interpretations of EU law by the European Court of Justice.

The common body of objectives, rules and procedures identifies on the one hand what the Union shall not do – the subsidiarity principle – and on the other what the Union ought to do as well as how it should do it. The 'subsidiarity' word was first mentioned in 1974 in connection with the Union, but it has an older ideological heritage dating back to the Roman Catholic social doctrine, as expressed, for example, in *Quadragesimo Anno* from 1931. The *principe de subsidiarite* governs the allocation of both exclusive and concurrent competences between the Union and the member states. In the preamble of the Maastricht Treaty it says that the Union shall 'continue the process of creating an ever closer union among the peoples of Europe, in which decisions are taken as closely as possible in accordance with the principle of subsidiarity'. Article 3b clarifies this by stating that the Union acts within the limits of the powers conferred upon it and that:

> In areas which do not fall under its exclusive competence, the Community shall take action, in accordance with the principles of subsidiarity, only if and in so far as the objectives of the proposed action cannot be sufficiently achieved by the

member States, and can therefore, by reason of the scale of the proposed action, be better achieved by the Community.

One may question whether the notion of subsidiarity implies efficiency or participation, as sometimes the former is the criterion and sometimes the latter. Sometimes subsidiarity involves nearness, democracy, decentralization and legitimacy. Sometimes it stands for effectiveness, necessity and transnationality.

The basic problem with the notion of subsidiarity is, however, not that it is ambiguous, but that the Union possesses a rule that tempers the principle, article 235 in the Treaty of Rome, which gives the Union requisite powers:

> If action by the Community should prove necessary to attain, in the course of the operation of the common market, one of the objectives of the Community and this Treaty has not provided the necessary powers, the Council shall, acting unanimously on a proposal from the Commission and after consulting the European Parliament, take the appropriate measures.

There is no simple yardstick to be applied in order to decide when Union action is called for and when decisions should be left or transferred to the member states. The use of the 'subsidiarity' term reflects more than guides the changing political acceptance of Union intervention. Yet, once the Union decides to act, then its decision-making and implementation institutions begin to operate, where the former are much stronger than the latter.

The European Union consists basically of four institutions: (1) the Parliament; (2) the Council; (3) the Commission; and (4) the Court of Justice. The Parliament is the assembly of the Union, comprising directly elected representatives of the peoples of Europe through special EU elections every fifth year. The Council is the legislative body of the Union, consisting of one minister from each member state, casting a number of votes. The Commmision can be identified as the executive arm of the Union, comprising some 20 commissioners who are responsible for various directorates. Finally, there is the Court which handles the judicial branch of the Union dealing with the interpretation of Community law as well as the adjudication of EU law including various kinds of actions to uphold and develop the legal order of the Union (see *Reports of Cases before the Court or European Court Cases*). The European Council on the other hand is only a mechanism for coordination between the heads of state and premiers of the member states, holding regular summit meetings where its decisions are not legally binding.

There are two recent important developments in relation to the institutional structure. First, the position of the Parliament has been strengthened, as it now not only has advisory and deliberative functions but also has been given some blocking powers. The Parliament may reject legislation by the Council and it must be consulted on all legislative proposals from the Commission or the Council. In the Parliament the representatives group themselves according to party criteria, but the number of representatives a country may send depends upon the size of its population, although not in a strictly proportional manner. The prerogatives of the Parliament include supervision of the Commission and Council as well as budgetary powers.

Second, decision-making within the Council has moved away from unanimity towards more frequent use of qualified majority voting, that is, requiring two-thirds of the votes with sometimes in addition two-thirds of the states supporting the proposal. The Council is the main legislative body of the Union as it may issue various kinds of rules: (1) regulations which are immediately binding; (2) directives which are binding when complemented; (3) decisions and recommendations which are not binding. The Council shifts the ministers involved in relation to the policy area concerned. The number of votes a minister may cast depends upon the size of the country population that he/she represents, although less in a strict proportional manner than is the case regarding the composition of the Parliament where various states have different numbers of mandates. Simple majorty voting is only used on procedural matters.

The move away from each country having a veto in the Council, in order to enhance the capacity of the Union to take swift decisions, as well as the strengthening of the Parliament in order to reduce the democratic deficit of the Union, has no doubt increased the federal characteristics of the Union. Supranationalism is clearly on the rise at the expense of intergovernmentalism as the guiding principle in the evolution of the institutions of the Union. The Commission and the Court of Justice are the chief federal organs of the Union, as the Union lacks defence as well as its own police.

The Commission is appointed by common accord of the governments of the member states, where the five large states – Germany, France, Italy, Spain and the United Kingdom – each nominate two Commissioners and the remaining small states each nominate one person. The Commissioners as agents of the Union act independently of the governments in order to further Union interests, because the Union, and not the member state governments, is their principal. The Commission has extensive agenda power in relation to the Council and the Parliament with regard to legislation and budgetary matters.

The Commission heads a bureaucracy in Brussels including some 20 000 employees. It submits proposals for Union legislation to the Council, negotiates international agreements between the Union and other states and it takes various steps in order to implement Union decisions, particularly with regard to the observance of Union legislation, as for instance the levelling of fines on member state governments in countries where Union law is not observed.

Even more federal is the European Court of Justice, situated in Luxembourg and consisting of 15 judges and nine advocates-general, appointed by common accord of the member state governments. The Court rules over the legal implementation of Union law and has interpreted the sources of Union law in a number of cases, in which the federal tone of Union legislation has been emphasized. The Court has consistently

Table 4.1 *Community institutions in 1995: votes or seats*

Country	Council of ministers	The Commission	Parliament	Court of Justice	Economic and social commission	Committee of the Regions
Austria	4	1	21	1	12	12
Belgium	5	1	25	1	12	12
Denmark	3	1	16	1	9	9
Germany	10	2	99	1	24	24
Greece	5	1	25	1	12	12
Finland	3	1	16	1	9	9
France	10	2	87	1	24	24
Ireland	3	1	15	1	9	9
Italy	10	2	87	1	24	24
Luxembourg	2	1	6	1	6	6
Netherlands	5	1	31	1	12	12
Portugal	5	1	25	1	12	12
Spain	5	2	64	1	21	21
Sweden	4	1	22	1	12	12
United Kingdom	10	2	87	1	24	24
Total	87	20	626	15	222	222

Note: There are nine advocates-general.

taken the position that Union law takes precedence over municipal law in the member states. Moreover, the Court has interpreted the Treaties and EU legislation in such a way that the scope or areas of activity for the Court to rule over is large. Its jurisdiction is compulsory and automatically binding on the member states. The Court represents the federal ambitions in the EU institutions in a most transparent manner.

Table 4.1 presents an overall picture of the main institutions of the Union in 1995, stating for each member state the number of votes it may cast in the Council and the number of seats or mandates it possesses in the other bodies.

The Economic and Social Commission (ESC) dealing with economic activities in a wide sense, and the Committe of the Regions handling regional matters, have a quasi-institutional status, which also applies to the Committee of Permanent Representatives (COREP), which prepares the meetings of the Council and acts as a liaison or mediator between national governments, the Commission and the Council. These bodies having their own budgets and administrative resources are consultative organs, commenting upon proposals by the Commission for decision-making by the Council.

Now, let us look more closely at two of the decision-making bodies of the EU, the Council and the Parliament. One may identify four decision-making procedures interlocking the Commission, the Council and the Parliament in a most complex fashion. First, the consultation procedure: this is the regular procedure covering, for example, agriculture, customs and transportation where the EU Parliament has only an advisory role in relation to the Council of Ministers. Second, the co-decision procedure: certain issues or aspects of issues concerning free movement of goods and services, research, environment, consumer protection, trans-European infrastructure, education, culture and public health. And third, the cooperation procedure: some aspects of issues in social policy, technology and environment. Major EU decisions require the assent procedure.

The cooperation procedure is a double reading system involving the European Parliament, the Commission and the Council acting in accordance with a strict time-scale for how the key players may express opinions on proposals introduced by the Commission. Under the cooperation procedure the Parliament has only a suspensive veto. The co-decision procedure (three readings) involves the use of a conciliation committee where differences between the three players can be ironed out, but in this procedure the Parliament has an absolute power of veto. It was not until the Maastricht Treaty that the position of the Parliament was strengthened, as it was only a body for deliberations during the 1980s. Now, which players exercise power in the Council and in the Parliament in the sense of casting a decisive vote, either for a 'yes' or for a 'no'? Let us look at decision-making power in the Council and in the Parliament, as the Commission exercises mainly agenda power.

Voting Power in the Council and Parliament

One may distinguish between two extreme allocation rules with regard to the assignment of votes to states. On the one hand we have the confederal mechanism that each state casts one vote independently of the size of the country, which would then also have veto status. On the other hand we have the opposite rule that the number of votes a state may control directly reflects the size of the country, measured in terms of its population. Such a proportional rule would provide the large states in Europe with many more votes than the small ones.

The exact number of votes each state may cast in the Council has changed for each enlargement, the EU now practising the principle that the allocation of votes to each state should be about proportional to the square root of its population. Table 4.2 shows the solution chosen for the Council.

The allocation rule linking country votes to country population takes the huge differences in population into account only to a slight extent. One may conduct a similar analysis of the European Parliament although now it is a matter of the allocation of seats to the member states. Table 4.3 illustrates the development in the number of seats allocated to each member state according to the year that EU elections have been held.

Comparing Table 4.2 with Table 4.3 one may establish that the differences in population are better reflected in the allocation of seats in the Parliament than in the allocation of votes in the Council. The former is more federal whereas the latter is more confederal, although it is never a

Table 4.2   *Composition of the EU Council: votes*

Country	Population, 1990 (millions)	Votes				
		1958	1973	1981	1986	1995
France	56.6	4	10	10	10	10
Germany	79.1	4	10	10	10	10
Italy	57.7	4	10	10	10	10
Belgium	9.9	2	5	5	5	5
Netherlands	15.0	2	5	5	5	5
Luxembourg	0.4	1	2	2	2	2
Denmark	5.2	–	3	3	3	3
Ireland	3.5	–	3	3	3	3
United Kingdom	57.4	–	10	10	10	10
Greece	10.3	–	–	5	5	5
Portugal	10.4	–	–	–	5	5
Spain	38.4	–	–	–	8	8
Austria	7.8	–	–	–	–	4
Finland	5.0	–	–	–	–	3
Sweden	8.6	–	–	–	–	4
Total	–	17	58	63	76	87

Table 4.3   *Composition of the EU Parliament: seats*

Country	1979	1984	1989	1994	1995
France	81	81	81	87	87
Germany	81	81	81	99	99
Italy	81	81	81	87	87
Belgium	24	24	24	25	25
Netherlands	25	25	25	31	31
Luxembourg	6	6	6	6	6
Denmark	16	16	16	16	16
Ireland	15	15	15	15	15
United Kingdom	81	81	81	87	87
Greece	–	24	24	25	25
Portugal	–	–	24	25	25
Spain	–	–	60	64	64
Austria	–	–	–	–	21
Finland	–	–	–	–	16
Sweden	–	–	–	–	22
Total	410	434	518	567	626

question about strict proportionality between votes or mandates on the one hand and population on the other hand. Now, what are the implications for voting power?

The development of the EU decision rules may be analysed by means of the power index method, which calculates the possibilities to be decisive in a choice group given a distribution of votes or mandates. In Tables 4.4–4.9 below we reproduce the power index scores for the different member states under alternative decision rules. The power index employed is the normalized Banzhaf index which has a straightforward interpretation as the percentage of swings a state may make, thus making it critical in a coalition that either says 'yes' or 'no' (Banzhaf normalized power index).

Four decision rules are feasible in the context of the EU: (1) unanimity or veto power; (2) qualified majority; (3) qualified majority with the additional qualification that two-thirds of the member states are in the coalition; and (4) simple majority voting. Voting in the Council is based upon quantitative voting, that is, a member state casts several votes whereas in voting in the Parliament each member casts one vote. The first three aggregation rules have been the critical ones in the debate about power in the Union.

The unanimity rule creates little difficulty in terms of calculating the power index scores, as each state will have the same power index measure. The crucial question in relation to unanimity is its existence, given the trend not to employ it unless it is a matter of exceptional things such as constitutional revisions. However, the derivation of the power scores for the other decision rules shows a few interesting results concerning the players in the EU power game.

The power index scores allow one to make conclusions about the development of formal power in collective choice institutions, where power depends upon the aggregation rules by means of which the preferences of players are summed up and transformed into a group decision. One may actually assume that real power tends to approximate formal voting power, as the voting power of a player, a state or a party, is the rational expectation of policy influence. In the EU setting one would need to take the interest organizations into account as EU lobbying is extensive and may have an impact upon policy-making (Andersen and Eliassen, 1993). Below we focus upon formal voting power.

First, the more countries that are entered as members in the Union, the less the voting power of each and every player, the major states included. In the 1958 EC the large West European states of Germany, France and Italy had more than 20 per cent of the voting power, which is now down to about 10 per cent in the 1995 framework and would shrink to less than 10 per cent in a future super EU, if indeed further enlargement eastward takes place. Power has become more diffused in the European Union than in the Community.

Second, the very special decision institution of the EU in the form of qualified majority voting, with the additional requirement that two-thirds of the players support a motion, increases the power of the small states somewhat. With 15 players in the 1995 union this special qualified majority voting rule implies a power distribution that decreases the power of the large states to only about 10 per cent of the total voting power. One may establish that the constitutional evolution of the Union with the successive

Table 4.4　*Voting power in the Council under qualified majority: states*

Country	1958	1973	1981	1986	1995
France	.238	.167	.158	.129	.112
Germany	.238	.167	.158	.129	.112
Italy	.238	.167	.158	.129	.112
Belgium	.143	.091	.082	.067	.059
Netherlands	.143	.091	.082	.067	.059
Luxembourg	.000	.016	.041	.018	.023
Denmark	–	.066	.041	.046	.036
Ireland	–	.066	.041	.046	.036
United Kingdom	–	.167	.158	.129	.112
Greece	–	–	.082	.067	.059
Portugal	–	–	–	.067	.059
Spain	–	–	–	.109	.092
Austria	–	–	–	–	.048
Finland	–	–	–	–	.036
Sweden	–	–	–	–	.048

Note: The power index scores are the Banzhaf normalized.

Table 4.5　*Voting power in the Council under qualified majority and two-thirds: states*

Country	1958	1973	1981	1986	1995
France	.214	.154	.134	.121	.101
Germany	.214	.154	.134	.121	.101
Italy	.214	.154	.134	.121	.101
Belgium	.167	.103	.091	.070	.061
Netherlands	.167	.103	.091	.070	.061
Luxembourg	.024	.026	.064	.025	.031
Denmark	–	.077	.064	.053	.043
Ireland	–	.077	.064	.053	.043
United Kingdom	–	.154	.134	.121	.101
Greece	–	–	.091	.070	.061
Portugal	–	–	–	.070	.061
Spain	–	–	–	.104	.085
Austria	–	–	–	–	.052
Finland	–	–	–	–	.043
Sweden	–	–	–	–	.052

Note: The power index scores are the Banzhaf normalized.

enlargement from 6 to 15 players has meant a sharp reduction in the power of the large states. What about power in the Parliament?

One may calculate power scores for the EU Parliament in two ways, theoretically speaking. Either one focuses upon the state as the collective player, casting a unanimous vote among all its representatives. Or one takes the party family as the collective player, allowing each member to vote according to party ideology along the left–right scale. In reality, one may expect to find that members vote sometimes according to state

Table 4.6 *Voting power in the Parliament: states*

Country	1979	1981	1986	1994	1995
France	.174	.170	.166	.161	.144
Germany	.174	.170	.166	.178	.166
Italy	.174	.170	.166	.161	.144
Belgium	.087	.064	.037	.037	.037
Netherlands	.087	.074	.037	.045	.044
Luxembourg	.043	.011	.004	.010	.009
Denmark	.043	.053	.027	.024	.024
Ireland	.043	.053	.025	.024	.022
United Kingdom	.174	.170	.166	.161	.144
Greece	–	.064	.037	.037	.037
Portugal	–	–	.037	.037	.037
Spain	–	–	.134	.126	.106
Austria	–	–	–	–	.031
Finland	–	–	–	–	.024
Sweden	–	–	–	–	.032

Note: Banzhaf normalized scores.

preferences and other times according to party ideology, when there is not idiosyncratic voting. The power scores for the states are given in Table 4.6.

The finding here is, on the one hand, that the larger states have more power in the Parliament than they have in the Council in relation to the small states. And on the other hand we note that the enlargement of the EU has not brought about any substantial reduction in the power of the larger states. Germany has almost the same power score in 1995 as in 1981.

Let us look at the power measures when the players in the Parliament are considered to be the party families where parliamentarians from each member state would vote according to party umbrella rather than state affiliation. Table 4.7 first states the composition of the party families from 1981 to 1994, which has been done by aggregating election outcomes using conventional criteria for how close various political parties are on the left–right continuum.

The largest block in terms of seats or mandates has clearly been the set of socialist parties. The set of Christian Democratic and the set of Conservative Parties were almost as large back in the early 1980s, but now they are only half the size of the set of socialist parties. The Green family has increased considerably, which is also true of the far-right wing and the regional-national parties. The power scores for the party families between 1981 and 1994 are presented in Table 4.8.

There has emerged over time one dominant player in the EU, the set of socialist parties. It has captured 41 per cent of the voting power independently. There is no similar group, as the shares of the voting power of the Conservatives and the Christian Democrats have decreased substantially. It seems as if the voting power of the left has increased at the expense of the voting power of the right, which may explain the increased attention of the EU to social issues and questions about rights.

Table 4.7   *The EU Parliament: seats of party families*

Party family	1981	1984	1989	1994
Communist-Left	50	44	46	45
Socialist	123	132	180	183
Green	–	9	26	21
Christian Democrat	98	92	93	86
Liberal	28	22	37	50
Conservative	116	108	92	96
Far Right	5	16	21	25
Regional-national	6	5	15	15
Other	8	6	8	46
Total	434	434	518	567

Note: Banzhaf normalized scores.

Table 4.8   *Voting power in the Parliament: party families*

Party family	1981	1984	1989	1994
Communist-Left	.010	.038	.088	.070
Socialist	.330	.340	.438	.409
Green	–	.009	.041	.035
Christian Democrat	.310	.264	.152	.139
Liberal	.010	.038	.060	.070
Conservative	.310	.264	.152	.139
Far Right	.010	.028	.032	.035
Regional-national	.010	.009	.023	.035
Other	.010	.009	.014	.070

Note: Banzhaf normalized scores.

In the EU Parliament the parties form groupings with special labels which varies over time. Table 4.9 presents a recent grouping in the extended 1995 Parliament (N = 626).

At present, the strongest group is the PES with a power share of 36 per cent. The EEP, comprising Conservatives and Christian Democrats, reaches only 16 per cent. There is a sizeable group of Independents with 6 per cent of the voting power. The ELDR has 12 per cent whereas the other groups score 5 per cent, where various left groups including the Greens are well represented. The decision-making in the Union results in the making of EU legislation, the structure of which we describe below. Actually, one may dare to suggest that EU legislation has become less orientated towards economic growth and more sensitive to redistributive matters, due to the strong position of the Left within the Parliament. The voting power that a player commands is the rational expectation of policy influence. And the general tendency is that the left has increased at the expense of the right since 1979, if the environmentalists are included in the former. What is the structure of European Law?

Table 4.9   *EU Parliament: party groups 1995*

	Seats	Voting power
PES: Party of European Socialists	217	.361
EPP: European People's Party	172	.155
ELDR: Liberal, Democratic and Reformist Party	52	.119
GUE: United Left – Northern Green Left	33	.062
FE: Forza Europa	29	.054
GRN: Green Group	28	.050
EDA: European Democratic Alliance	26	.054
ERA: European Radical Alliance	19	.042
EN: Europe of Nations Group	19	.042
N: Non-attached	31	.058

Note: Banzhaf normalized scores.

Union Law

The expression 'European Law' stands for a variety of rules including not only EC law or Union law but also the human rights framework of the Council of Europe as well as other treaties between European states. In addition, there is European customary law comprising principles about the rule of law, democracy and equity. Yet, what used to be called 'EC law' has a special position, as it is not simply public international law as is the case with other kinds of European law. EC law or Union law is closer to municipal law than international law, as it is immediately applicable in the member states without the need for any transformation or adoption by the member states into municipal law and it holds for national authorities as well as the courts in the member states. However, EC law lacks one typical characteristic of municipal law in that it requires the cooperation of the member states in order to be implemented, because the Union has few if any centralized means of execution. Responsibility for the implementation of Union law rests with the Commission, who may impose sanctions in the form of economic penalties on a member state which does not respect the legal order of the Union.

Union law is based on principles of supranationality. The rule of Union law has priority over all national law dealing with areas within which the Union has legislated (supremacy of Community law) and it applies directly to individuals in each member state (direct effect). The European Court of Justice (EJC) laid down in 1963 that the legal system of the Union:

> constitutes a new legal order of international law for the benefit of which the States have limited their sovereign rights, albeit within limited fields, and the subjects of which comprise not only Member States but also their nationals.

Thus, the jurisdiction of the Court of Justice is obligatory in cases between member states, between the organs of organizations and between the organs and individuals and member states. The sources of Union law include the treaties, the legislation by the Council, the precedents by the

Court as well as general norms of reason. The Community possesses legal personality, meaning that it can enter into all kinds of juristic relationships. Its operations are regulated by the *Acquis Communautaire*, or the Community patrimony of rules, practices and opinions accepted by the EU institutions, covering not only EU law but also fundamental objectives accepted in the course of institutional evolution.

From a formal point of view there are the following types of EU legislation: (1) Regulations which are directly applicable on all states in its entirety; (2) Directives which are binding on states named, who decide the form of implementation at the national level; (3) Decisions that are administrative acts which are binding for only those states that are addressed; and (4) Recommendations expressing only EU preferences, as they are not binding; finally (5) Opinions that are not binding legally speaking. The European Court has built up a huge body of case law in relation to these distinctions. From a policy point of view they are not absolutely essential, because countries may wish to adopt EU principles despite the fact that they may not be legally binding.

Public policies within the Union are driven by two opposing tendencies. On the one hand, there is the wish among the member states for common new policies in several areas of social life as well as a demand for the harmonization of existing rules in these areas. A common or harmonized framework of rules all over Europe is both an end in itself and a means to other objectives such as reducing transaction costs. On the other hand, there is the problem of the implementation deficit, meaning that intentions in Brussels are not matched by realities at the member state level, as countries may not be able to deliver outcomes that accomplish policy goals. One may divide Union law proper into four main sections besides a number of other areas: (1) competition policy; (2) social policy; (3) agricultural policy; and (4) transport and infrastructure policies. Let us look at each of these shortly (El-Agraa, 1990; Andersen and Eliassen, 1993; Bueno de Mesquita and Stokman, 1994; Jachtenfuchs and Kohler-Koch, 1996; Pappi, König and Knoke, 1995).

Market and Competition Rules

Among the rules that establish the common market within the Union one may mention the following: (1) the customs union; (2) the fundamental freedoms; (3) prohibition against discrimination; and (4) rules about competition and subsidies. The four components which make up the common market framework call for uniform rules among the member states in relation to trade with outside countries as well as with regard to trade within the Union. Thus, the common market regime includes both a customs union and an internal market for the free movement of goods and services, labour and capital.

The customs union carries rules against any tariffs and quotas for the trade between the countries within the Union. Thus customs duties, quantitative restrictions or any charges on trade or hidden trade barriers in the form of, for example, technical provisions are completely ruled out. The Union has adopted a common customs policy including rules that all member states have to comply with. The Union negotiates for the member states international agreements about changes in the tariffs and quotas, as for instance within the GATT (General Agreement on Tariffs and Trade) framework or in relation to Third World countries. The member states are only allowed to introduce restrictions on the trade in goods and services on the grounds of public morality, security and health. The EU has worked out a common commercial policy, which covers general rules about tariffs, trade agreements, export policy and trade protection.

A number of rules regulate the freedom of movement of the so-called factors of production. First, Union law provides for the freedom of movement across country boundaries of workers when they acquire a new job, as well as the right to stay after employment has been ended. Despite the fact that Union law comprises numerous rules about the rights of employees when they have moved to another country within the Union, for example with regard to social security, Union law does not contain a European citizenship.

Second, Union law comprises rules that enhance the opportunities for the self-employed to take jobs in other member countries. Thus, numerous attempts have been made to harmonize different qualifications and diplomas that hinder the free movements of persons within professions such as medicine and law.

Third, there are the rules that provide for the freedom of capital movements, including both tangible assets and financial ones. For all these regulations of the four freedoms – goods, services, labour and capital – hold that there is a general prohibition of discrimination, not only on the basis of nationality but also hidden ones as for example when certain criteria have been laid down which only one group can satisfy.

The competition law of the Union includes a network of regulations concerning agreements or mergers that enhance horizontal or vertical integration or the use of a dominant position in a market strengthening monopoly power, as well as rules about franchising and rights in industrial property such as patents, trade marks and copyrights. Although the Commission may not be able to do much with regard to merger control, it remains the case that the Commission has contributed over the years to the opening up of several sectors in the European economy: airlines and transport, banking and insurance, telecommunications for instance (Goyder, 1992).

European law is to a large extent competition law. The purpose of EU competition rules is to: (1) prevent the formation of cartels; (2) stop state aid to enterprises; and (3) to enhance the opportunities for bidding for contracts in the private or public sectors. The anti-trust legislation includes a procedure for EU acceptance of major firm aquisitions as well as a mechanism for enquiries into the abuse of a dominant market position involving the levelling of fines. State aid to firms is in principle prohibited, but there are exceptions as when payments have a social character. Public contracts over a certain size have to be announced over the entire Union so that the bidding process includes all willing participants. The Commission monitors developments with regard to EU competition law and has the competence to impose fines without hearing the Court.

Social Policy

The Maastricht Treaty reoriented EU law from the enactment and implementation of market rules towards the introduction of social legislation. Thus, in the early 1990s the EU has become more active in legislation concerning labour and social policies, including besides working conditions and gender questions also the environment and regional matters.

The Union now allocates substantial sums of money to its three regional funds, which operate according to a system of regulation dividing the member countries into various types of support areas. The regional funds are allocated to areas that face difficulties of uneven development resulting in regional disparities in terms of affluence or employment. There are three large funds from which funds may be sought for specific projects. The regional funds are to be allocated in accordance with a set of regional policy criteria, dividing Europe into six different support areas based on a number of considerations such as regional disparities in agricultural structure, in unemployment and in income: projects and networks.

The allocation of money from these funds is a major Union activity where many actors send applications from projects often involving several countries. One may calculate how much resourcing each country receives through these EU projects and relate them to how much each country pays into the Union in the form of membership fees. Thus far, the allocation of regional funds have benefited Southern Europe the most, but also regionally deprived areas in Northern Europe have been among the beneficiaries. A major problem is the control of the vast sums of money floating through these regional policy programmes, as auditors have discovered that money is sometimes not properly accounted for.

Agricultural Policy

The agricultural sectors in the various member countries are regulated by special rules, which enter the EU agricultural policy together with a substantial financial mechanism for paying for the commitments that the policy and its regulations entail. The so-called CAP – Common Agricultural Policy – involves a number of market arrangements for the protection against imports from third countries as well as price guarantees for producers in order to provide farmers within the Union a secure income.

The CAP as a whole utilizes roughly 50 per cent of the EU's yearly budget. So-called intervention authorities in the Commission were obliged to buy agricultural products at a fixed price, and this practice has resulted

Table 4.10   *Types of expenditures in 1994 (billions of Ecu)*

Member state	Agricultural guarantee	Structural funds	Structural aid	Total
Belgium	1 174	208	265	1 647
Denmark	1 288	118	127	1 533
Germany	5 272	1 815	2 040	9 126
Greece	2 724	1 689	1 876	6 288
Spain	4 427	2 549	2 799	9 774
France	8 049	1 298	1 402	10 749
Ireland	1 527	682	707	2 917
Italy	3 481	1 379	1 485	6 346
Luxembourg	13	14	14	40
Netherlands	1 936	265	275	2 475
Portugal	713	1 832	1 976	4 521
UK	3 002	1 595	1 727	6 324
Total	33 605	13 443	14 692	61 740

Source: *Official Journal of the European Communities* 14/11 1995: 89, 159, 160. The remaining unallocated funds includes payments for overseas aid and administration.

in butter mountains and wine lakes. The CAP, however, also includes guidance in order to promote structural reforms, such as compensation for taking land out of use.

The place of the costs for the two main CAP programmes (EAGGF) in the structure of the EU budget is illustrated in Table 4.10. The agricultural policy under its two headings is the most costly programme on the Union budget. Attempts have been made to reform the CAP on several occasions, including the 1992 major change towards an entirely different support system, but it has proven difficult to cut costs (Fries, 1995).

Table 4.11 has the data for the income side of the Union, which is labelled 'Own Resources' in order to identify the money as strictly Union property. The most important revenue item is the VAT tax that the Union may levy on its member states. Own resources of the Union may not surpass 1.2 per cent of the total GNP of the member states.

The VAT taxes make up the bulk of the Own Resources of the Union, but the income from the GNP-based contribution and the customs duties is not marginal in the Union budget. There has been much debate about which countries gain and lose respectively on the budget. Table 4.12 contains a clue to the answer to this question about how much a country pays and how much it receives. It is obvious from Table 4.12 that the Union involves considerable redistribution, mainly from Germany to the Southern European countries. A few countries break even, for example Denmark and the United Kingdom.

A common fisheries policy has been on the agenda of the Union for a number of years. Such a policy would include regulations of catchment areas in the Union, including the amount of fish that various country fleets may bring up from the sea.

Table 4.11　*Types of income in 1994 (billions of Ecu)*

Member state	Levies		Customs duties	GNP-based own resource	VAT-based own resource	Total
	Agriculture	Sugar				
Belgium	46	90	929	637	1 227	2 822
Denmark	15	51	240	375	646	1 296
Germany	162	412	3 730	5 537	11 956	21 366
Greece	11	25	132	267	575	992
Spain	73	69	517	1 393	2 733	4 718
France	67	394	1 409	3 601	7 267	12 551
Ireland	2	12	229	123	297	639
Italy	136	150	997	2 370	4 234	7 760
Luxembourg	0.2	–	20	45	102	165
Netherlands	98	99	1 522	898	1 801	4 255
Portugal	103	0.4	122	279	734	1 216
UK	208	80	2 575	2 132	1 708	6 417
Total	923	1 382	12 420	17 657	33 280	64 189

Source: *Official Journal of the European Communities*, 14/11 1995: 56. The difference between the various items of income and total income is a small cost item relating to the collection of the Union's own resources.

Table 4.12　*Payments from and contributions to the EU in 1994 (percentages)*

Member state	Payments	Contribution	Difference
Belgium	2.7	4.4	−1.7
Denmark	2.5	2.0	0.5
Germany	14.8	33.3	−18.5
Greece	10.2	1.5	8.7
Spain	15.8	7.4	8.4
France	17.4	19.6	−2.2
Ireland	4.7	1.0	3.7
Italy	10.3	12.1	−1.8
Luxembourg	0.1	0.3	−0.2
Netherlands	4.0	6.6	−2.6
Portugal	7.3	1.9	5.4
UK	10.2	10.0	0.2

Sources: Tables 4.10 and 4.11.

Transport Policy

The EU has broadened its focus on the conditions for establishing a competitive market economy to include infrastructure and the transport sector. Common regulations now apply to transport by rail, road and inland waterway with the purpose of ruling out discrimination on grounds of origin of goods in regard to transport rates or conditions. Furthermore, state subsidies on transport are not allowed in general. The Union has committed itself to do away with all kinds of charges or duties in respect of the crossing of frontiers.

In the area of electricity and gas the Union has recommended that the principle of *Third Party Access* be applied in relation to infrastructure. This involves the deregulation of the transmission and distribution of electricity and gas in favour of competition in supply, where producers and consumers may ask for permission to employ distribution facilities that neither owns.

Harmonization and Economic Policy

Both the market rules and the social rights are conducive to unification of institutions in the Union. Besides these two sets of regulations, there are other harmonization policies as well as other forms of cooperation. Thus, the Union has empowered the Council to work for the harmonization of the whole of national economic law, including safety regulation. The same endeavour applies to taxation, where the Union upholds the principle that tax rules cannot discriminate between domestic products and products from other member countries. The Union has succeeded with this objective in so far as it has introduced a common value-added tax system.

The Union has extended its coordination ambitions to include general economic policy. The most spectacular format is the economic and monetary cooperation. Although the first policy of a monetary union including the EMS and fixed exchange rates as well as the introduction of common currency failed in the early 1990s, new mechanisms have been launched in order to make possible a monetary union with one central bank and one single currency from 1999 onwards. Membership in the monerary union depends on country convergence on criteria concerning total state debt (60 per cent of GDP) and current yearly deficits (3 per cent of GDP). Such a monetary union would equalize interest rates among the member states. However, a country that fails to comply with the current convergence criteria remains a member of the Union. It may also negotiate an agreement with the new monetary institute about a successive procedure for complying with the criteria for membership in the monetary union.

The creation of an Economic and Monetary Union (EMU) would be a major step in the direction towards a federal state in Europe. It would not only be based on one single currency but would also entail the arrival at a more or less common fiscal and monetary policy for the entire set of member states entering the EMU, including one chief central bank. The critical question is whether all member states are prepared or willing to take such a step, especially since few meet the Maastricht convergence criteria. Next, what about political cooperation in foreign policy and defence matters?

Foreign Policy Cooperation in Europe

The Union has recognized the need for political cooperation besides the policy coordination with regard to economic and social objectives since 1969. Thus, the EPC (European Political Cooperation) is institutionalized mainly through the European Council and attached institutions including the meetings of foreign ministers as well as a permanent secretariat. However, the EPC remains outside of the proper institutions of the Union, as it is not based on enforceable legal obligations. Its ambition to formulate and implement a common European foreign policy belongs to the *Acquis Communautaire* though.

Informal mechanisms for the collaboration between the states in Western Europe on foreign policy questions emerged shortly after the end of the Second World War in 1945. They were partly institutionalized between the countries that entered the European Community. In 1959 the foreign ministers of the six member states of the Community committed themselves to holding regular meetings on foreign policy matters. These talks paved the way for the creation of the European Political Cooperation in 1969, which further institutionalized cooperation between the member states in foreign policy matters.

The EPC remained an informal mechanism outside of the Community framework up until the Single European Act in 1987, which laid a legal foundation for the EPC. In the Act the member states committed themselves to take full account of the positions of the other member states and give due consideration to the desirability of adopting and implementing common European positions. Moreover, it was decided that member states have a formal obligation to consult each other on foreign policy issues. The purpose of the frequent contacts and the information duty is to enhance coordination, the convergence of positions as well as the implementation of joint action.

Since the 1987 Act the EPC mechanism has worked in close contact with EC institutions such as the Commission, the Council and the Parliament. The Presidency of the EPC goes to the foreign minister of the member state which holds the office of the Presidency of the Council of the European Union. This presidential office rotates every six months in alphabetical order of the member states. The Presidency of the EPC is assisted by a group of assistants.

The Maastricht Treaty of 1992 effectively integrated the EPC into the Union framework. The treaty commits the member states to a common foreign and security policy in order to safeguard common values and fundamental interests. The Council of Ministers may take joint action and request the Western European Union (WEU) to implement actions which have defence implications.

As the situation now stands, the EPC has been integrated into the EU and it has been broadened to cover security questions. However, the capacity of the EPC to bring about coordinated action is a contested issue in the Union. There are provisions for qualified majority voting in matters in relation to foreign policy and security issues, but several states claim an individual veto. Furthermore, the relations between the Union and the military organization WEU is not quite clear, as not all the member states of the Union particpate in the WEU. However, there is an unambiguous ambition among many member states to extend European cooperation to the security area, including the setting up of a joint European defence force. Yet, convergence on security policies must take into account the existence of other mechanisms for defence cooperation, such as the NATO alliance and the Organization for Security and Cooperation in Europe.

Finally, it should be mentioned that the member states have started to coordinate certain policies in the field of internal order, for example the police and immigration concerning the rights of asylum seekers and foreign labourers – the third pillar of the Union.

Military Cooperation

The key questions regarding security matters in Europe involve what forms cooperation takes as well as between which countries a common defence policy is definied and implemented. In reality, we find on the European scene all kinds of cooperation on security matters between a large number of states, including countries who are not on the European continent, strictly speaking. What used to dominate the European scene was quite naturally the confrontation between the NATO and the Warsaw alliances, but with the 1989 system collapse in the East this situation changed dramatically within a few years. Let us begin at the beginning, that is, when the war ended in 1945.

NATO

The North Atlantic Treaty Organization came into existence in 1949 as a collective defence for the following West European countries: Belgium, Denmark, France, Iceland, Italy, Luxembourg, the Netherlands, Norway, Portugal and the United Kingdom. Greece and Turkey entered NATO in 1952 and West Germany in 1955. Spain did not join until 1982, whereas France withdrew in 1966 from the military command of NATO though staying on as a member of the organization. Thus, Sweden, Finland, Ireland, Switzerland and Austria have stayed outside of NATO as formally neutral states.

NATO is based on the agreement of the parties to the Organization to come to each others' assistance in the event that one of them is attacked in Europe or North America. This includes all kinds of assistance, also the use of armed force. The original purpose of NATO was to maintain security in the North Atlantic area, and this aim was extended to include the Mediterranean Sea.

NATO is formally run by the North Atlantic Council, which is made up of ministerial representatives of the member states who meet at least twice a year. For the conduct of military matters there is a military committee, consisting of the chiefs of staff of the member states, under which operate three major commands: (1) the European command; (2) the Atlantic Ocean command; and (3) the Channel command.

NATO kept expanding its number of troops until they were in excess of those of the military organization, which it was primarily directed against, that is the Warsaw Pact. Following the breakdown of the Warsaw Pact NATO has reduced its number of troops considerably. The core of the NATO troops comes from the key member countries. The very same troops may, however, act under different command, as for instance when they form part of the troops of the Western European Union.

NATO has not only been occupied with creating credibility of the nuclear deterrent against the Warsaw Pact countries, that is mainly the Soviet Union, but it has all the time had to face internal dispute about the organization of military cooperation in Western Europe. One key question has been the rearmament of West Germany. Another is the deployment of nuclear warheads in Western Europe. Finally, the West European powers have demonstrated suspicion of the United States for making bilateral agreements with the Soviet Union or Russia.

Warsaw Pact

In 1955 the Warsaw Treaty Organization came into being, or as it was called: Warsaw Treaty of Friendship, Cooperation and Mutual Assistance. It included the following countries: the Soviet Union, Bulgaria, Czechoslovakia, East Germany, Hungary, Poland and Romania, as Albania withdrew in 1968.

The Warsaw Pact comprised a unified military command as well as the presence of Red Army troops in the other member states except Romania. At its height the troops under the Warsaw Pact command numbered some 4 700 000.

However, the presence of Soviet Union troops in particularly Poland and Czechoslovakia became a source of contention. When Czechoslovakia was invaded in 1968, the Warsaw Pact was involved formally. After the Pact had been dissolved the withdrawal of Russian army units became a new source of dispute, as in some countries like the Baltic states it proved cumbersome to bring the army units back to Russia.

Several of the former Communist countries have expressed a wish to join NATO but Russia thus far has objected to such a dramatic reversal of the military alliances map. Some countries such as Poland, Hungary and the Czech Republic have signed a collaboration agreement with NATO. What is to fill the gap after the dismantling of the Warsaw Treaty Organization in 1991 is an open question, as it involves different aspects about security and defence in Europe referring both to the future of CSCE (which became the OSCE in 1994) as well as the future of WEU and the ambitions of the European Union in foreign policy matters.

Western European Union

WEU, or the Western European Union, came into existence in 1955 when Belgium, West Germany, Italy, Luxembourg, the Netherlands and the United Kingdom decided to coordinate their defence. It actually dates back to the 1948 Brussels Treaty which provides for mutual aid in military, economic and social matters. The headquarters of the WEU is located in London and includes a council, a secretariat, an agency for the control of armaments and a standing armaments committee. The WEU used to be subordinate to NATO, but it has become more active in the last decade, as the West European powers attempt to formulate a common defence policy on their own terms. It is an open question whether the WEU will develop into the military organization of the European Union, because many members of the European Union, as formally neutral states, wish to downplay military cooperation within the Union, and some members of the Union oppose too much coordination in foreign policy and security questions. It was NATO and the UN that acted in Bosnia.

OSCE

Given the existence of many states on the European continent, of which some possess considerable military capacity, as well as the occurrence of two world wars on the same continent, the search for some kind of security framework after 1945 is not surprising. The drive for an international regime peacefully regulating the interaction between states seems all the more plausible in a world drawn up according to the superpower agreements in Yalta and Potsdam, dividing Europe into two camps, both heavily armed and in possession of nuclear capacity. The interesting thing is that the need for an international regime regulating the states of Europe persisted with the collapse of the Communist states and the dismantling of the Warsaw Pact. Thus, the security system created at the 1975 Helsinki meeting is still on the agenda as a mechanism for European convergence, although it did little in the Yugoslavian civil war.

The initiative to the Helsinki Conference goes back to the 1950s when the Soviet Union and the Warsaw Treaty Organization repeatedly called for a conference about Europe's security. Despite differing views between NATO and the Warsaw Pact on the ends and means of European security, it was possible to come to an agreement: the Final Act on Security and Cooperation in Europe, which started a sucession of meetings with the CSCE framework increasingly institutionalizing the efforts to make Europe safe from war between states.

The Helsinki Declaration lays down some guiding principles concerning relations between participating states. These rules include: sovereign equality, territorial integrity, political independence, non-intervention in internal affairs, inviolability of frontiers, peaceful settlement of disputes, respect for human rights and fundamental freedoms as well as equal rights and self-determination of peoples. Basically, the Helsinki Declaration confirms the relevance of public international law and commits the signatories to respect these principles. The members of the OSCE include all the member states of NATO and the Warsaw Pact and in addition the non-allied countries in Europe. Today the Organization for Security and Cooperation in Europe has more than 50 member countries.

The Helsinki Declaration aims to increase cooperation between states, secure the fulfilment of obligations under international law and introduce confidence building measures between member states. The CSCE process has been continued after the Helsinki Conference by a number of consecutive conferences and the setting up of a CSCE secretariat.

At the 1990 Paris meeting of the CSCE the central ambition was no longer to overcome the suspicion between two military blocks, but to enhance peace and security in Europe under a common denominator, namely human rights, democracy and the rule of law. Thus, a number of common institutions were now introduced: (1) a Council with the ministers of foreign affairs; (2) a Permanent Secretariat in Vienna; (3) a Conflict Prevention Centre in Vienna; (4) an Office of Democratic Institutions and Human Rights in Warsaw; and (5) a Parliamentary Assembly. The Council meets regularly as a mechanism for consultation and cooperation in relation to emergency situations.

Over the years since the 1975 Helsinki Act the CSCE has organized a number of meetings with the countries that are connected with questions of peace in Europe, which has resulted in a number of agreements institutionalizing procedures for enhancing collective security among member states. These agreements do not have the position of international law being only statements of intent, but they do contribute towards the arrival at institutions that are conducive to the peaceful settlement of conflicts between states. The OSCE though can do little with regard to internal conflicts such as civil wars.

Conclusion

The institutionalization of European convergence has come a long way since the first proposals of a united states of European peoples were suggested in the middle of the twentieth century. Cooperation, as well as coordination, have taken place mainly in Western Europe in several areas, though chiefly concerning human rights and economic matters. It may be expected that Eastern Europe is to be drawn into the process of harmonization of rules and the establishment of common institutions. It is also likely that other areas such as foreign policy and security will see more of coordination, if not straightforward integration (Fries, 1995).

As the institutions of the European Union appear to be the most spectacular phenomena of integration in Europe, this chapter has dealt at length with the Union. But one must not forget the activities of the Council of Europe as well as those of the WEU, or OSCE and NATO. Institutional convergence is no doubt strongest with regard to the creation of a common market all over Western Europe, to which a few East European countries have been associated. Yet, institutional convergence also covers other aspects such as human rights and social rights. The Council of Europe with its European Court of Human Rights covers the entire Europe, from Iceland to Russia.

The processes of formal European integration have thus far created one single European market for goods, services, labour and capital. Will it also lead to the establishment of a federal state in Europe with common political institutions of a *supranational* character? Or will European integration remain an *intergovernmental* phenomenon? In whichever way one chooses to answer this question about the future of Europe, one still must come to grips with the existence of European law. EU legislation in combination with the interpretation by the European Court of Justice in the form of precedents has resulted in the creation of a mass of rules common to all the member states. The creation of a huge bulk of European law is a most profound event of legal harmonization and political integration. It applies not only in the member states but also in the countries that signed the EEA treaty between former European Free Trade Association countries and the EEC.

In a legal approach one may wish to distinguish between various elements in the *Acquis Communautaire* or the Community patrimony of rules and objectives isolating those that have the specific federal property, of being directly applicable and having direct effects both horizontally between individuals in the Union and vertically between individuals and member states. But European integration also works outside of these rules which lie at the foundation of the concept of the Supremacy of Community law. Thus, member states often seek to adopt rules that the Union has recommended, because uniformity in institutions enhance interaction and reduce transaction costs. Also states that are not members of the Union may accept rules emerging out of the policy process in Brussels, either because they wish to join in the process of harmonization or because they anticipate a future membership for themselves. At the same time one must warn against any naïve belief that implementation of EU law is straightforward or willingly forthcoming.

The Union has mainly been seen as a rule maker, establishing a distinct European law as a major element in the fabric of the legal systems in 15 European countries. However, the Union has become more important recently in allocating and redistributing money through its regional funds. Together with the CAP the regional policy programmes take rather large sums of money, which may benefit particular target groups. It remains to be seen whether the regional policies will significantly hasten the process of equalizing regional disparities in income and employment.

But one still needs to assess how similar real political processes and behaviour are between the countries in Europe, whether they have been inside or outside of the Community. Institutional convergence in a number of legal frameworks is one thing, real life convergence in country politics is another, and which Chapters 5 to 9 examine more closely. The data on political institutions and behavioural patterns as well as political culture follows the classification of West European countries according to the EU format, where member states of the Union have been separated into those that formed the Community in 1958 (CORE EC and those that entered between 1973 and 1986 (OTHER EC). The remaining West European countries have been identified as OUTSIDE EC, although a few entered the Union in 1995. Perhaps the classification of East European countries into CORE EAST and EAST PERIPHERY also reflects the presence of the Union, because the former would be the most likely candidates for the further enlargement of the Union. But can we detect any differences between these five country sets when it comes to the analysis of politics?

Appendix 4.1   *Political/economic cooperation in Europe*

Country	Council of Europe membership			EC/EU membership			Any member of:		
	1950	1990	1995	1960	1990	1995	EFTA	CEFTA	CMEA
Albania			•						(•)
Austria		•	•			•	•		
Belgium	•	•	•	•	•	•			
Bulgaria			•						•
Croatia									
Czechoslovakia			•					•	•
Denmark	•	•	•		•	•	•		
Estonia			•						
Finland		•	•			•	•		
France	•	•	•	•	•	•			
Germany	•	•	•	•	•	•			GDR
Greece	•	•	•		•	•			
Hungary		•	•					•	•
Iceland	•	•	•				•		
Ireland	•	•	•		•	•			
Italy	•	•	•	•	•	•			
Latvia			•						
Lithuania			•						
Luxembourg	•	•	•	•	•	•			
Netherlands	•	•	•	•	•	•			
Norway	•	•	•				•		
Poland			•					•	•
Portugal		•	•		•	•	•		
Romania			•						•
Slovakia			•					•	
Slovenia			•						
Spain		•	•		•	•			
Sweden	•	•	•			•	•		
Switzerland		•	•				•		
United Kingdom	•	•	•		•	•	•		
Yugoslavia									(•)

Appendix 4.2 *Military cooperation in Europe*

Country	NATO membership			PFP	WEU		CSCE/OSCE		WTO Any member
	1950	1990	1995	1995	1960	1995	1975	1995	
Albania				•				•	(•)
Austria				•			•	•	
Belgium	•	•	•		•	•	•	•	
Bulgaria				•			•	•	•
Croatia								•	
Czechoslovakia				•			•	•	•
Denmark	•	•	•				•	•	
Estonia				•				•	
Finland				•			•	•	
France	•	•	•		•	•	•	•	
Germany		•	•		•	•	•	•	GDR
Greece		•	•			•	•	•	
Hungary				•			•	•	•
Iceland	•	•	•				•	•	
Ireland							•	•	
Italy	•	•	•		•	•	•	•	
Latvia				•				•	
Lithuania				•				•	
Luxembourg	•	•	•		•	•	•	•	
Netherlands	•	•	•		•	•	•	•	
Norway	•	•	•				•	•	
Poland				•			•	•	•
Portugal		•	•			•	•	•	
Romania				•			•	•	•
Slovakia				•				•	
Slovenia				•				•	
Spain		•	•			•	•	•	
Sweden				•			•	•	
Switzerland							•	•	
United Kingdom	•	•	•		•	•	•	•	
Yugoslavia							•	(•)	

Note: CEFTA = Central European Free Trade Agreement; PFP = Partnership for Peace.

5

Political Institutions

The dismantling of Communist institutions in Eastern Europe offered a unique opportunity for institutional redesign. Given the almost universal search for more of democracy it is little wonder that the new governments in Eastern Europe copied political institutions in Western Europe. Institutional convergence looms large in Europe in the 1990s, but the key question is: by how much?

The making of constitutions is the most conspicuous form of institutional design. However, one must be aware of the danger of drawing conclusions about real life institutions from simply reading constitutional documents. The process of implementing a new constitution is far from a top-down one, because constitutional practice as well as institutional inertia limit the possibilities of implementing constitutional blueprints. Moreover, constitutional documents, with their sometimes contradictory paragraphs, need to be interpreted implying that the gulf between the written constitution and the real or actually practised constitution may be vast.

The purpose of this chapter is to try to identify how similar political institutions are in Europe following the extensive processes of institutional reorientation in the early 1990s. On the one hand, we have to take into account onlingering differences between the states in Western Europe. On the other hand, there are the outcomes of constitutional policy-making in Eastern Europe (Hesse and Johnson, 1995). Surely, the abandoning of the Communist regimes must have made states in Eastern Europe more similar to states in Western Europe (Pridham and Vanhanen, 1994). What are the chief differences between states in Europe today then?

Variety of State Institutions

The state is basically a set of institutions for the regulation of the employment of physical force. In order to monopolize the use or threat of use of physical force the state identifies public authorities that are entrusted with the task of using physical force in a determinate way. The fundamental tasks of the state are internal and external defence. Once public authorities for these purposes are in place the state may set itself other tasks such as the allocation of infrastructure and the provision of welfare state services. The setting up of a set of public authorities requires that the territory and the population of the state be identified.

The first source of institutional variation concerns the distinction between unitary and federal states. The separation between these two forms of state refers to whether the state is one and indivisible or consists itself of several states. In unitary states the public bodies exercise authority over the population in a direct manner whereas in federal states the central government not only faces the population but also other states within its own territory.

The legitimacy of public authorities requires that authority be exercised by special and separate institutions that handle the three basic functions of legislative, executive and judicial tasks. The second source of institutional variation is the various manners in which the *trias politica* separation may be identified. Three aspects of institutional variation may be mentioned. First, some states are monarchies and others are republics, depending upon whether the head of state is a monarch or a president. Second, cutting across this distinction between two types of heads of state is the separation between parliamentary regimes and real presidential regimes, which refers to whether the body that exercises legislative powers also has control over the body that handles the executive powers in the special form of political and not only legal accountability. Finally, the judiciary may or may not have the special power of legislative review, or a capacity to interfere in politics quashing laws or regulations that are not in accordance with the constitutions. States that accept judicial review tend to have a special judicial body, a constitutional court.

The third source of institutional variation is to be found in the way democratic accountability is exercised. Democratic accountability may be handled in various ways: (1) Direct democracy versus representative democracy, or the extent to which countries rely upon the referendum for handling political issues; (2) The electoral system used for translating the votes of the electorate into seats in Parliament where the polar types are plurality formulas on the one hand and proportional techniques on the other; (3) The composition of the main representative institution, Parliament, with respect to whether it has one or two chambers.

The emphasis below, when mapping institutional variety, is on behavioural patterns, because reading formal constitutional documents is not enough. In real life constitutional principles may be bent in various directions, often under conflicts of interpretation between the major players. Constitutional practice may be messy, because political élites are often not in agreement on how constitutional paragraphs are to be interpreted. Simply quoting constitutional documents is not a reliable source of information about real life institutions. One has to examine how the state is actually run. The distance between constitutional *formalia* and institutional practice exists in any state, but it may be smaller or larger as well as more or less transparent.

Constitutional ambiguity is no less in Western Europe than in Eastern Europe, although the reasons for it are different. There is bound to be institutional uncertainty when a major overhaul of the political institutions is attempted. It may even prove difficult to introduce a definite constitution as for example in Poland, because the political élite is not in agreement about the fundamental rules of the state. But there will also be constitutional ambiguity when a formal constitution has been in place for many years, because many of its key paragraphs may have become obsolete. For example, the 1814 Norwegian constitution still stipulates that executive powers rest with the monarch, although constitutional practice since 1884 fully recognizes the principles of parliamentarism.

The distinction between constitutional *formalia* and institutional *realia* has particular relevance with regard to two facets of the state: first, the extent of decentralization of state powers between various levels of government within federal and unitary systems; and second, the division of executive powers between the president as head of state and the Premier in systems with the special European blend of presidentialism and parliamentarism.

One may assume that federal systems by their very nature are more decentralized than unitary systems; however, one has to look at the actual distribution of competencies beween central, regional and local governments, which may not coincide with the constitutionally prescribed one. Moreover, one cannot in Europe find any example of the American version of presidentialism, where there is no Premier and the members of the government are not accountable to the national assembly except under legal norms of control. But when there is both a strong presidential office and a Premier, then who is actually in charge? Constitutional documents cannot tell, actual behavioural patterns being crucial.

Thus, we arrive at the following list of aspects of sources of variation in state institutions in Europe, which are emphasized in the literature (Lijphart, 1984, 1994b; Huber et al., 1993):

- unitarism versus federalism;
- presidentialism versus parliamentarism;
- structure of Parliaments;
- the referendum;
- the degree of electoral proportionality;
- the extent of judicialization of politics.

The empirical analysis below looks at the extent to which some 30 states in Europe differ on these six institutions.

Unitary or Federal Format

Federalism is the state doctrine that argues that a federal state format is more congenial than a unitary one. The critical question is congenial for what and under which circumstances? Federalism would argue that the federal framework is the only type of state that can accomplish a decentralized polity. Furthermore, it would claim that the federal format is appropriate to any society, whether small or large (Elazar, 1987, 1995; Ostrom, 1991; Villiers, 1994).

Table 5.1   *Unitary and federal states*

	Unitary format	Federal format
CORE EC	4	2
OTHER EC	6	0
OUTSIDE EC	4	2
CORE EAST	6	0
EAST PERIPHERY	6	1
All	26	5

Sources: EB (1995), *Statesman's Yearbook 1995*.

Although this divergence model contrasting the unitary and the federal state is a challenging one, we must ask whether it holds up in relation to present European realities. Perhaps the federal state should be interpreted less pretentiously? A federal framework could bring about decentralization, but it may not be the only state type that will do so. A federal format could be the most suitable format only for a special set of states, that is large states which face so-called divided societies, meaning that they are characterized by deep-seated cleavages along ethnic or religious lines.

Table 5.1 gives information about the occurrence of the two basic state formats in Europe. Evidently, European statehood favours the unitary model ahead of the federal model. It is true that in 1993 Belgium shifted from the unitary to the federal format (Witte, 1992) as the final outcome of a long constitutional crisis involving a major overhaul of the constitution commenced in 1980. But all the new regimes in Eastern Europe chose the unitary format when the Communist regime was dismantled with the exception of the 'Federal Republic of Yugoslavia' (FRY), comprising Serbia and Montenegro and established in 1992, which looks more like a confederation as its real leader, Šlobodan Miloševíc, is the president of Serbia.

There used to be two federal states in Eastern Europe, namely Czechoslovakia, which was divided peacefully into two unitary states in 1993, and the former Yugoslavia, which collapsed into a number of states in the early 1990s: Croatia, Slovenia, Bosnia and Herzegovina, the Former Yugoslav Republic of Macedonia (FYROM) and FRY, the borders among some of these states still remaining unsettled as a result of the civil war.

There has been talk about a semi-federal model in Southern Europe, that is, in Spain and Italy. However, it is not clear what such a hybrid between the unitary and federal format would actually involve for various levels of government in terms of the two critical things in the centralization/ decentralization nexus: the exercise of competencies on the one hand and the allocation of financial resources on the other hand.

One may observe that the federal states in Europe occur in what Lijphart (1977) described as deeply divided societies, that is societies characterized by a historical legacy of strong ethnic and/or religious cleavages. In Belgium it is ethnicity whereas in Germany and Austria it is religion. Switzerland has the most fragmented society in Europe, combining ethnicity and religion as cleavages.

The relevance of the divergence model contrasting the unitary against the federal format decreases still further when one acknowledges that federal states could be centralized – such as Austria – as well as that unitary states can be decentralized – such as Denmark and Sweden – or regionalized such as France. After all, the unitary framework has worked well in many countries in Europe, especially when admitting extensive local or regional government discretion, or even constitutional autonomy to its subunits.

The local governments in Europe differ much in terms of size, competences and power (Norton, 1994). Speaking generally, the local governments in Northern Europe have more discretion and functions than local governments in Southern Europe, reflecting different state legacies. And it is also true that local governments in federal states have less autonomy, being under the authority of the states, than local governments in a unitary state, if indeed that unitary state practices a decentralized state format (Page and Goldsmith, 1987; Batley and Stoker, 1991; Chandler, 1993). Typical of local governments, whether they are so-called communes or regional governments, is that they derive their mandate from below, being directly elected.

If decentralization of power or state competencies is the critical issue in the debate between the federalists and unitarists, and if fiscal indicators may be used to tap the centralization/decentralization dimension, then Table 5.2 has relevant data on two indicators on the amount of fiscal decentralization around 1990. The idea behind the fiscal indicators on the distribution of powers between various levels of government is that the more resources lower levels of government can raise themselves by taxation, the larger their discretion vis-à-vis the central or federal government. The first fiscal decentralization indicator (D1) measures regional/local government revenue as a proportion of central government revenue. The second indicator (D2) presents the opposite information, namely the proportion of grants from other levels of government in relation to the total revenue of regional/local governments.

Interestingly, only in OUTSIDE EC is there real extensive fiscal decentralization, that is in countries where either state, regional or local governments have considerable independent taxation power (D1). Consider briefly the countries with an extensive degree of fiscal decentralization having large taxation power at lower levels of government, namely: federal Switzerland and Germany as well as unitary Denmark, Finland and Sweden. And then move to compare them with the countries where most of the taxes are raised by the central or federal government, namely the following: Italy, the Netherlands, Czechoslovakia, Belgium, Ireland, the United Kingdom and France.

The other indicator (D2) in Table 5.2 hints that with a few exceptions all

Table 5.2 *State format and fiscal decentralization*

	Own taxes/central government revenue (D1)	Grants from other levels of government/total revenue of provincial or local government (D2)
CORE EC	16.3 (6)	52.4 (6)
OTHER EC	18.5 (5)	54.9 (5)
OUTSIDE EC	43.3 (6)	26.8 (6)
CORE EAST	14.0 (3)	47.9 (3)
EAST PERIPHERY	26.6 (2)	35.3 (2)
All	24.8 (22)	43.7 (22)

Source: IMF (1993).

states in Europe are rather centralized, because in most countries lower levels of government receive considerable grants from the central or federal government. This applies to both federal Germany and Austria as well as to unitary Norway where local governments are strong. The data in (D2) offer ample evidence of the Fritz Scharpf idea of *Politikverflechtung*, or how various levels of government tend to be interwoven in a complex pattern of reciprocities (Scharpf et al., 1976). The transfer of money from the central or federal government to provincial or local governments is one thing and the amount of discretion exercised by the latter in relation to the former is another thing though. It is not necessarily true that who pays the piper calls the tune, especially in intergovernmental interaction where the central government employs framework legislation to unify state practices (Hesse, 1978).

In any case, the major finding in Table 5.2 is that the amount of decentralization varies independently of the state format. Decentralization is a real possibility within the unitary model and centralized federal states are practically feasible. The extensive processes of regionalization in Southern Europe and local government decentralization in Northern Europe have taken place without changing the indivisible nature of the unitary state (Keating and Jones, 1985). In fact, the only exception to the general decentralization trend among unitary states in Western Europe is the United Kingdom where there has been a pronounced process of centralization initiated in the late 1980s and carried on into the early 1990s (Rhodes, 1992), turning it into one of the most centralized states in Western Europe. Whether the unitary states in Eastern Europe will embark upon a decentralization trend is doubtful though, given the weakness of the often numerous local governments in these countries (Clark, 1993; Coulson, 1995; CDLR, 1995).

In relation to the theory that the federal type of state is employed in segmented societies, that is countries with high levels of ethnic and/or religious cleavages, one may make the counter observation that not all countries that are heterogeneous have a federal framework. Spain, the

Netherlands, Italy and Finland must be classified under the unitary category, in terms of constitutional law. If federalism is appropriate for divided societies, then the federal format could be relevant for Slovakia, Romania and Bulgaria, for example, where there are substantial ethnic minorities. But there seems to be much hesitation in introducing the federal format in these countries, as some fear that this state format could fuel conflict along ethnic and religious lines instead of appeasing them, the main danger being that of secession if indeed the ethnic or religious cleavages have an underlying territorial dimension.

A distinction is often made between symmetrical and asymmetrical federalism, depending upon whether the states of the federation have the same competences or status (Burgess and Gagnon, 1993). A similar distinction is also relevant in relation to unitary states, where certain regions may be granted a special status or separate regional autonomy, sometimes called home rule. We find this asymmetrical state structure in Italy and Spain where certain provinces have separate constitutions granting them competencies – the so-called autonomous regions in Italy. In the Spanish state there is an asymmetry between the so-called nationalities and the remaining provinces, as the former have more discretion than the latter, which is recognized in the constitution by the employment of different paragraphs for introducing decentralization (Heywood, 1995). However, we cannot find any cases of asymmetrical federalism in Europe. Instead we note that a few unitary states have granted special regional autonomy, as for example France to the island of Corsica and Finland to the island of Åland. In the United Kingdom the Isle of Man and the Channel Islands have separate status, which also applies to the Azores and Madeira in Portugal.

Often asymmetrical state structures give rise to regional conflicts, because not all regions may be willing to grant special powers to a few regions, giving rise to a special status for these. The conflict in Spain between the so-callad nationalities and the provinces is a telling case, as they face alternative routes to establishing autonomy but it is far from obvious that the competences arrived at would be different. One may question whether asymmetrical federalism is really a viable option. The success of German and Swiss federalism appears to rest upon the symmetry between the member states. Asymmetrical federalism may lead to *dual* federalism, where one state or region is entirely distinct from the others. The emergence of dual federalism could be conducive to the creation of two separate states as was the case in former Czechoslovakia splitting into the Czech and Slovak Republics. Will the new Belgian federation, comprising three different language communities, develop towards a kind of confederation or perhaps the separatist forces in Flanders will prevail?

To summarize, the unitary model prevails in Europe, as the number of federal states according to constitutional law include only Germany, Switzerland, Austria, Belgium and the FRY. Perhaps Switzerland is the only true federation in Europe, as the degree of fiscal decentralization is exceptional in this state on both indicators used above (D1 and D2). The 26 Swiss cantons and demi-cantons and local governments raise as much money as the federal government in the form of taxation and they receive only 20 per cent by means of grants from the federal government. Whereas German federalism is heavily based upon intergovernmental interaction, the federal government both creating legislation which the *Länder* are free to implement and transferring huge grants to the *Länder*, Swiss federalism distinguishes in a more clearcut fashion between central and regional government competences. Austrian and Belgian federalism on the other hand must be classified as harbouring a rather centralized form of state. There are unitary states where lower levels of government possess considerable amounts of autonomy such as in Scandinavia. Even France with its tradition of centralization has moved towards regionalization. Each *département* has a General Council which is elected for six years and it is responsible for the chief departmental services such as welfare, health and local regulations (Stevens, 1992). Earlier the *préfet* exercised extensive fiscal control and veto power over the affairs of local governments, but the 1982 reform involved that the prefects would only see to it that departmental activities are in agreement with the law.

The Executive

The definition of the head of state, the office itself and its competences as well as the identification of the person, is handled in each constitution by a few very important rules. The classical distinction between kings or queens on the one hand and presidents on the other hand is of little relevance in the European context, because what matters is the actual power of the head of state which is practically nil in the European monarchy. Pure presidentialism as an institution connects the tasks of the head of state with those of the head of government or cabinet, meaning that the president is the premier. However, there are no pure presidential systems in Europe. In the European republics presidents and premiers exist side by side, but their respective powers differ in various republics.

Since there exist no real monarchies in Europe any more, the king or the queen is a mere figurehead, a national symbol, and he or she can only play a political role under exceptional circumstances. One should, of course, not underestimate symbolic institutions, which the events in Greece and Spain prove, where one king was drawn into politics to a much too large extent (Konstantin) and another refused to be involved in a *coup d'état* against democracy (Juan Carlos). There is no real threat against the remaining royal houses in Europe, but at the same time it is very unlikely that the number of monarchies will grow in the future. When the East European states changed their political institutions in a radical fashion around 1990, none seriously contemplated abondoning the republican form of government.

The European republics are more numerous than the monarchies. They

Table 5.3   *Heads of state and government*

Country set	Monarchy	Republic	Strong	
			President	Premier
CORE EC (6)	3	3	1	5
OTHER EC (6)	3	3	1	5
OUTSIDE EC (6)	2	4	2	4
CORE EAST (6)	0	6	3	3
EAST PERIPHERY (7)	0	7	4	3
All (31)	8	23	11	20

Sources: Shugart and Carey (1992), McGregor (1994).

all have a presidential head of state, but the presidential institutions in Europe are very different from American presidentialism. What is decisive is the position of the head of the cabinet, the premier. In all monarchies the premier is the head of government, whereas in the republics presidents as heads of state existing alongside premiers may exercise certain executive functions. There are two versions: weak presidentialism where the premier is the head of government and the president as the head of state is merely a symbol of national unity on the one hand; strong presidentialism, on the other hand, where the president and the premier share executive powers. Table 5.3 provides data on two aspects of the institutions surounding the head of state.

One may argue that there is only one example of true presidentialism, which is an institution where the head of state is at the same time the head of government and not responsible to Parliament in accordance with the principles of parliamentarism. This would be Switzerland with its special government institution, where the cabinet forms a collegial presidency, which rotates yearly between the seven ministers, elected from seven different cantons for four years. The Swiss presidency thus has seven heads, as it were, since there is a permanent grand coalition government comprising seven ministers among which the presidency rotates yearly.

Strong presidentialism of the European type including both a president and a premier is to be found in about half of the republics, although the distinction between strong and weak presidentialism is not crystal clear in Europe (Moe and Caldwell, 1994). In Eastern Europe strong presidentialism is frequent whereas in Western Europe weak presidentialism occurs more often. Speaking generally, the institution of premier is the most typical institution for defining the head of government in Europe. And premiers are always more powerful than kings or queens and have more power than presidents most of the time. Strong presidentialism is to be found in France, Portugal, Finland, Poland, Romania, Lithuania, Albania and Yugoslavia. However, in all the cases of European presidentialism except Switzerland the president as head of state has to share power with a premier as head of government.

It is not possible to make judgements about the power of the president by simply reading the formal constitution. In Slovakia, Hungary and Bulgaria for instance there are different views about the competences of the president and the premier, respectively, although the constitution favours weak presidentialism (Baylis, 1996). The general pattern is that weak presidents tend to be elected by the national assembly whereas strong presidents are elected directly by the people. But there exist exceptions to this pattern. Typical of strong presidentialism in Europe is the tension between the president and the premier, as for example in France during the so-called cohabitation: Mitterand and Chirac 1986–8 and Mitterand and Balladur 1993–5 (Cole, 1993), as well as in Poland between president Walesa and the premiers Pawlak and Olesky (Karpinski, 1995). Finally, one may mention the conflict between premier Meciar and president Kovac in Slovakia (Fisher, 1995).

The problem in classifying executives as either presidentialist or premier based in Europe is that there are several possible presidential prerogatives, but European presidents do not exercise all of them. Some presidents have certain legislative powers such as the veto in Portugal and the competence to issue decrees or by-laws in France. Presidents may also have the power to appoint or dismiss cabinet members or to dissolve Parliament, as in Lithuania, Poland and Romania. How such presidential prerogatives limit the powers of premiers and Parliaments depends more upon constitutional practice which scholars may judge differently.

From Table 5.3 it is apparent that monarchies have strong premiers and republics have strong premiers when they have weak presidentialism. The power struggle between a strong president and a strong premier can be conducive to executive stalemate as with problems of cohabitation in France and Finland. In Greece the constitution was amended in 1986 to clarify that the executive powers were to rest with the premier. Yet, it must be emphasized that European politics does not harbour any case of American presidentialism involving the separation of powers between one head of state, who is also the leader of the government, and the legislature. Parliamentarism reigns in Europe with the sole exception of Switzerland, where the cabinet is elected by the national assembly, but it cannot be dismissed by Parliament nor can it dissolve Parliament.

Parliamentarism is the set of institutions that anchor the power of cabinets to rule a country on their being tolerated by Parliament. As soon as Parliament, by means of a majority vote, expresses its lack of confidence in the government, then the existence of the government is at stake. In parliamentary democracies the trust mechanism between the national assembly and the government is handled by the political parties, which is the institutional foundation of party government.

Although all the countries in Europe except Switzerland express their adherence to parliamentarism, there is an interesting institutional variation in how parliamentarism is practised from one country to another. The institutions of parliamentarism may vary in relation to the requirements for: (1) cabinet investiture, or the procedure for appointing a premier or government; (2) a vote of non-confidence by Parliament in relation to the government; (3) the request for a vote of confidence by the premier; and (4) the dissolution of Parliament in order that new elections be held. The rules governing these mechanisms of parliamentarism differ from one country to another, as different players may take the initiative or make the final decision concerning points 1 to 4.

In the United Kingdom there are few restrictions on how these four mechanisms of parliamentarism may be employed, whereas in other countries they are more regulated. The German requirement of a 'constructive vote of non-confidence' is one example, practised also in Spain where Parliament is restricted to bringing down a government only if it can support a new one. Another instance is the French institution of block vote, where the premier may demand that a bill be voted on in its entirety and that its rejection by Parliament entails that the cabinet will step down. Finally, the prerogative of the premier to dissolve Parliament may be restricted by rules that either stipulate specific circumstances, such as a successful motion of non-confidence, or place the final decision with someone else such as the president in countries with strong presidentialism or Parliament (Döring, 1995).

If one relates the findings in Table 5.3 above to the debate about the pros and cons of presidentialism and parliamentarism (Linz, 1990, 1994; Linz and Valenzuela, 1994), then one may argue that it is not possible to have such a blunt dichotomy. The phenomenon of European presidentialism, which provides the head of state with some but certainly not many executive prerogatives in relation to Parliament, does not fall neatly into the divergence model of US presidentialism versus UK parliamentarism. In any case, although the president may have certain prerogatives in legislation, finance and budget-making on the one hand and/or in government formation and the dissolution of Parliament on the other hand, he/she has to accept the coexistence of the institution of premier everywhere except in Switzerland.

Legislatures

Democratic legitimacy provides legislatures with a prominent symbolic role, representing the will of the people as it were. How powerful national assemblies are in reality vary from one country to another. Legislatures are elected every fourth or fifth year on a regular basis, but the election period may be shorter due to institutions that make it possible to dissolve Parliament and call for standby elections.

The composition of the national assembly is a function of the chamber system and the election method employed. Table 5.4 gives information about the construction of the legislature, whether there are one or two chambers as well as whether the two chambers have equal competences.

Table 5.4 *The chamber system of the legislature*

Country set	One chamber	Two chambers	
		Unequal	Equal
CORE EC (6)	0	3	3
OTHER EC (6)	3	2	1
OUTSIDE EC (6)	4	0	2
CORE EAST (6)	3	1	2
EAST PERIPHERY (7)	5	1	1
All (31)	15	7	9

Sources: Laundy (1989), Norton (1990), Hibbing and Patterson (1994), Mény (1994), Remington (1994).

There are as many one-chamber Parliaments as two-chamber Parliaments in Europe.

The federal states have without exception a bicameral legislature as the second chamber represents the states. However, a large number of unitary states adhere to bicameralism, having besides a national assembly that is directly elected also a senate. Unicameralism is more frequent in two country sets, OUTSIDE EC and EAST PERIPHERY. Although all the states in Eastern Europe are unitary states except Yugoslavia, many of them have two chambers such as Poland, Slovenia, the Czech Republic and Romania.

Bicameralism is so frequent in Europe that it is necessary to look at the relationship between the two chambers. The critical question is whether they have the same powers or status. One speaks of symmetrical and asymmetrical bicameralism in relation to whether the competences of the two chambers are the same or not. Federal states tend towards the first type but unitary states may display either symmetrical or asymmetrical bicameralism. As well as the United Kingdom and Ireland, the Netherlands and France constitute examples of the latter, whereas Spain and Italy could be considered as examples of the former. In Eastern Europe there is symmetrical bicameralism in Poland and Romania (Olson, 1994; Agh, 1995).

Bicameralism has thus two sources. On the one hand, federal states have two chambers. The construction of the federal chamber may vary both with regard to the number of representatives each state may send and in relation to the status of the representative. Swiss federalism applies the principle that each canton sends two representatives independent of the size of the canton, which means that the Council of States is made up of 46 members from 23 cantons. In German federalism the 68 members of the *Bundesrat* represent the state governments, the small states sending three and the large six representatives. Austrian federalism applies the rule that each state legislature sends to the federal council of 64 members representatives in accordance with the size of the population of the state.

Bicameralism may be employed in unitary states where a senate or upper

Table 5.5 *Referenda, 1990–4*

Country set	Average
CORE EC (6)	2.3
OTHER EC (6)	1.0
OUTSIDE EC (6)	9.3
CORE EAST (6)	.5
EAST PERIPHERY (7)	1.9
All (31)	3.0

Sources: Brady and Kaplan (1994), Butler and Ranney (1994), Kobach (1994), *Keesing's*.

house complements the national assemby or lower house. The senate may be recruited in different ways – by appointment, direct election and indirect election. The upper house may be regarded as a special body of excellence and wisdom, as in Ireland and the United Kingdom where it moderates the lower house if necessary, or it may exercise the same political prerogatives as the lower house. The UK House of Lords is in addition a supreme court of appeals. It is not the case that only federal states have a chamber system where the two chambers have equal competences.

The Referendum

The position of legislatures in the political system of a country is affected by whether it faces competition from the referendum. In several European countries there are institutions for calling a referendum and in some of them referenda are employed as a mode for making decisions that restricts the power of Parliaments. The referendum may be obligatory or facultative and its outcomes may be decisive or advisory. Finally, there exists the possibility of a people's intitiative, that is, a group of citizens or a group of parliamentarians may ask for a referendum.

The referendum is an important political institution in Switzerland, Italy, Denmark, Ireland and France. Switzerland is the referendum democracy *par préférence* in Europe with constant activity involving referenda at either the federal or cantonal level stimulated by the raising of people's initiatives. A number of referenda have been held in the early 1990s concerning the entrance to the European Union. Yet, only with regard to the case of Swiss democracy is it possible to argue that the referendum institution is a threat to the institutions of representative democracy in Europe which Parliaments confirm. Table 5.5 illustrates one indicator on the importance of the referendum, namely the actual referenda held between 1990 and 1994.

The explanation for the high score for OUTSIDE EC is the almost unbelievably large number of referenda in Switzerland, or 53 referenda during a five-year period. The only country that comes anywhere near to that score is Italy, which had 13 referenda between 1990 and 1994.

Another interesting observation in relation to Table 5.5 is that the referendum institution is as relevant in EAST PERIPHERY as in CORE EC and OTHER EC. Thus, Estonia and Lithuania have had 3 referenda each; Croatia and Yugoslavia 2 each; and Latvia, Romania, Slovakia and Slovenia 1 referendum each. In Western Europe Ireland scores a high 4 referenda whereas Denmark has had 2; Sweden, Norway, Finland and France 1 each, almost all of which pertain to membership in the European Union.

One may argue that some referenda are more important than others and that consequently counting the number of referenda is not enough. One single referendum may shape the future of a country, becoming critical moment in the history of politics of the country when events are interpreted some years after the referendum in question. Yet, the referendum institution is in effect only a real alternative to Parliaments when it is employed in the Swiss style. One must recall that Swiss democracy is founded on a large number of referenda also at the cantonal level. Now, the composition of representative institutions is decided primarily by the election techniques.

Election Systems

Perhaps the most well-known model about institutional effects in politics is Maurice Duverger's hypothesis about the consequences of the framing of the rules for the electoral system, or more specifically that plurality electoral formulas are more likely to enhance political stability in the form of government durability than proportional election formulas.

Duverger's *Political Parties: Their Organization and Activity in the Modern State*, published in English for the first time in 1954, comprises two parts: 'Party Structure' and 'Party Systems', the latter starting out from the divergence between two-party systems and multi-party systems. Two-party systems are described as:

> for practical purposes only two parties share the parliamentary seats: the one assumes the entire responsibility for government, the other limits itself to the free expression of criticism in opposition; a homogeneous and powerful Cabinet has at its disposition a stable and coherent majority. (Duverger, 1964: 207)

This is the typical feature of adversarial politics when operating under its optimal institutions. Duverger goes on to describe the multi-party system in the following way:

> In the other case a coalition between several parties, differing in their programmes and their supporters, is required to set up a ministry, which remains paralysed by its internal divisions as well as by the necessity of maintaining amidst considerable difficulties the precarious alliance on which its parliamentary majority is based. (Duverger, 1964: 207)

Thus, twopartism goes together with government durability whereas multipartism is linked with government instability. What made Duverger's distinction between two kinds of party systems well known is his explanation of the institutional cause of the separation, the impact of the election system: '*the simple majority single ballot system favours the two-party system*. Of all the hypotheses that have been defined in this book, this approaches the most nearly perhaps to a true sociological law', states Duverger (Duverger, 1964: 217).

Although the first part of the argument, linking the electoral formula with the party system, has gone down as Duverger's law, the second part is as important. In the conclusion Duverger emphasizes the connection between the party system and government authority: 'the two-party system too has strengthened the authority of the government but without destroying the apparatus of democracy' (Duverger, 1964: 403), versus: 'Internally weak, multi-party governments are also weak in their relations with parliament' (Duverger, 1964: 408).

Duverger paid much attention to explicating why the electoral formula shaped the party system, but said little about why multi-party systems would tend to produce unstable governments. The basic idea is that proportional representation (PR) formulas result in multi-party systems where a large number of parties find it difficult to form and uphold a stable government. The model raises several questions as to how election rules affect political behaviour through various mechanisms.

The Duverger model stimulated a whole body of research into the political consequences of electoral systems (Rae, 1971; Nohlen, 1978; Lijphart and Grofman, 1984; Grofman and Lijphart, 1986; Lijphart, 1994a), focusing first on the connection between election techniques and the party system, and second on the relationship between multipartism and political instability. Duverger was more explicit on the former than on the latter, arguing in favour of the so-called Duverger's law:

> (1) Proportional representation tends to lead to the formation of many independent parties . . . (2) the two-ballot majority system tends to lead to the formation of many parties that are allied with each other . . . (3) the plurality rule tends to produce a two-party system. (Duverger, 1986: 70)

Duverger's law has been examined at length, testing whether PR election formulas produce multipartism and plurality twopartism. Here we note that Duverger's model is of the divergence type positing a sharp separation between majoritarian formulas including the two-ballot procedure and PR techniques, which is translated into the party system and moves further into the pattern of government formation and durability. How valid is the starting-point of Duverger, the sharp distinction between PR and plurality formulas, in relation to European politics today?

When looking at how election formulas vary across Europe, then one could first look at which election formula a country employs and then estimate how close to strict proportionality between votes received and seats allocated the political parties in a country come. One must keep in mind that electoral outcomes depend on factors other than simply the election formula used. Thus, the size of the constituencies, the occurrence of formal thresholds and malapportionment also impact upon the degree of

Table 5.6   *Election systems*

Country set	Plur	Mixed	PR	Disproportionality
CORE EC (6)	1	2	3	13.2 (6)
INSIDE EC (6)	1	0	5	9.5 (6)
OUTSIDE EC (6)	0	0	6	5.1 (6)
CORE EAST (6)	0	1	5	18.3 (6)
EAST PERIPHERY (7)	0	2	5	12.9 (6)
All (31)	2	5	24	11.8 (30)

Note: The index of disproportionality measures how closely the allocation of seats (mandates) mirrors the allocation of votes by measuring the percentage difference between votes and seats for the parties.

Sources: McGregor (1993), Lijphart (1994a); see also Appendix 6.1.

disproportionality between votes and seats (see Lijphart's (1994a) analysis). The impact of the election technique on politics tends to be transmitted through the degree of disproportionality (Lijphart, 1994a: 139–41).

Examples of the plurality formulas could be found in the United Kingdom and France, the latter country using the two-step procedure with a few exceptions where a PR method was employed (d'Hondt). The d'Hondt method is used in the BeNeLux countries, Finland, Spain, Switzerland, Portugal and Iceland; the Saint-Lague formula in the Scandinavian countries; and the Largest Remainder (Hare/Droop quota) in Austria, Greece and Italy (before the 1994 election) would exemplify the proportional formulas, which also cover the Single Transferable Vote (STV) in Ireland. Mixed election formulas combine the plurality techniques with the use of some proportional method. Thus, in Germany the so-called Hagenbach-Bischof method involves two votes, the *Erst-Stimme* for choosing candidates in 328 single-member constituencies and the *Zweit-Stimme* in relation to party lists where the states (*Länder*) are the constituencies. A most interesting change in the electoral formula was made in Italy in 1994, replacing the Imperiale quota method with a mixed system. Thus, three-quarters of the seats for both the Chamber of Deputies and the Senate are to be filled from single-member districts by First-Past-the-Post, while the remaining quarter are to be reserved as proportional compensation seats subject to a 4 per cent threshold.

The new democracies in Eastern Europe employ PR techniques with the exception of Hungary, Albania and Lithuania which employ mixed election systems (Furtak, 1990; McGregor, 1993; Gonzales Enriques, 1995). Table 5.6 has the overview of election systems.

Thus, there is no considerable variation in the employment of various election institutions across Europe. The proportional electoral formulas are much more often used than the plurality formulas. This observation holds for both Western and Eastern Europe, which reflects the strong institutionalization of multi-partism in Europe. In the set of OUTSIDE EC countries the adherence to proportional election rules is total.

Although it is a fact that the plurality methods overexaggerate the differences between parties on the allocation of seats in Parliament, one needs to emphasize that there may be a lack of proportionality also in countries which employ proportional methods. The countries characterized by a large difference between electoral outcomes and the allocation of mandates include the following: France, Croatia, Poland, the Czech Republic, Hungary, Slovakia, Estonia and the United Kingdom. The rather low proportionality score for Spain reflects the many small constituencies in the rural areas.

It is a surprising finding that the proportionality index shows such large differences between votes and seats for the new democracies in Eastern Europe. In some of these the average percentage difference between votes and seats is as high as 20 per cent, which is far from the ideal of strict proportionality. Only the Netherlands, Austria, Sweden and Denmark come close to this ideal with a 3 per cent average difference between votes and seats. Yet, what Table 5.6 shows is that it is hardly meaningful to classify the European election systems into the simple dichotomy of plurality versus PR systems. Actually, the relationship between election formula and the amount of proportionality is far weaker in this data set than earlier results have shown ($r = .44$), as PR-systems may vary extensively in terms of proportionality. The Duverger divergence model seems not particularly illuminating in relation to the realities of the 1990s.

European democracy focuses much upon the national assembly and its composition deriving from it crucial implications for government formation, in accordance with the prevailing model of party government (see Concluding Chapter). Yet, legislative supremacy in Europe is increasingly being challenged from the judicial branch of government.

The Judicial System

In the *trias politica* model, or the separation between executive, legislative and judicial powers, the judiciary has a special status. Its separation from the other powers is considered vital, as its engulfment is looked upon as the hallmark of the existence of a *Rechtsstaat*. Whereas the principle of parliamentarism to some extent obliterates the sharp separation between executive and legislative powers, the importance to create stable and firm barriers between the judiciary and the other powers has never been called into question.

The legal system may be organized in different ways. In some countries there is a sharp separation between public and private law – the Roman-Germanic tradition – the former being handled by administrative courts and the latter by ordinary courts. In countries belonging to the Common Law tradition ordinary courts are more important than the many public tribunals. In federal states there is explicit recognition of the need for some type of court review of the division of competencies between the federal and the provincial governments.

Table 5.7   *Countries which accept legal review*

Country set	Judicial review	
	Supreme court	Constitutional court
CORE EC (6)		3
INSIDE EC (6)	1	2
OUTSIDE EC (6)	1	1
CORE EAST (6)		6
EAST PERIPHERY (7)		4
All (31)	2	16

Sources: Blaustein and Flanz (1972–), Duhamel and Mény (1992), Schwartz (1993), International Institute for Democracy (1995), Stone (1995).

Now, the increasing influence of judges upon politics stems from two sources. On the one hand there is the large expansion of public law that has attended the growth of the public sector since the Second World War. On the other hand, we have the increasing use of judicial review, or the growing legitimacy for the reliance upon courts to test the constitutionality of first and foremost acts of Parliament, but also executive decisions and then possibly to quash them.

Legal review is a much contested institution, because it makes often life-time appointed judges politically influential, although there is no mechanism for holding them accountable in a democratic fashion. In some countries judicial review is entrusted to a separate constitutional court that may either test for constitutionality before a law is enacted (France) or after legislation has taken place (Germany). Some countries reject entirely the notion of judicial review, upholding the principle of parliamentary sovereignty as in the United Kingdom, Sweden, Denmark and Finland. Legal review may also be entrusted to the ordinary courts, such as a supreme court as in Norway. Table 5.7 maps the existence of judicial review in various European countries. It is noteworthy that Switzerland as a federal state lacks not only a formal constitutional court, but also that its Supreme Court does not have the general competence of legal review, although it must guard the division of powers between the federal and cantonal governments. All in all 18 countries practise strong judicial review.

Interestingly, the constitutional revolution in Eastern Europe has been so much driven by the ideal of institutionalizing human rights protected by the judiciary that almost all the former Communist countries have introduced a separate constitutional court. In the following 16 countries the constitution provides explicitly for a constitutional court: Austria, Germany, France, Italy, Portugal, Spain, Albania, Poland, Slovenia, the Czech Republic, Hungary, Romania, Yugoslavia, Slovakia, Bulgaria and Croatia. The fact that there are few constitutional courts in Western Europe reflects the distrust in many countries of judicial review, because of the danger of the judicialization of politics, although in some of these countries the ordinary courts exercise a kind of softer form of legal review.

The standard impression that unitary states reject judicial review whereas federal states welcome it is not corroborated in the European case. The supreme court for administrative matters in unitary Greece engages in legal review whereas the supreme court in federal Switzerland cannot test for the constitutionality of all kinds of legislation. How could strong legal review be compatible with Swiss referendum democracy?

Institutional Patterns

In his seminal text *Democracies*, Lijphart's basic argument is that there are very strict limits on institutional variation in the European states. The Westminster model favours a unitary state, unicameralism or asymmetrical bicameralism, indirect democracy and parliamentarism, the plurality election method and no judicial review. The Consensus model opts for federalism, symmetrical bicameralism, power separation, the use of proportional election formulas and legal review (Lijphart, 1984).

Lijphart was well aware of the fact that the institutions, formal and real, of democracy vary considerably in both space and time. But he claimed that his ambition was to:

> discover patterns and regularities, and I will argue that both the variations and the regularities can be interpreted in terms of two diametrically opposite models of democracy: the majoritarian model (or the Westminster model) and the consensus model. (Lijphart, 1984: 3)

How valid is this institutional classification after the system transitions which occurred around 1990, incorporating a number of East European countries into democratic Europe? How much of the variation in political institutions in Europe conform with the two regularities identified in these ideal-types?

Analytically speaking, the Lijphart divergence model covers two basic dimensions of the state institutions: the nature of the state with regard to the unitary or federal format on the one hand, and *trias politica* or the separation of powers on the other hand between the executive, legislature and judiciary. A country may be federal, practise parliamentarism but recognize judicial review (Germany). Or a country may be federal and have full separation of powers (Switzerland). And a country may be unitary but have a presidential form of government and a constitutional court (France, Romania). Finally, a country may be unitary but practise parliamentarism and no legal review (the United Kingdom).

Empirically speaking, Appendix 5.1 shows the correlations between a number of political institutions, which allow us to estimate the degree to which the Lijphart aspects of the state tend to go together according to his two ideal-types of democracy. The overall finding in Appendix 5.1 is negative, as the correlations between the institutional features are much too low to substantiate the claim that there are two, and only two, fundamental state models in Europe. Actually, there seem to be very few real constraints on institutional variation in the political institutions in the countries of Europe.

Conclusion

The transition to democracy in Eastern Europe has added institutional variety to European political institutions. Although all the new democracies are almost exclusively unitary states, some of them have a parliamentary regime whereas others belong to the special brand of European presidentialism. They use proportional or mixed election formulas at the same time as emphasizing the independence of the legal system, entrusting a special constitutional court with the power of judicial review.

There are few restrictions on institutional variety in Europe looked at from a constitutional point of view. Federal states may be either parliamentary or presidential – the same is true of unitary states. Constitutional courts operate not only in federal systems or in countries with European presidentialism, but they are also important in some unitary systems with parliamentary regimes. A variety of chamber systems is employed, where it is not the case that unitary states only have one chamber or exclusively tend towards asymmetrical bicameralism. Direct democracy is practised in but a few countries in Western and Eastern Europe.

Divergence models employing simple dichotomies such as Westminster versus Consensus democracy, or countries with plurality election formula versus countries with PR election techniques, appear to be less relevant to the realities of the 1990s than earlier. Instead of a sharp separation between two kinds of election system we see the increasing employment of mixed systems. And mixed as well as proportional election formulas may result in very different degrees of proportionality between the votes and seats of a party. One may even question the distinction between unitary and federal states, as both types may vary extensively in terms of fiscal decentralization which tends to be an appropriate indicator on institutional autonomy. To overexaggerate somewhat, the only truly different political system in Europe today is Switzerland with its special executive and its strong commitment to fiscal decentralization in combination with the numerous referenda.

One may look at an index that taps the extent of democracy in a country taking into account the institutionalization of various civil and political rights (Table 5.8). The index on democracy measures the institutionalization of civil and political liberties and the scores, ranging from 0 to 10, show the convergence in Europe towards the democratic regime.

It is true that there is institutional variation between the European democracies in the early 1990s, but the countries do not tend to diverge systematically into two neat sets, however delineated. Politics is much more than the constitutional framework. Perhaps there is more of a

Table 5.8   *Index on democracy, 1989–95*

Country set	DEMO89	DEMO90	DEMO92	DEMO94	DEMO95
CORE EC	9.9	9.7	9.6	9.6	9.6
OTHER EC	9.7	9.6	9.7	9.4	9.4
OUTSIDE EC	10.0	10.0	10.0	10.0	10.0
CORE EAST	2.7	6.6	7.5	8.1	8.2
EAST PERIPHERY	2.1	2.5	6.1	6.4	6.8
All	7.8	8.6	8.5	8.6	8.7

Sources: Freedom House (1990, 1991, 1993, 1995, 1996).

clearcut pattern of variation between countries in the information about important political aspects such as the party system, government formation and public expenditures?

With the strong evolution of the Union some see federalism as the future state format in Europe. Perhaps it is more appropriate to talk about *regionalism* as the new form of territorial politics. In the 1990s regionalism affects both the nation-states and EU, but it does not necessarily mean decentralization (Keating and Hooghe, 1996). Regionalism turns European policy-making into a multi-level game (Keating and Jones, 1995; Keating and Loughlin, 1996).

Appendix 5.1   *Institutional patterns*

	Fed	Decen	Chasys	Pres	Elecdis	Concourt
Fed	1.0	.49	.61	.04	−.28	.07
Decen		1.0	.00	.14	−.26	−.21
Chasys			1.0	.01	−.02	.31
Pres				1.0	.26	.31
Elecdis					1.0	.47
Concourt						1.0

Sources: Federalism (Fed) = Table 5.1; Decentralization (Decen) = Table 5.2; Chamber System (Chasys) = Table 5.4; (Unicameralism = 0; asymmetrical bicameralism = 1; symmetrical bicameralism = 2); Strong President (Pres) = Table 5.3; Electoral Disproportionality (Elecdis) = Table 5.6; Constitutional Court (Concourt) = Table 5.7.

6

Party Systems

When one examines the party systems in Europe, then one is at the heart of politics on this continent, because these political systems all adhere to the principles of party government. The political parties are the main so-called *players*, as they put up the candidates for competition in elections and they provide the cabinets of the European governments. It is true that there are occurrences of entrepreneurial politics in a few countries providing single personalities with some opportunities for charismatic behaviour, but party politics is the dominant mode.

The purpose of this chapter is to describe how the electorate aligns itself in relation to the political parties. According to Giovanni Sartori party systems tend to diverge according to two dimensions. On the one hand there is the number of parties (fractionalization) and on the other hand there is the ideological distance between the parties (polarization) (Sartori, 1976: 126–9). How useful are these concepts for an understanding of the party systems in both Western and Eastern Europe in the early 1990s?

Below we will analyse the party systems in Europe along a couple of dimensions drawing upon recent research on party systems (Mair and Smith, 1989; Janda, 1993; Katz and Mair, 1995). We cover the period since the introduction of free and fair elections in Eastern Europe. The first elections with limited or full competition took place in Poland on 4 and 16 June 1989, in the DDR on 18 March 1990, in Hungary on 25 March and 8 April 1990, in Romania on 20 May 1990, in Czechoslovakia on 8–9 June 1990, and in Bulgaria on 10 and 17 June 1990 (Butler and Särlvik, 1990).

As well as examining the set of European multi-party systems from the distinction between fractionalization and polarization we also describe the content of these party systems, or which parties fill up the spectrum from the left to the right. Thus, we describe which parties make up the Right and the Left as well as whether there are centre parties in between the left and the right parties. Finally, we discuss volatility, or how stable the voter support for parties tends to be over time.

Electoral Availability and Parties

The European electorate votes regularly with a rather high turnout. Table 6.1 shows that between 75 and 80 per cent of those eligible to vote use their rights in both Western and Eastern Europe.

There is immense variation in political participation between different

Table 6.1   *Electoral turnout, 1990–5*

Country set	Turnout	High	Low
CORE EC (6)	82.1	91.9	68.5
OTHER EC (6)	76.2	83.5	67.4
OUTSIDE EC (6)	74.6	87.3	44.1
CORE EAST (6)	75.8	90.9	47.6
EAST PERIPHERY (6)	82.0	94.6	68.3
All (30)	78.1	94.6	44.1

Source: Appendix 6.1.

countries, but the variation has nothing to do with the West–East or North–South divisions. Turnout in the early 1990s has been very low, that is below 50 per cent, in Switzerland and Poland as well as rather low in Hungary, Estonia, Portugal, Ireland, France and Finland, that is around 68 per cent. Turnout has been high, or in the region of 90 per cent, in Albania, Belgium, the Czech Republic, Latvia and Luxembourg.

A number of hypotheses have been suggested in order to account for differential voter participation rates (Grofman and Lijphart, 1986; Lewis-Beck and Lockerbie, 1989), including: (1) Institutions: a publicly sanctioned obligation to vote, registration law, PR election formula; (2) Party system characteristics: the degree of competition, the extent of polarization, the support for new parties; (3) Societal conditions: affluence, education (Powell, 1986; Blais and Carty, 1990; Crepatz, 1990; Jackman and Miller, 1995).

It is argued that political competition in the form of adversarial politics drives up electoral participation whereas a high degree of disproportionality in the election system drives down participation in elections. But adversarial politics tends to feed upon disproportionality as in twopartism. Compulsory voting cannot be a necessary condition for a high turnout as the cases of Austria, Iceland and the Netherlands show. And it is not a sufficient condition as the case of Greece shows. Some highly affluent countries, such as the Scandinavian countries, have above the average turnout rate whereas rich Switzerland has the lowest figure. If one critically examines the hypotheses explaining country differences in electoral participation, then no single hypothesis really stands up. Probably one needs to focus on specific factors in the few countries that are so-called outliers – that is, they diverge clearly from the average score which is about 78 per cent for all the European countries.

It has been debated whether the rate of turnout is going down (Topf, 1995). Such a trend towards a lower rate of electoral participation would be regarded as evidence of a system crisis or as a questioning of the legitimacy of representative democracy. However, there are at the same time contradictory signs about the nature of political involvement, because there is growing support for new social movements and an increase in political action outside of the Parliamentary arena. What is called 'New

Politics' in Europe is channelled to a large extent through groups that act outside of the established political parties (Kriesi et al., 1992; Rohrschneider, 1993). Fuchs and Klingemann argue that new forms of political participation are spreading at the same time as the system legitimacy remains high:

> Citizens use non-institutionalized forms of action because these forms offer their own possibilities for attaining political goals – not because citizens are dissatisfied with conventional forms of action. (Fuchs and Klingemann, 1995: 432)

Yet, despite the emergence of new social groups and many mechanisms for direct political participation (Aarts, 1995), European politics is, basically, party government. The behaviour of the key players is institutionalized in the form of parties, and the political parties in the European democracies operate, as we saw in Chapter 5, under the institutions of parliamentarism. Let us first examine what this entails, as this is one of the major characteristics of all European party systems, the second being their multi-party nature.

Party government is fostered by the institutions of parliamentarism, which links the executive to the legislature on the basis of political trust. Parties discipline their parliamentarians in order to be able to act as one player, maximizing their bargaining strength in the allocation of rewards and costs in the policy-making process. In the electoral process the parties serve as intermediaries between citizens and Parliament. Thus, parties tend to handle both the process of articulating the interests of the citizens and the process of forming a cabinet that has the confidence of Parliament.

Parties may be challenged by political entrepreneurs in their claim for controlling entry to politics. In a few countries, such as France and Greece, political leaders may have the upper hand in relation to the political parties, giving birth to new parties or terminating old parties. However, in most European countries politics is in the hands of the political parties, which even major politicians like Margaret Thatcher, Felipe Gonzales and Helmut Kohl cannot do without.

Running a democracy is time consuming, claims vast resources and requires formal organization. Managing the electoral process if possible is costly. Only very exceptional politicians can manage to fund and organize a candidacy on their own. Even a charismatic politician like Charles de Gaulle had to rely on political parties (RPF, UNR) in order to give more stability to his ambitions.

Political parties are transaction cost minimizing devices in a democracy. If each and every issue were to be decided by the electorate by means of the referendum, then people would have to be engaged in politics almost hour by hour on a daily basis. Political parties package issues and offer support for certain sets of programmes on the condition that they can collect the votes of the electorate. How faithful political parties are to their electoral promises is another matter, but the electorate has the possibility in the next election to punish politicians who fail to deliver. The evolution of new forms of political participation in the form of New Politics and numerous social groups at the grassroots level has complemented representative democracy rather than superseded it (Klingemann and Fuchs, 1995).

At the same time political parties employ strategies to safeguard their own interests. Large parties pursue a catch all strategy searching for positions where the median voter is placed. Small parties define a niche which they attempt to penetrate. Whether parties pursue a strategy of truly maximizing their payoffs, or if they merely satisfy some objectives, is a contested problem in party research. The institutional setting may make a crucial difference, as a two-party system tends to stimulate maximization behaviour, whereas multi-party systems harbour satisficing activity. Uncertainty increases as the number of parties go up meaning also that risks are augmented. With many players the stakes are higher as a failure to identify and maintain a niche may result in annihilation in elections. More and more parties are becoming sensitive to media coverage of politics. Their tactical and strategic efforts may be furthered or hindered by the media, testing the popularity of parties in recurrent polls.

Multipartism and Party Types

European politics is to a large extent multi-party politics. There exists no single pure two-party system. It used to be argued that the United Kingdom and Germany belonged to a special kind of two-party system: the so-called 2.5 party system, if one can talk about the absolute number of parties as something other than integers (Blondel, 1968). But fractionalization has increased in both countries, at least with regard to the number of parties that receive support in elections. At the moment the United Kingdom has more political parties than Germany, if one takes into account the ethnic and regional parties

Yet, multipartism is the typical characteristic of the party systems in Europe, that is, for all the countries it holds good that they adhere to the multi-party format. But is party fractionalization more excessive in Eastern Europe where the party systems are in the process of being formed, compared with Western Europe where they have been long established? Besides number, a party system may be analysed with regard to its composition – that is, what kinds of parties it harbours and how their relative strength compares.

This is the main thrust of Sartori's argument. He stated:

> The point is to show that the traditional multi-party category grievously muddled two radically different cases and that the more-than-two party systems cannot be lumped together in a single package. (Sartori, 1976: 140)

There are, according to Sartori, entirely different types of multi-party systems depending on the number and strength of what he calls 'anti-system' parties, that is, parties which question the legitimacy of parliamentary democracy. Sartori's basic distinction is that between party systems with moderate pluralism and party systems involving polarized pluralism, the applicability of which we can only probe by looking not only at the number of parties but also at their ideological orientation. Thus, we must try to understand the programmatic orientation of parties.

There is, no doubt, a certain amount of idiosyncrasy in the European party systems, as in some countries there are parties with labels that have no correspondence in most other countries. However, party idiosyncrasy is not a pervasive phenomenon. On the contrary, the political parties in the European countries tend to cluster into a limited number of distinct party types, to be identified by criteria such as party labels or ideology (Janda, 1980; Seiler, 1992). One may disagree about the classification of some of the parties, but certainly not the bulk of them.

It is true that the classification of some parties in the new democracies in Eastern Europe presents difficulties. The party systems in Eastern Europe are still in a process of formation which means that there will be much instability both with regard to the kind of parties that are formed and the fate of the parties at the polls. Yet, instability is on the increase also in several West European party systems including the formation of new parties and the transformation of old established ones. Extensive processes of electoral dealignment and realignment have taken place in several West European party systems.

For the analysis of the new party systems in Eastern Europe Klaus von Beyme lists the following party types (in German): Forumparteien, Christdemokraten, Liberale, Sozialdemokraten, Reformkommunisten, Grüne, Nationalisten, Ethn/Regionale and Funktionelle (Beyme, 1994: 298–9). One may argue that such a classification is adequate in relation to European politics, because issues and party support express more than the left–right dimension. There is evidence that other dimensions show up in the alignment of the electorate around political parties. Thus, Ronald Inglehart has pointed out the relevance of post-materialist values, which involve a different set of attitutes towards economic growth and environmental concerns from those of both the left and right (Inglehart, 1977, 1990). Besides, there is the ethnic or nationalist dimension and in addition gender. However, the general impression is that the left–right dimension is the dominating one in almost all party systems in Europe, which is the reason that we employ it as the basis for the presentation of the political parties in Europe (Lindström, 1991; Kitschelt, 1992, 1995a; Mink, 1993; Roskin, 1993; Szajkowski, 1994; Whightman, 1995; Rivera, 1996). In addition, one may create a few special party family labels such as religious, environmental and forum parties.

We have thus opted for the following scheme for classifying the political parties in Europe into party-types or families of parties: religious, ethno-regional, agrarian/centre, socialdemocrats, communist/post-communist, left-socialist, liberal, conservative, populist, green, forum, and a residual: Other parties. Any attempt to map the political parties in Europe according to this scheme meets, needless to say, with difficulties. Still, there is a general understanding about what to count as religious parties (Madeley, 1982; Karvonen, 1993b; Hanley, 1994; Durand, 1995), ethno-regional parties (Coakley, 1992; Seiler, 1994; Malmström, 1995), socialist parties (Dreyfus, 1991; Karvonen and Sundberg, 1991; Gillespie and Paterson, 1993; Anderson and Camiller, 1994; Kitschelt, 1994; Waller et al., 1994), communist or post-communist parties (Gotovitch et al., 1992; Bull and Heywood, 1994; Ishiyama, 1995), liberal parties (Kirchner, 1988; Roussellier, 1991), conservative parties (Layton-Henry, 1982; Morgan and Silvestri, 1982) and green parties (Rüdig, 1988; Müller-Rommel, 1991; Kaelberer, 1993; Frankland, 1995).

What we call 'populist' parties stands for parties that from a mainly right-wing position deliver demands upon the state to take drastic action in various fields such as taxation, immigration and welfare state retrench-ment. Since it is almost unfeasible to differentiate between discontent parties, ultra-right parties or nationalist parties we have assembled them all under one heading: Populist parties (Beyme, 1988; Ignazi, 1992; Held, 1993; Gärtner, 1995; Kitschelt, 1995b; Taggart, 1995).

When following any scheme for classifying political parties according to party types, one is always confronted with how to identify a particular party. Some critical cases are the Irish parties Fine Gael (religious) and Fianna Fail (liberal) and the French Front National (populist). How to classify the Italian right-wing parties including a former fascist party and the Partito Democratico della Sinistra (post-communist) on the left-wing? The Austrian FPÖ was considered liberal in 1990, but populist in 1994 and 1995.

The newly formed parties in the Baltic party systems seem almost to resist any attempt at classification. Still, for Estonia we have opted for: Coalition Party and Rural Union (KMUE; agrarian-centre), Center Party (K; forum); Estonian Reform Party (RE; liberal); Pro Patria and ENIP Union (I & ERSP; conservative); Better Estonia/Estonian Citizen (PE/EK; populist); Justice (communist). Our choices in the Latvian party system are as follows, if we quote some cases: Saimnieks (agrarian); Latvia's way (conservative); Union for the Fatherland and Freedom (populist); Ziegerist's Party (populist); Unity Party (communist); National Conservative Party (LNNK; conservative); National Harmony Party (TSP; liberal). In Poland The Alliance of the Democratic Left (SLD) is considered post-communist, while the tiny Democratic Social Movement (RDS) is classified as socialdemocratic. These cases indicate that an attempt to classify the political parties in Europe into some 12 party types remains a provisional one that subsequently will need to be revised.

Fractionalization

Distinctive of European politics is that the party systems harbour the most important political players and that there is a multiplicity of parties. The first party system model underlined the implications of the sheer number of

Table 6.2 *Fractionalization, 1990–5*

Country set	Electoral fractionalization	Parliamentary fractionalization
CORE EC (6)	6.2	5.0
OTHER EC (6)	3.5	2.9
OUTSIDE EC (6)	4.9	4.4
CORE EAST (6)	6.1	3.9
EAST PERIPHERY (6)	5.7	4.3
All (30)	5.3	4.1

Source: Appendix 6.1.

players, that is, the fractionalization approach (Rae, 1971). How many parties or players there are varies from one country to another, but the average scores on the indices that measure party system fractionalization all validate the impression of well-developed multi-party systems.

One may employ a few standard indicators on party system fractionalization. The most simple indicator is to look at the absolute number of political parties, whereas other more complex indicators take the votes for the parties into account. Thus, in some countries there may be as many as 15–20 parties, but the size of several small parties may be so tiny that they matter little. An overall fractionalization index such as the effective number of parties weights the number of parties according to their electoral support (Laakso and Taagepera, 1979).

Looking at the absolute number of political parties is beset with some uncertainty, because one may not agree upon what constitutes a political party. How firm or large must an organization be to qualify as a political party? This problem is relevant not only in relation to East European party systems but may also be raised concerning party systems in Western Europe, such as the Italian and Dutch party systems. Tiny parties come and go as they fail to elect any representatives to Parliament. In a few countries the formal threshold is very effective in keeping small parties from getting representation.

Table 6.2 has the data on two indices on party system fractionalization, the first looking at the effective number of parties in national election outcomes and the other on the effective number of parties in the national assembly. The interesting finding in relation to Table 6.2 is that the party systems in Eastern Europe are hardly more fractionalized than those in Western Europe on both indices. When one consults the two indices, then the finding is that fractionalization, electoral and parliamentary, tends to be rather extensive in all country sets except OTHER EC. Parliamentary fractionalization in the set of CORE EC countries is larger than that of CORE EAST and EAST PERIPHERY.

One may note that electoral fractionalization and Parliamentary fractionalization are not the same thing, because the electoral institutions play a role in translating voter support for a party into Parliament support. The average fractionalization in Parliaments (4.1) is substantially lower than the electoral fractionalization (5.3). The party systems that score high on electoral fractionalization include: Poland, Belgium, Estonia, Slovenia, Switzerland and Italy – all having more than seven effective political parties. And the countries that are high on Parliamentary fractionalization are roughly the same: Belgium, Slovenia, Poland, Switzerland, Italy and Estonia – all having more than five effective parties in Parliament.

There is much less electoral fractionalization in Albania, Greece, Portugal and the United Kingdom, with less than three effective parties in the elections. Parliamentary fractionalization is low in Albania, Portugal, Croatia, Greece, the United Kingdom, Bulgaria, Spain, the Czech Republic and Germany, with less than three effective parties. Perhaps one could call these party systems '2.5' party systems today, but then one is not talking about the absolute number of parties. In any case, such a relative number as the effective number of parties does not contain the whole truth, as one must remember that the number of parties that receive electoral support is considerably higher also in these countries.

Polarization

In party system research it has been considered that it is not enough to look at the sheer number of players. A classical dimension in European party systems is the left–right one, which refers to party ideology. In every party system there has been the confrontation between class-based parties with the possible exception of the Irish party system, which though houses a labour party. The relevance of the left–right dimension may be measured by several indicators which help us shed light on the extent to which the party systems in Europe differ in terms of polarization, or the ideological tension between the left and the right.

One index is the strict polarization index, which measures the weight of left-wing and right-wing parties in the party system in terms of electoral support (Sigelman and Yough, 1978). Party systems with large centre parties score low on this index. A second index looks at the overall support for political parties that are conventionally considered to be placed at the extremes of the left–right scale: Populist, Communist and Left-Socialist parties.

Yet, in relation to both these measures it is today an open question whether these left-wing or right-wing parties really constitute so-called extreme parties that are fundamentally different from the other parties, constituting a set of so-called anti-system parties in the Sartori framework (Sartori, 1976). Not only Communist parties have reorientated themselves in relation to democracy and the market economy, but also ultra-right parties have toned down their ideological heritage from the 1930s.

A third index is the left–right index which starts from the placement of the political parties on a left–right scale aggregating them to a party system measure with due consideration of the size of the electoral support of the

Table 6.3   *Polarization, 1990–5*

Country set	Polarization index	Extreme party support	Left–right index
CORE EC	3.7 (5)	14.9 (6)	5.6 (5)
OTHER EC	2.7 (5)	8.2 (6)	5.7 (5)
OUTSIDE EC	3.1 (6)	13.4 (6)	5.5 (6)
CORE EAST	3.8 (5)	37.1 (6)	5.2 (5)
EAST PERIPHERY	0.3 (1)	29.8 (6)	4.5 (1)
All	3.2 (22)	20.7 (30)	5.5 (22)

Note: The polarization index goes from 0 to 25, higher scores meaning a more polarized party system. The left–right index ranges from 1 to 10, the lower the score the more left orientated is the party system.

Source: Appendix 6.1.

various parties. This index is also sensitive to how the ranking of the political parties is done, this time along a left–right continuum. We have employed a party identification suggested by Huber and Inglehart (1995) – see also Castles and Mair (1984). One could also employ information about how the voters themselves rank the parties on the left–right scale (see Chapter 9), but expert judgements do not always coincide with the voters' ranking.

Table 6.3 gives the information for the party systems according to these three indices, first the strict polarization scale and then the extreme party support and the left–right score.

The data on polarization in Table 6.3 must be interpreted with care, as the three indices show different things. The strict polarization index displays that no party systems in Europe are really polarized in a strong sense. This finding reflects the declining relevance of extremist ideologies since the fall of Communism in 1989. Although there have emerged new nationalist movements in the last decade, these parties are not as ultra-right as the fascist parties of the 1930s. Actually, the country that scores highest on the polarization index is the Czech Republic, reflecting how its former Communist Party is classified by experts, which only shows that the identification of the programmatic orientation of parties is far from self-evident. Other countries with a high level of polarization include: Hungary, France, Italy, Denmark and Sweden.

Yet, there is a clear difference between the party systems in Western and Eastern Europe here, which shows up in the indicator on the support for extreme parties. There is nothing similar in Western Europe to the extreme party support in both CORE EAST and EAST PERIPHERY, except for Italy and France. The countries with the largest support for extreme parties are, not surprisingly, Romania, Slovakia, Lithuania, Bulgaria, Albania and Italy. Countries with a low level of polarization or support for extreme parties are the United Kingdom, Ireland, Belgium and Portugal.

However, the crucial left–right index does indicate a very small difference between the party systems in Western and Eastern Europe with

Table 6.4   *Support for left-wing parties, 1990–5*

Country set	Entire left	Post-communist	Social Democrat	Other left
CORE EC (6)	30.2	6.4	23.3	0.6
OTHER EC (6)	41.7	5.0	34.7	2.0
OUTSIDE EC (6)	36.8	5.4	29.3	2.0
CORE EAST (6)	31.6	26.2	3.9	1.4
EAST PERIPHERY (6)	25.7	20.9	4.1	0.8
All (30)	33.2	12.8	19.1	1.4

Source: Appendix 6.1.

regard to where the main ideological profile of the major parties, as the parties in Western Europe tend to be somewhat more to the right than the parties in Eastern Europe. The polarization index and the left–right scale indicate convergence whereas the index on extreme party support indicates divergence. In order to understand the relevance of the left–right continuum in party systems one must look more closely at the composition of the flanks as well as the centre of party systems.

Programmatic Orientations of the Party Systems

It would be a very strong case for the convergence theme if the only substantial and telling party system difference between Western and Eastern Europe were to be found in the continued and strong support for the former Communist parties. Surely there must be other differences in the political orientations of the parties in the party systems of Western and Eastern Europe? Let us look more closely at how the left, the right and the centre of these party systems are constituted.

The Left-wing Flank

Looking at the variety of left-wing parties in a broad sense one observes that today the support may go to either the Social Democratic parties, to left-Socialist parties or the former Communist parties. Table 6.4 shows the distribution of votes for these different left-wing parties.

There is little variation between the country sets with regard to the overall strength of the left-wing parties. What does vary systematically as well as strongly between these sets is the relative strength of the two main contenders for the left-wing vote, Social Democracy and Former Communism. In Western Europe Social Democracy prevails whereas in Eastern Europe former Communist parties predominate. The crux of the matter is that many former Communist parties now claim that their programmatic orientation is in reality that of Social Democracy. The old Social Democratic Parties in Eastern Europe have received weak support in the first democratic elections, where the Czech Social Democrats (CSSD) constitute an exception as they have risen to the position of second largest party in the 1995 polls (Kettle, 1995).

Table 6.5 *Support for right-wing parties, 1990–5*

Country set	Conservative	Populist
CORE EC (6)	9.1	7.9
OTHER EC (6)	23.1	1.2
OUTSIDE EC (6)	15.9	5.9
CORE EAST (6)	2.7	9.4
EAST PERIPHERY (6)	16.7	8.2
All (30)	13.5	6.5

Source: Appendix 6.1.

Only in a few countries do we find strong left-Socialist parties that are not former Communist parties such as in Denmark and Norway. At the same time as one observes that the traditional large Communist parties in Western Europe have shrunk considerably in voter support since 1989 despite efforts to change their profile (Bull and Heywood, 1994), one must recognize that the former Communist parties have staged a real comeback in many East European countries. This is true not only of the peripheral countries but also of core East European countries like Poland and Hungary (Ishiyama, 1995; Mahr and Nagle, 1995).

The overall position for left-wing parties is close to or over 50 per cent in the following countries: Romania, Greece, Lithuania, Spain, Denmark, Sweden and Norway. In the following countries the left-wing parties whichever they may be are weak: Latvia, Slovakia, Croatia, Switzerland and Ireland with an average support of 20 per cent. It is true that former Communist parties receive much electoral support in Eastern Europe, but one must emphasize that not all East European party systems have strong former Communist parties. An interesting observation is the high score for overall Left support within OTHER EC, in which set of countries also the Social Democrats have their highest scores. In the early 1990s the strongest Social Democratic Parties are to be found in Southern Europe (Spain, Portugal and Greece) and not in Northern Europe (Scandinavia, Germany and Austria), as it used to be.

The Right-wing Flank

Turning to the right wing side, the question is again which types of parties here receive most support, as there tends to be a few chief contenders on the right side of the spectrum. Thus, one must make a distinction between, on the one hand, conservative and on the other hand, discontent, populist or utra-right parties. It is not always crystal clear where one party fits in this classification, particularly in relation to the last three mentioned party types. The recent rise of nationalist parties presents a classification problem, as they may be placed in either of these categories. Table 6.5 suggests one answer.

Large conservative parties are to be found in three country sets: OTHER EC, OUTSIDE EC and EAST PERIPHERY. On the other hand, such parties meet with little support in both the CORE EC set and the CORE EAST set. The largest conservative parties are to be found in Greece, Croatia, France, the United Kingdom, Iceland, Spain and Latvia as well as Estonia, where they score above 30 per cent.

Populist parties may be found in all sets, although they are marginal within OTHER EC countries where traditional conservative parties completely dominate the right-wing flank. Populist parties show up within the CORE EC, CORE EAST and EAST PERIPHERY sets, as Populist parties tend to be strong in Slovakia, Estonia, Poland and Luxembourg with 10 per cent support or even more. The same is true of Austria in the OUTSIDE EC set. However, one must underline that the classification of some of these parties as populist may be questioned. Although, for example, the placement of Le Pen's National Front is unambiguous, one may hesitate about how to classify the Italian right wing comprising Forza Italia (conservative), MSI/Alleanza Nazionale (populist), the Lega Nord (ethno-regional).

One may establish that the similarities between the five country sets are just as limited concerning the composition of the right as was the case in relation to the composition of the left. Only populist parties operate with roughly the same support in all the sets except OTHER EC, whereas conservative parties are not significant players in all the countries entering the sets of CORE EAST and CORE EC countries. And what about the composition of the centre in the party systems?

The Centre

The much discussed left–right continuum may give the impression that the major parties are to be found either to the right or to the left. Such an interpretation would, however, entail a neglect of the centre (Daalder, 1984). Bypassing the fractionalization and polarization concepts it has been argued in recent party system research that a key feature of party systems is whether they are balanced or not (Smith, 1979, 1989a). Party systems may comprise *core* parties which although not large may have much bargaining power in policy-making and government formation – so-called *pivot* parties (Keman, 1994). Centre placed parties, such as Christian Democracy in the West and the Centre Parties in the Nordic countries, may constitute core parties which balance the left-wing and the right-wing flanks. Liberal parties as well as ethnic parties may at times be able to exercise pivotal power.

This is not to deny that a balanced party system could be made up of two major parties on the right and the left wings such as a big conservative and a large social democratic party. Nor can one always take for granted that the core parties in a party system are made up of small pivot parties. Large Social Democratic or Conservative parties have at times been able to play the role of state parties, bringing balance, stability and coherence to the party system at the same time that the opposition has been fragmented and internally split, as for example in Norway and Sweden as well as in the United Kingdom and France.

Table 6.6   *Support for centre-based parties, 1990–5*

Country set	Agrarian parties	Christian parties	Liberal parties	Ethnic parties
CORE EC (6)	0.0	24.6	15.1	3.7
OTHER EC (6)	3.2	5.6	18.7	2.9
OUTSIDE EC (6)	13.8	11.0	8.7	1.1
CORE EAST (6)	8.0	6.1	12.3	5.0
EAST PERIPHERY (6)	8.8	5.1	9.5	1.5
All (30)	6.7	10.5	12.9	2.8

Source: Appendix 6.1.

Yet, there is certainly a case for arguing for the relevance of centre parties in European politics with regard to simple facts. Table 6.6 shows that there are indeed many kinds of centre parties and that some of them may be rather large in terms of electoral support, at least at certain times.

In fact, only one type of centre-based party tends to be tiny, namely the ethnic type. Of the other kinds of centre-based parties it is possible to find many examples which are large or medium-sized parties such as the CDU/CSU in Germany and the Christian Democratic parties in Luxembourg, Austria, the Netherlands, Belgium, Ireland and Switzerland. Large or medium-sized liberal parties are to be found in Portugal, Ireland (Fianna Fail), the Netherlands, Hungary, Switzerland, Slovenia and the Czech Republic. The following countries have medium-sized Agrarian parties: Finland, Iceland, Denmark and Norway – all running under the label 'centre party'. These centre parties or former agrarian parties are to be found within the OUTSIDE EC set, mainly the Nordic countries, as well as in Eastern Europe. It should be pointed out, however, that ethnic parties score around 10 per cent in Belgium, Spain, Slovakia and Italy.

What is conducive to party system divergence in the way various types of centre orientated parties receive support is mainly the differences in support for the former agrarian parties. The other types of centre-based parties tend to be represented in most countries. Perhaps one can argue that there are more similarities between the country sets in how centre-based parties occur than was the case with either left-wing or right-wing parties. Christian Democratic, Liberal and Ethnic parties exist in several of the European party systems and although their levels of support vary, the variation is not exceptional as is true of the former Communist and Populist parties.

New Politics

Most of the political parties in Europe may be classified according to their programmatic orientation as belonging to the left, right or to the centre. The only distinctively new parties formed in Europe from the 1970s and onwards are the Green Parties and the so-called Forum Parties. Common to these parties is that from the beginning they have refrained from identifying themselves in terms of the left–right scale, which is the reason

Table 6.7   *Support for new politics, 1990–5*

Country set	Forum parties	Green parties
CORE EC (6)	0.0	6.7
OTHER EC (6)	0.0	0.5
OUTSIDE EC (6)	0.0	5.1
CORE EAST (6)	17.9	1.8
EAST PERIPHERY (6)	15.6	1.5
All (30)	6.7	3.1

Source: Appendix 6.1.

that one may consider these two party types to constitute the representatives of new politics. However, as these parties have developed over time one may note that the Green Parties have tended to orient themselves increasingly in a left-wing direction, whereas the Forum Parties, once the introduction of a new political system in Eastern Europe has been accomplished, have tended to disintegrate into different parties with various political orientations, mostly to a centre-oriented kind of party. Thus, although it is still possible to identify parties in Europe today as adhering to some kind of new politics, it is an open question whether in the future they will remain parties located outside of the traditional left–right scale. The support for the New Politics in Europe of today is outlined in Table 6.7.

A few Green parties have managed to reach a 10 per cent level of support in Belgium, Luxembourg and Iceland. Green parties are to be found within the CORE EC and the OUTSIDE EC set. On the other hand, the Forum parties constitute a special set of parties to be found in CORE EAST and EAST PERIPHERY, where they were a response to the need for new parties to channel the system transition in a legitimate fashion. Forum parties are large or medium-sized in Albania, Bulgaria, the Czech Republic, Lithuania, Hungary and Poland, but their electoral trend is downwards.

Any discussion about the party system of a country would be incomplete if it did not contain information about volatility, or the change in electoral support. Some party systems are in more of a state of flux than others.

Volatility

According to Stein Rokkan and Seymour Martin Lipset the West European party systems tend to be stable as the shares of the major parties remain intact from one election to another as if the electorate was frozen into fixed patterns of alignment (Lipset and Rokkan, 1967). Much research has dealt with the so-called frozen party system hypothesis, the relevance of which to Western Europe has been confirmed by research using data up to the late 1980s (Bartolini and Mair, 1990; Mair, 1993). However, it is of little use when analysing the emerging party systems in Eastern Europe. What is its general relevance to the interpretation of party systems in the

Table 6.8 *Volatility, 1990–5*

Country set	Volatility in votes	Volatility in seats
CORE EC (6)	15.1	19.3
OTHER EC (6)	10.9	12.0
OUTSIDE EC (6)	11.3	12.7
CORE EAST (6)	26.0	32.5
EAST PERIPHERY (5)	36.3	40.0
All (29)	19.4	22.7

Source: Appendix 6.1.

entire Europe? Are the European electorates firmly aligned behind a fixed set of political parties?

One must distinguish between two kinds of volatility, gross and net volatility. Gross volatility is the same as the summation of all voter shifts from one party to another. Although gross volatility is important to the political parties, it is net volatility that counts at the end of the day. In the net volatility index voter gains cancel out voter losses for the single party measuring the resulting net change. Net volatility has an impact upon the changes in the allocation of seats in the representative assembly, which is a most fundamental concern of political parties. It is this kind of electoral change that we focus on here.

It has been argued that West European politics is in a process of deep *dealignment* and *realignment*. If so, then the scores on volatility for the three sets of West European countries would not be entirely different from those for the two sets of East European countries, where the party systems hopefully move towards more stability. Table 6.8 has the net volatility scores for both votes in the election and seat allocation in the national assembly.

One may observe two things in these volatility data. On the one hand, the level of volatility is high in particular with regard to the allocation of seats. This is evidence to the effect that the Rokkan-Lipset model about party system stability is questionable. On the other hand, the data indicate that volatility is a much more pervasive phenomenon in the emerging party systems in Eastern Europe, where the average measures on both volatility indices run as high as 30 per cent, than in Western Europe.

There are two different processes at work here which have the same result, one of which is the search for party system stabilization in Eastern Europe and the other is the weakening of party attachments in Western Europe. The figure of about 20 per cent volatility in seat allocation in the set CORE EC in the early 1990s must be considered high, revealing a much less firm commitment of the electorate to their political parties. Several party systems have experienced the phenomenon of an earthquake election, involving considerable voter dealignment and realignment: Denmark and Norway in 1973; Sweden in 1991; Italy, Austria and the Netherlands in 1994.

The following countries have exceptionally high levels of electoral volatility: Estonia and Latvia with 47 per cent, Romania with 36 per cent, Poland with 34 per cent, Croatia, Albania, Slovenia and Italy with around 30 per cent and Hungary with 27 per cent. The net volatility score is a high 20 per cent for the Netherlands, France and the Czech Republic. Very high levels of seat volatility are to be found in Poland (57 per cent), Estonia and Latvia (55 per cent), Hungary (45 per cent), Albania (41 per cent), France (38 per cent), Romania and Italy (33 per cent). The electoral system translating votes into seats increases the amount of seat volatility over and above that of electoral volatility when other electoral formulas than PR are employed. At the same time the use of a formal threshold in PR systems may make seat volatility smaller than electoral volatility.

Volatility is on average rather low in OTHER EC and OUTSIDE EC, where we find the following countries with the lowest scores on electoral volatility: the United Kingdom, Luxembourg, Germany, Switzerland, Greece, Portugal and Spain – all with a score below or around 10 per cent. Perhaps it is premature to predict the occurrence of an earthquake election also in these countries during the late 1990s. Some countries that have had an election involving a major dealignment move towards more stability, the electorate realigning itself firmly again. Other countries become stuck with high levels of volatility from one election to another.

Conclusion

How much is there to be said for using a divergence approach to the interpretation of data about the party systems in Europe? Undeniably, there is a gulf between the party systems in Western Europe and those in Eastern Europe, at least so with regard to the support for extreme parties – that is, the former Communist parties as well as in relation to the support for so-called Forum parties. Volatility is excessive in Eastern Europe whereas it is only considerable in Western Europe. Yet, there are also signs of convergence, especially if one focuses upon the key party system properties of fractionalization and polarization in the Sartori framework.

It is true that there are examples of all four possible combinations: low polarization and low fractionalization (the UK), low polarization and high fractionalization (the Netherlands), high polarization and low fractionalization (Czech Republic) and high polarization and high fractionalization (Italy). But the main characteristic of almost all the party systems is a medium degree of fractionalization and a low extent of polarization.

One may venture to argue that the party systems in Europe have more in common than things that set them apart. The indications of party system convergence in Europe are that many party systems share certain traits such as a medium degree of fractionalization, a moderate extent of polarization and fairly extensive volatility.

They differ somewhat in relation to which parties constitute the bulk of the left and the right wings as well as how the centre-based bloc is composed.

Table 6.9   *West European party systems, 1950–94*

Year		Mean	CV		Mean	CV
1950–54	VOL	9.4	.719	EFF	3.9	.279
1955–59	VOL	7.1	.729	EFF	3.6	.288
1960–64	VOL	7.4	.628	EFF	3.7	.276
1965–69	VOL	7.5	.311	EFF	3.9	.297
1970–74	VOL	10.8	.686	EFF	4.4	.398
1975–79	VOL	9.4	.573	EFF	4.1	.293
1980–84	VOL	12.3	.687	EFF	4.1	.380
1985–89	VOL	10.0	.553	EFF	4.5	.336
1990–94	VOL	12.5	.468	EFF	4.9	.398

Note: VOL = volatility; EFF = effective number of parties.

These differences involve mainly that large Social Democrat parties as well as large Conservative parties are to be found in Western Europe, while the reformed Communist parties belong mainly to Eastern Europe.

There is a certain likelihood that the East European party systems will stabilize in the second half of the 1990s, or at least some of them. But the evidence for Western Europe indicates increasing instability. Taking a long-run perspective on fractionalization and volatility Table 6.9 shows that instability is on the rise, because the number of parties has increased and volatility has gone up. Note that the CV-scores are rather low or are declining, also indicating convergence.

Whereas net volatility, as measured by the Mogens Pedersen index, was as low as 7 per cent in the 1950s, it has now risen to 13 per cent, reflecting the occurrence of earthquake elections in many countries. In addition to processes of electoral dealignment new parties have been formed increasing the probability of electoral realignment. The effective number of parties, as measured with the Laakso-Tagepeera index, has risen from 3.7 parties in the early 1960s to 5 parties in the early 1990s. Surely instability has increased in Western Europe profoundly, although certainly not to the levels that characterize the newly formed party systems in Eastern Europe.

The evolution of New Politics in Western Europe is the explanation behind much of the rise in electoral instability. On the one hand, new parties and new social movements have been formed. On the other hand, new cleavages have emerged in the electorate, sometimes called 'post-materialism' or 'post-modernism'. These two change processes are inter-related, as the new parties and social movements draw support from the emergence of new issues and values in the electorate. However, the traditional parties have also adapted to the new cleavages in the electorate, drawing support by underlining environmental values and/or libertarian ones (Knutsen, 1995a).

Recalling the Duverger analysis of twopartism versus multipartism from Chapter 5, he claimed that the party system is the basis for the formation of governments. What is left of that part of the Duverger argument once one realizes that there are very few examples of two-party systems in Europe, if indeed any? How are governments formed in Western and Eastern democracies? Surely Duverger must have been correct in predicting that multipartism fosters the making of coalition cabinets?

Appendix 6.1   *Documentation of the electoral outcomes in Europe, 1990–5*

Albania: Szajkowski (1992a, 1992b).
Austria: Mackie (1992); Pulzer (1995); Internet.
Belgium: Deruette and Loeb-Mayer (1992); *Keesing's*; *Electoral Studies*.
Bulgaria: Kostova (1992); Mackie (1992); Karasimeonov (1995).
Croatia: Cohen (1993); Glaessner (1994); Jovic (1995); *Keesing's*.
Czech Republic: Mackie (1992); Brokl and Mansfeldova (1993).
Denmark: Mackie (1992); Fitzmaurice (1995); *Keesing's*; *Electoral Studies*.
Estonia: Fitzmaurice (1993); Arter (1995); *Electoral Studies*; Internet.
Finland: Sundberg (1992); *Keesing's*; *Electoral Studies*; Internet.
France: Ysmal (1994).
Germany: Mackie (1992); Philips (1995).
Greece: Mackie (1992); Mavrogordatos (1994).
Hungary: Mackie (1992); *Keesing's*; *Electoral Studies*.
Iceland: Hardarson (1992); *Keesing's*; *Electoral Studies*.
Ireland: Marsh (1993).
Italy: Ignazi (1993); Donovan (1994); Lo Verso and McLean (1995); *Keesing's*.
Latvia: Bungs (1993); *Keesing's*.
Lithuania: Girnius (1992).
Luxembourg: Hearl (1994); Smart (1995).
Netherlands: Wolinetz (1995); *Keesing's*.
Norway: Heidar (1994); *Keesing's*.
Poland: Jasiewicz (1992, 1994); Sanford (1993); Vinton (1993).
Portugal: Stock (1992); *Keesing's*; Internet.
Romania: Mackie (1992); Shafir (1992a, 1992b).
Slovakia: Mackie (1992); Brokl and Mansfeldova (1993); *Keesing's*; Internet.
Slovenia: Cohen (1993); Glaessner (1994).
Spain: Castillo and Lopez-Nieto (1994).
Sweden: Pierre and Widfeldt (1992); Aylott (1995).
Switzerland: Ladner (1992); *Keesing's*.
United Kingdom: Mackie (1993).

7

Governments

In a representative democracy candidates offer policy alternatives to the electorate, whose choices become decisive for the recruitment of the national assembly. Once the electoral outcomes are final and the seats in the legislature have been allocated according to some rule in relation to the votes cast, then the process of forming a government begins. In European politics the political parties put up politicians to the electorate and political parties have the major say in how governments are formed. They may also be critical in bringing down a government before the next regular election.

Government formation in democracies has been much researched especially from a coalition building perspective inspired by game theory (Budge and Keman, 1990; Laver and Schofield, 1990; Laver and Budge, 1992). In this literature one may contrast one convergence focus with a few divergence perspectives. The convergence theme maintains that governments will tend to have one chief format, that is, they constitute a minimum winning coalition (MWC), or governments will not last long if another format is employed. If cabinets only need 51 per cent support in Parliament in order to govern, then it is not rational to form any other type of government.

The divergence themes argue that government formation tends to be radically different in various European countries, reflecting historical legacies and institutional differences (Bogdanor, 1983; Pridham, 1986; Strom, 1990). Not all countries practise the minimum winning model, as several countries resort to radically different formats for the formation of government: either the grand coalition involving oversized coalition governments or the minority cabinet format, whether by one party only or a coalition of parties.

The purpose of this chapter is to shed light upon government formation by examining data about the composition and durability of governments between 1990 and 1995. Are governments in various parts of Europe – West, East, North, South – very different from each other or is there a clear tendency towards convergence on to the format that game theory or rational choice predicts: the minimum winning coalition format? Do the three different formats for governments – minority, simple majority and oversized cabinets – also differ in terms of durability?

Kinds of Governments

Surveying how governments are formed, a number of distinctions have to be kept in mind, as one may classify governments in different ways. Several of these distinctions stem from coalition theory, which has became the foundation for the analysis of government formation.

From a theoretical point of view, the concept of a coalition is very helpful when discussing the formation of governments, because all governments may be regarded as one type of coalition government or another. In Europe governments frequently involve more than one party or several so-called players, which makes it necessary to bring in coalition theory. In fact, one may look at each government as a virtual coalition, where a single party government may simply be regarded as being in a coalition with itself. Empirically, one needs data about the following in order to survey the pattern of government formation in the early 1990s.

First, one would wish to know about each and every government in Western and Eastern Europe whether it is of one of the following possible types: minority governments; small majority governments; grand coalitions; and caretaker governments. Second, in addition to this information about the level of support in Parliament for the government, one would need information about how many players are involved in each government. Third, one requires data about the length of time that a government is in power, that is, if it is a coalition between two or more players, then how long does the coalition last.

Now, coalitions in politics are any short-run or long-run pact involving two or more parties or groups in Parliament. Temporary coalitions typically focus on a specific problem, the resolution of which makes the coalition unneccesary whether it lost or won. Long lasting coalitions often involve cooperation in governments. For how long formal governmental coalitions really last is open to question.

Thus, coalitions may be based on loosely connected ties between the parties or there may be formal cooperation defined in terms of some institutional mechanism. Ad hoc coalitions form in Parliament in relation to specific issues where a temporary coalition may be successful in winning a critical roll call. Government coalitions, however, require a firm collaboration between the parties. Typically, there is a joint declaration of a platform of some kind when a coalition government is formed as well as a mutually binding commitment among the parties to work for the implementation of the programme of the government. How much agreement there really exists is again open to question.

The less long lasting coalitions tend to be in a country the lower the government durability score is. It has been argued that government instability has risen in the last decade, reflecting the increase in voter volatility. Yet, one should not prejudge the question about the length of time a coalition may hold together or a government may last. There exist many cases where one government or a coalition has governed a country for more than the normal period of time of a government, namely, an uninterupted full election cycle period with no extraordinary elections in between.

Kinds of Coalitions

Speaking of governments from a theoretical point of view, rational choice theory approaches any government as a coalition, where a one-party government is also considered to be a coalition, as the party in government is in a coalition with itself. In rational choice one makes a distinction between two types of coalition models in relation to the analysis of government formation – (1) office-seeking models; and (2) policy-pursuit models – depending upon whether the actors or players in government formation games focus rationally upon the acquisition of cabinet posts or the making of policies.

Governments are critically dependent upon support from parties in Parliament. William Riker's (1962) coalition model is of type (1) and it involves two profound ideas. First, in the formation of a government coalitions tend to be as small as is strictly necessary from the point of view of receiving simple majority support in Parliament:

> A *minimal winning coalition* is a winning coalition such that the defection of any member will make the coalition no longer winning. (Gamson, 1961: 376)

In reality, coalitions will tend to be minimum sized so that the gains that the coalition may reap can be divided in larger shares for each player participating in the coalition:

> The *cheapest winning coalition* is that minimal winning coalition with total resources closest to the decision point. (Gamson, 1961: 376)

Second, minority governments or grand coalitions are more vulnerable to shifts in opinions in Parliament than minimum winning coalition (MWC) governments meaning that only MWCs will be durable (Riker, 1962). Now, what is the relevance of Riker's size principle in relation to today's realities in Europe?

The fact that minority governments and grand coalitions are formed and do endure in some countries testifies to the viability of formats other than the minimum winning one. Perhaps coalition models of type (2) derived from the policy-pursuit approach should be resorted to in order to understand them, because in addition to the office-seeking approach, coalition governments may be examined for their overall policy profile.

For multi-party systems one may expect that a certain fraction of all governments formed would be formal coalitions between two or more parties. This entails the possibility that a government may include parties with very different programmatic and ideological orientations, but one would assume that coalitions are more likely to constitute the basis for governments when parties are not at a large policy distance from each other. This is the gist of the well-known De Swaan government coalition model (De Swaan, 1973).

In order to examine the relevance of the policy-pursuit approach to government formation one can employ the left–right scale trying to pin down the programmatic profile of a government. Here we look at the occurrence of the following categories: (a) right-wing governments, (b) left-wing governments and (c) balanced governments which comprise both left or right wing parties. One might expect that coalitions of type (a) and (b) are more frequently occurring than type (c), if indeed the left–right scale taps the different policy orientations among the political parties.

There are two additional models of government formation that figure prominently in the literature and which are not strictly accountable for in terms of either the Riker or the De Swaan approaches, or some combination of them. First, in the so-called consociational camp, the emphasis is upon the relevance of grand coalitions or oversized governments in relation to what is needed for survival in terms of support in Parliament. The consociational model suggests that grand coalitions are the suitable format in divided societies, that is, societies with sharp ethnic and/or religious cleavages (Lijphart, 1977). The majoritarian format of minimum winning coalitions works well only in homogeneous societies. Although a grand coalition could conceivably be a minimum winning coalition, it holds true that when it constitutes an oversized government, then it falls outside of both the office-seeking and the policy-pursuit perspectives, strictly speaking.

Second, there is the model of a minority government which is durable (Strom, 1990). Such a government may consist of more than one party but whether it is a one-party government or a coalition of several parties, the government receives less than 50 per cent support in Parliament. The minority government model falls outside of the office-seeking approach, because a minority government is not a minimum winning coalition. Yet, one could argue that minority governments, if durable, tend to secure enough Parliamentary support by informal coalition-building at the floor or in the committees of Parliament. Minority governments may consist of parties that are close to each programatically in accordance with the policy-pursuit approach, but strictly speaking the minority coalition model falls outside of this approach, because minority governments are not large enough to carry through their policies. Durable minority governments occur in societies where class cleavages separate socialist from non-socialist parties at the same time as neither camp being strong enough to secure a majoritarian position.

Gordon Smith has pointed out one chief difficulty in the models of government formation discussed above. He argues that one needs to distinguish between social cohesion and governmental cohesion in relation to European realities. Cohesion in government as witnessed in government durability may be low whatever the institutions and the historical legacies may be (Smith, 1989b). Government cohesion may not only be low in fragmented countries with extensive and intensive cleavages despite a long-term commitment to consociational devices, but it may also be low in homogeneous countries whether they employ the plurality election formula or PR. Government cohesion may be difficult to bring about even when there is social cohesion, because the sentiments among the political

Table 7.1 *Number of parties in government, 1990–5*

Country set	Average number of parties in government
CORE EC (6)	2.8
OTHER EC (6)	1.6
OUTSIDE EC (6)	2.7
CORE EAST (6)	2.9
EAST PERIPHERY (7)	2.1
All (31)	2.4

Source: Appendix 7.1.

élites in a country may be such that governments easily break-up. If the parties in a multi-party system are highly self-interest seeking with guile, then it may be difficult to form any government, even if the players come from the same flank along the left–right scale.

Thus, one may question whether government formation always results from a rational choice process. Here, we investigate if there are systematic differences between European countries in relation to a few key questions concerning cabinets in office between 1990 and 1995, namely: (1) the number of parties participating in governments as well as the number of governments; (2) the status of the government in terms of Parliamentary backing; and (3) the policy profile of the government. What about the actual occurrence of the different models of government, namely, the minimum winning, grand coalition and minority types of government? Our analysis of government formation in Europe during the period 1990–5 is based on the information in Appendix 7.1, which was gathered from reports in *Keesing's Record of World Events* (1990–5) and from Woldentorp et al. (1993).

Number of Parties in Governments

Since the party systems in Europe are prevailingly of the multi-party type (see Chapter 6), one may expect that single party governments are not that numerous, at least not in the position as single majority governments. One may make a first description of the kinds of governments that tend to be formed in Europe by looking at either a measure on the number of players participating in government coalitions or at a measure of the percentage time of the period 1990–5 during which either a single party government or a multi-party government has been in power, with the remaining time allocated to caretaker governments, if any that is.

The formation of governments in Europe in the early 1990s displays a rich variation. Between 1990 and 1995 there were no less than 91 cabinets in office, of which 19 were single-party governments, 68 multi-party governments and 4 caretaker governments. Real coalition building between two or more parties is thus frequent in Europe. Table 7.1 contains the information about the average number of parties in governments.

Table 7.2   *Types of government: single or multi-party governments in percentages of the time period 1990–5*

	Single-party government	Multi-party government
CORE EC (6)	0	97.2
OTHER EC (6)	50.5	49.5
OUTSIDE EC (6)	22.7	77.3
CORE EAST (6)	8.1	91.1
EAST PERIPHERY (7)	31.9	64.8
All (31)	22.9	75.6

Source: Appendix 7.1.

European governments are very often coalition governments with two or more parties in formal coalition. Only a few countries have governments with one player, which may be either a majority or minority government. This applies to all country sets with the exception of OTHER EC. In the early 1990s the average number of players in governments in CORE EC, OUTSIDE EC and CORE EAST has been about three parties. This empirical observation is, of course, the starting-point for modelling government formation as a coalition building game with several so-called players.

In multi-party systems governments will be formed under the constraints of coalition building, either in terms of formal participation in cabinets or through negotiations in Parliament. If states are not to be run by means of caretaker governments, which is in agreement with the principles of party government only under exceptional circumstances, then coalition governments will have to be formed. Even in countries which practise minority governments there is often a process of coalition building resulting in a coalition government. Table 7.2 corroborates the generalization that European governments tend to be real coalition governments with two or more players involved.

About 75 per cent of all cabinets in office in the early 1990s were multi-party governments – that is the ultimate scope for coalition building. Speaking generally, coalition governments in the East are no different from those in the West with regard to the number of parties participating. In CORE EC all governments have included two or more players, which is certainly the main trend also in CORE EAST and OUTSIDE EC.

Within OTHER EC there are a few countries where single-party governments prevail including the United Kingdom, Spain and Greece, as the party in government has majority or near majority support in these countries. One-player governments are to be found also in Lithuania and Croatia. Norway and perhaps also Sweden tend to have governments with only one party, but these governments are minority ones.

On the contrary, there are numerous countries where there have been as many as four or more parties participating in governments, including: Poland, Belgium, Italy and Switzerland. The Swiss case is different, because Switzerland is the only country in Europe with a permanent coalition government by means of its seven member Federal Council, elected for a fixed four-year term by the Federal Assembly on a party proportional basis. The consequence is, of course, that government stability is very high in the Swiss case, especially since there exists no vote of non-confidence. Compare this with Slovenia, where the government formed in early 1993 contained five parties, but it was reduced to three in 1994 when one party declined from the government partly due to an amalgamation of some of the other parties in the cabinet into a new Liberal party.

One may note that caretaker governments occur very seldom. This form of government is resorted to when no party government can be formed. Thus, the absence of this type testifies about the validity of party government all over Europe. In fact, caretaker governments have occurred in only three countries in Eastern Europe, namely Estonia, Albania and Bulgaria, which is evidence about the hold of parties on government formation in the new democracies. The most well-known caretaker government in the early 1990s has been the Dini government in Italy, which stayed in power for a surprisingly long time, partly as a result of low government cohesion in the Smith interpretation.

Let us now pursue the analysis of governments by looking at the size of their parliamentary support and then examine the policy orientation of cabinets in office.

Size of Governments

One chief method for classifying governments is to look at how large the parliamentary support for the government is. This involves looking at the size of the parties, measured by the number of parliamentarians, who support the government in terms of formal collaboration between political parties. One may distinguish between three kinds of governments, whether they are single- or multi-party governments, in terms of their parliamentary status: (1) minority or less than 50 per cent support; (2) small majority or more than 50 per cent and less than 60 per cent support; and (3) grand coalitions or oversized governments with more than 60 per cent support. The cut-off point of 60 per cent is, strictly speaking, arbitrary, as it may occur that large coalition governments are not only minimum winning but also minimum-sized coalitions.

We have already seen that governments in Europe tend to include more than one party. In most countries governments are multi-party governments, as in around 75 per cent of all governments two or more players are involved in formal cabinet collaboration. Table 7.3 gives data about how frequent the three kinds of governments identified above according to support in Parliament tend to be, as measured in terms of the percentage time that they have been in power during the years 1990–5.

There are several observations to be made in relation to the data in Table 7.3, which clearly indicate that all three types of governments occur

Table 7.3 *Types of governments, 1990–5: size of support*

Country set	Minority governments	Small majority governments	Grand majority governments
CORE EC (6)	8.8	54.6	34.8
OTHER EC (6)	31.0	57.9	11.1
OUTSIDE EC (6)	33.3	25.7	41.0
CORE EAST (6)	26.4	42.8	30.1
EAST PERIPHERY (7)	23.1	17.6	56.1
All (31)	24.5	39.0	35.3

Source: Appendix 7.1.

frequently. The pattern is actually a very heterogeneous one with almost no trace of an East–West division. Small majority governments remain the most frequently occuring type of government all over Europe, except in EAST PERIPHERY and OUTSIDE EC. A few systematic observations may be made in relation to Table 7.3.

First, minority governments are often formed in two country sets – OUTSIDE EC and CORE EAST – where such governments have been in place for roughly 30 per cent of the time period covered. The occurrence of minority governments is significantly less only in the set of CORE EC countries. The countries with frequent minority governments are especially Latvia and Estonia in Eastern Europe as well as Sweden and Norway in Northern Europe. France, Denmark and Poland have resorted to minority governments though not to the same extent as the former countries. What needs to be underlined is that grand coalitions are more frequent than minority governments.

Second, the grand coalition format is especially used in the following sets: EAST PERIPHERY, OUTSIDE EC and CORE EC, but it occurs almost all over Europe regularly. Oversized coalitions are very frequent in countries such as Slovenia, Switzerland, the Netherlands, Austria and Yugoslavia. In Croatia and Albania one party has been able to receive more than 60 per cent in electoral support which means that these governments are classified as oversized coalitions. And oversized governments have been in power about half of the time between 1990 and 1995 in countries such as: Portugal, Romania, Finland and Belgium.

If oversized cabinets really indicate élite cooperation and élite accommodation through grand coalitions is a typical consociational mechanism, then one may establish that consociationalism is no longer restricted to the classical central European cases of Switzerland, Austria, Belgium, the Netherlands and Luxembourg. The only set of countries where oversized governments occur seldom is OTHER EC, which adheres more to the simple majoritarian or Westminster ideal of an effective although not strictly representative government.

Third, the small majoritarian form of government is no doubt frequent but this type of government does not prevail. Only in countries in OTHER EC do simple majority governments dominate as the typical model of running the executive. Here we have the following countries that employ this type of government often: Italy, Iceland, the United Kingdom, Lithuania, Greece, Luxembourg and Hungary. In addition small majority governments tend to occur often in Spain, Germany, the Czech Republic and Slovakia. About half of the governments in CORE EC and CORE EAST have been small majority governments. Belgium has left the consociational camp and employs simple majority governments instead of grand coalitions.

Thus, at the same time as one may emphasize that there are in Europe many minority governments as well as oversized coalition governments, it is also worth observing that small majority governments make up more than 50 per cent of the governments in CORE EC and OTHER EC. But generally speaking small majority governments are not the only mode of conducting the business of government in Europe. Actually, there is an interesting case of a country that may be classified as having both minority and simple majority governments, namely Ireland. Two Irish governments in the early 1990s (Haughey and Reynolds) have had exactly a 50 per cent level of support in the Dail, but that did not entail that the government possessed a majority in Parliament. Thus, we have classified these Irish governments as minority ones.

Now, what then about the occurrence of minimum winning coalitions, whether in the form of a multi-party government or in the form of a single-party government, which then is in a coalition with itself? In office-seeking theories this form is considered as the standard one, with the minority and oversized types of governments relegated as pathologies in need of special explanation. A grand coalition could be a minimum winning coalition, but only under very special circumstances could it also be a minimum sized coalition government or the cheapest winning coalition.

Laver and Schofield (1990) examine the evidence in favour of the theory of minimum winning coalitions. They state in relation to a measure on the frequency of various types of governments between 1945 and 1987 in 12 European democracies:

> it can be seen that the prima facie evidence is that, of the 218 governments considered, 'only' 77 – a mere 35 per cent – were minimal winning. Critics such as Bogdanor, von Beyme, and Pridham cite such figures as evidence of failure, but there is another way of looking at them. (Laver and Schofield, 1990: 92)

Basically, Laver and Schofield argue that predicting correctly once every third time is not bad for a social science theory, especially given the large number of possible governments which may be formed theoretically, if one places no restrictions on either size of support or policy commitments of the parties. Yet, there is still another way to interpret the data.

When there is a one-party government and it has simple majority support, then it is a minimum winning coalition, because it may be regarded as in a coalition with itself. Grand coalitions could be minimum winning, if for instance two dominating parties are in coalition as has been the case in Austria and the Netherlands. However, most minimum winning

Table 7.4   *Governments, 1990–5: minimum winning coalitions*

Country set	Minimum winning coalitions
CORE EC (6)	76.6
OTHER EC (6)	63.2
OUTSIDE EC (6)	33.3
CORE EAST (6)	45.4
EAST PERIPHERY (7)	35.2
All (31)	50.2

Source: Appendix 7.1.

coalitions are minimum sized – that is, they include the least necessary number of players. Typically, a minimum winning government has about a 51–60 per cent support base in Parliament. Why should a government be either less or larger than that?

Well, the minimum winning format could be the type of government towards which there is convergence, if there are no exceptional conditions at work, which favour either the minority government format or the oversized government format. The former would occur to the extent that a minority government would be successful in striking minimum winning coalitions in Parliament on a short-term basis, for example in various Parliamentary committees. And the latter could be operating in countries where governmental consensus is a major consideration, either because several of the key players are close to each other or because the major parties are very distant from each other from a policy point of view, at the same time as no one single player has enough Parliamentary support in order to form a viable government by itself.

The crucial question in the office-seeking approach is: how frequently do minimum winning coalitions occur in Europe? Considering a single-party government with majority support as a minimum winning coalition Table 7.4 provides the answer with the calculation of the percentages of the time period for this type of government.

The game theoretical prediction that governments will be mimimum winning or not receive more support than is needed for being in majority is correct for about 50 per cent of all governments formed in the early 1990s in the whole of Europe. Within the CORE EC and OTHER EC countries governments clearly tend to be minimum winning coalitions. For the other country sets one may conclude that coalition mechanisms other than the simple minimum winning institution are at work. Note the low number of governments that are minimum winning coalitions in both OUTSIDE EC and EAST PERIPHERY, where some practise the minority format and others the oversized format.

The following countries have had minimum winning coalitions all the time in the early 1990s: the Netherlands, Austria, Croatia, Germany, Luxembourg, Iceland, the United Kingdom and Lithuania. In Greece, Portugal, the Czech Republic and Slovakia it has been very frequent.

However, in a number of countries there has been no minimum winning coalition or it is employed only infrequently – why?

One could regard the minimum winning format as the model towards which there is a convergence trend, since it covers 50 per cent of all governments in Europe. Why would governments be different from a MWC if normal circumstances prevail? If one takes this position, then one must examine the countries that adhere to the other two patterns of government formation in order to enquire into the special circumstances that enhance the occurrence of the minority or grand coalition formats. One such condition for deviating from the MWC-format could be historical legacies in the form of strong social heterogeneity, or deep-seated cleavages.

Let us now turn to the other major coalition framework – policy pursuit, where we will focus upon the content of the coalition by examining to which party families the parties that make up the government belong. Although party ideology is not quite the same as the policy orientation of the party, they tend to be fairly close in the long run. Let us follow this line of research by examining what kinds of government are formed in CORE EC, OTHER EC, OUTSIDE EC, CORE EAST and EAST PERIPHERY.

Policy Orientation of Governments

Another method of classifying governments is to focus on their programmatic orientation. If the first main question in coalition theory is to predict the size of the support in Parliament for the government, then the second major problem in coalition theory would be to predict the character of the government in terms of its policy composition. According to the median voter model launched by Downs (1957) governments would form along the left–right continuum reflecting the distribution of the electorate in the very same dimension. Furthermore, the De Swaan (1973) model entails that coalitions tend to be compact meaning that the policy distance between the players will be minimized.

One may note that the office-seeking framework is easier to apply than the policy-pursuit approach. So, how to handle the concept of policy distance? Students of politics are well aware of the possibility that parties may adopt one stance in their general party platform and quite another one when in government. One method for analysing the policy distance between parties is to use the ranking of the parties along the standard left–right scale. In the following discussion 'right-wing' parties include Populist, Conservative, Liberal, Centre and Christian Democratic parties. 'Left-wing' parties are the remaining ones along the left–right scale.

Starting from the policy-pursuit approach we would expect the following empirical realities in a multi-party setting: (1) normally governments would tend to be either left-wing orientated or right-wing orientated; (2) coalition governments would never comprise both extreme left-wing and right-wing parties; (3) coalition governments would not consist of a large left-wing

Table 7.5   *Governments, 1990–5: right-wing coalitions*

Country set	Right-wing governments
CORE EC (6)	26.8
OTHER EC (6)	59.3
OUTSIDE EC (6)	23.9
CORE EAST (6)	35.0
EAST PERIPHERY (7)	35.2
All (31)	36.0

Source: Appendix 7.1.

Table 7.6   *Governments, 1990–5: left-wing coalitions*

Country set	Left-wing governments
CORE EC (6)	8.8
OTHER EC (6)	23.4
OUTSIDE EC (6)	22.7
CORE EAST (6)	13.8
EAST PERIPHERY (7)	30.1
All (31)	20.1

Source: Appendix 7.1.

and right-wing party simultaneously, because major left-wing or right-wing parties would only include small adjacent parties whenever necessary. Let us look at the data about the composition of governments in the early 1990s to test these key predictions from the policy-pursuit approach.

Table 7.5 gives information about the occurrence of right-wing governments – that is, governments based on one large right-wing party or on a coalition among right-wing parties, measured in terms of percentages of all governments for the entire time period.

Governments formed with right-wing parties as major players do occur in all the sets of countries, but at the same time right-wing governments are the dominant type only in one set of countries: OTHER EC. The frequent use of the MWC format in OTHER EC results partly from these right-wing governments in countries such as the United Kingdom and Portugal. Several right-wing governments consist of one major right-wing party in coalition with one or more small moderate right-wing parties. The CORE EC countries are the deviating ones, as right-wing governments are less frequent, except in Germany. Table 7.6 has the corresponding data about left-wing governments.

Governments based on left-wing parties have occurred significantly less frequently than right-wing governments. It is only in the set EAST PERIPHERY that left-wing governments have been usual whereas they have been

Table 7.7   *Governments, 1990–5: balanced coalitions*

Country set	Right and Left governments
CORE EC (6)	61.8
OTHER EC (6)	17.4
OUTSIDE EC (6)	53.5
CORE EAST (6)	50.5
EAST PERIPHERY (6)	31.4
All (31)	42.5

Source: Appendix 7.1.

marginal in CORE EC. In OTHER EC and OUTSIDE EC left-wing governments have been in power about one-fifth of the time span studied here.

Generally speaking, it is striking how weak left-wing parties have been in government formation in the different sets of West European countries compared with right-wing parties, although left-wing governments play a major role in a few West European countries such as the Scandinavian countries, Spain and Greece. However, the picture of right-wing governments prevailing over left-wing governments must be qualified by the occurrence of a third type: balanced governments. Europe is actually ruled more often by this type of government than by either pure right-wing or left-wing governments.

Looking at Left–Right governments, one may designate them 'balanced' or 'even' coalitions. Such governments could consist of a large moderate left-wing party such as a Social Democratic party as well as a moderate right-wing party like the Liberal Party or the Christian Democratic Party. Or they could be made up of a large moderate right-wing party and small left-wing parties. Table 7.7 records the occurrence of such balanced or even coalitions.

The surprising finding is that more governments in Europe belong to this category of coalitions than to any of the other types of government, or some 42 per cent. Whereas the occurrence of left-wing or right-wing governments is in accordance with the policy-pursuit framework, balanced governments are not easily accounted for by the same coalition theory.

Among one set of countries, CORE EC, this kind of balanced coalition is the most prevalent type of government. It is also common in the set OUTSIDE EC, for example in Iceland. One must also observe that this type is rather frequent in CORE EAST. Balanced governments may be MWCs, as in the Netherlands and Luxembourg. Or they may be oversized coalitions, as in Switzerland. In fact, Austrian governments tend to have all three properties, that is, they are balanced, oversized and minimum winning coalitions.

The frequent use of balanced governments offers a challenge to the policy-pursuit approach to the interpretation of government formation. Which parties are close to each other from a policy standpoint? Is there a clear-cut dividing line between left-wing and right-wing parties meaning that coalitions tend to occur within either the first set or the second set? Or are moderate left-wing and right-wing parties closer to each other than to the parties on their respective flanks?

The coalition governments that enter this type include the Austrian and Finnish grand coalitions, the Dutch and Belgian centre-based coalitions as well as what used to be the classical Italian coalition of the Democrazia Cristiana with small socialist parties. The set of countries OTHER EC has a totally different coalition pattern, meaning that governments in these countries will be either based on right-wing or left-wing parties, but not both. Is policy distance between the parties different among these countries with a more sharp separation between the Left and the Right? In few countries do we find coalitions covering both a large left-wing party and a large right-wing party simultaneously, as for instance in the Finnish Rainbow government that came to power in 1995.

A balanced coalition could be MWC where the policy distances between the parties are minimal although it bridges the gap between the Left and the Right. Such coalitions occur, for example, in Denmark and Belgium, as the policy-pursuit approach entails. But an even coalition may aim at incorporating the major players coming from rather different political angles as long as these parties are not anti-system parties. The latter case would be an application of the consociational idea that the main political contenders would benefit from an institutionalized framework for élite cooperation. The problem is that it is far from clear whether balanced governments belong to the former or to the latter types.

If balanced governments are conducive to political stability and social order, then the prospects for Eastern Europe should be encouraging, because right and left governments are frequent there. This holds in particular for Slovenia, Albania and Poland but also for the Czech Republic and Slovakia to some extent. Yet, balanced coalition governments failed to bring stability to Italy, and the Austrian right and left government broke up in 1995. The occurrence of many balanced governments casts doubts upon the general validity of the principle that coalitions minimize the policy distance between the partcipating players or political parties. Not only is it difficult to measure policy distance, but coalitions may be formed not because the policy distance is to be minimized but because the policy distance between the parties may be so large that élite cooperation becomes a necessity for the purpose of political stability.

Perhaps one could point out that the wide occurrence of balanced coalitions has not been observed quite accurately in the literature on government formation in Europe. Balanced governments are common not only in CORE EC countries but also in Eastern Europe. They are not the same as the consociational form of government, because these balanced coalitions may not only be MWCs but also minority governments. And they may include players that are close to each other on the left–right continuum, bridging the gap between left and right, as it were. It may actually be difficult to classify balanced governments, as for instance the Dutch grand coalitions or the Luxembourg governments. Are these really consociational governments in deeply divided societies or are they to be seen as coalitions that minimize the policy distance between players located in the centre of the left–right continuum?

Government Durability

Can one account for the variety of European governments by means of two basic approaches: the office-seeking and the policy-pursuit perspectives? From the former come the concepts of a minimum winning coalition government as well as of a minimum sized government. The deviations from the MWC model government would then be either a minority government or an oversized government in the form of a grand coalition. One may use the policy-pursuit perspective to classify governments along the left–right scale starting from the location of the parties that form the government along the same scale. Then we arrive at the following additional types of governments: left-wing, right-wing and balanced governments.

The basic principle in the office-seeking approach is the so-called size mechanism, which entails that governments will be only large enough to secure support in Parliament. Why would governments include players that are not strictly necessary? The size principle predicts that minority governments will fall down easily by a vote of non-confidence in Parliament as well as that oversized governments will break down internally, as they are after all too big. One may test the size hypothesis by means of calculations of the average survival rate of the seven different types of governments identified above.

Government durability is measured as the number of months a cabinet stays in office as a proportion of the entire election period (survival rate). The standard election cycle is almost everywhere four years. The United Kingdom, France, Ireland, Italy and Luxembourg have five years and Sweden practised three years for a short time. Presidential election cycles may last longer than four years as in France and Portugal. But four years is the normal time for a government to stay in power, if it does not have to step down prematurely. It may lose the confidence of Parliament and it may respond by dissolving Parliament. Norway and Switzerland are the only countries in Europe where Parliament cannot be dissolved. And Austria is the only country where the legislature may decide to dissolve itself (Döring, 1995). The way the institutions of Parliamentarism (Chapter 5) are structured in a country impacts upon the formation and dissolution of governments. Table 7.8 provides data about government durability.

There is in the data no support for the size principle derived from the office-seeking approach that governments which do not adhere to the MWC format would be unstable. Actually, none of the various types of governments are more durable than any of the other types. This is a very negative finding for the office-seeking approach.

Let us look at the data about government durability from another angle,

Table 7.8   *Average government durability, 1990–5*

Types of governments		Survival rate
Minimum winning coalitions	(40)	50.2
Small majority governments	(33)	50.9
Minority governments	(25)	42.9
Grand coalitions	(29)	48.7
Left-wing governments	(18)	46.5
Right-wing governments	(31)	49.4
Left–right governments	(38)	47.2
Caretaker governments	(4)	11.8
All	(91)	46.2

Source: Appendix 7.1.

Table 7.9   *Government durability*

Country set	Survival rate
CORE EC (6)	53.3
OTHER EC (6)	59.5
OUTSIDE EC (6)	75.8
CORE EAST (6)	36.5
EAST PERIPHERY (6)	33.0
All (31)	51.0

Source: Appendix 7.1.

that of country averages (see Table 7.9). Government durability tends to be lower in the two East European sets than in the three West European sets. One set is clearly different from the others, namely OUTSIDE EC, where government stability is very high. Here we have the Scandinavian countries with their minority governments as well as Austria and Switzerland with their characteristic grand coalitions.

The following countries have had a very high number of governments during this short time priod: Bulgaria, Albania, Poland, Slovakia, Croatia, Italy and Lithuania – from five up to eight governments, which fact shows up in the low survival rates for the East European sets. On the other hand few governments are to be found in Spain, Portugal, the Netherlands, Luxembourg and Iceland. Concern has been expressed about the consolidation of the new democracies in the Mediterranean basin (Lijphart et al., 1988; Pridham, 1995). In terms of governmental stability only Italy scores low among the South European democracies though. Then there is more cause for concern about the low level of government stability in Eastern Europe, where most countries are still in the transition phase (Pridham et al., 1994).

Conclusion

When one examines the way governments are formed in Europe, then there are few traces of any East–West differences. All kinds of governments occur in the five country sets. The standard model of a viable government, a minimum sized MWC, is mostly to be found in CORE EC and OTHER EC. But it is not the prevailing government format in Europe, because there are several minority governments and grand coalition governments, occurring in the countries in OUTSIDE EC, CORE EAST and EAST PERIPHERY.

Looking at similarities and differences when cabinets are formed and break up in our five sets has given us an opportunity to examine a few of the specific hypotheses in the coalition literature. Coalition theory is neatly classified as either focusing on office-seeking or policy-pursuit. The size principle argues that coalitions will be bare majority coalitions, whereas the policy distance principle claims that coalitions will exhibit ideological coherence along the left–right dimension. Although we did find clear traces of the workings of these two basic mechanisms, one referring to the size of the parliamentary support for the coalition and the other to the policy positions of the government players, the data about government formation in Eastern and Western countries do not fully corroborate these implications. The MWCs are neither more frequent nor more durable than minority or oversized governments. And the frequent occurrences of balanced governments bridging the policy gap between left-wing and right-wing parties may make the notion of minimizing policy distance questionable.

What must be underlined in all the diversity in patterns of government formation is that there is hardly any divergence between Western Europe and Eastern Europe except for the fact that the survival rate of cabinets in office is clearly lower in the latter than in the former.

One could argue that there is a convergence process at work, as half of all the governments do constitute MWCs. This convergence process in the pattern of government formation becomes even more pronounced, if one interprets stable minority governments as adhering to the same format although coalition building is done elsewhere than in the government. Yet, in the data for the early 1990s there reappears the basic separation between three types of government:

1 Small majority governments;
2 Grand coalitions;
3 Minority cabinets.

Type (1) is always an MWC and type (2) could be an MWC, whereas type (3) is never an MWC. Perhaps the divergence between countries in relation to patterns of government formation reflects on lingering historical traditions of conflicts and cleavages though fading?

The minority model tends to prevail in the Scandinavian countries, whereas grand coalitions are to be found in the so-called consociational countries in Central Europe on the one hand and in the new democracies in Eastern Europe on the other hand. The argument in favour of grand coalitions or so-called *Konkordanzdemokratie* underlines the necessity to bring all the major players on board in order to promote political stability (Lehmbruch, 1992). The theory of minority governments points out that such cabinets may strike short-run majority agreements in parliamentary committees (Strom, 1990). Small majority governments are formed in countries which adhere to the Westminster model of majoritarian government: the United Kingdom, but also Germany, Italy, Greece and Spain.

Against such an interpretation that focuses upon onlingering historical legacies of cleavages or institutions, one may point out that many countries move between various formats for governments even during such a short time period as five years. It seems as if those governments are being formed which can at all be formed, given a substantial lack of government cohesion, as pointed out by Smith. After all, government durability is not high in Europe with the exception of Switzerland, Luxembourg and perhaps Austria with their institutionally sanctioned grand coalition governments (Abromeit, 1993; Schmidt, 1995).

In any case, the office-seeking and policy-pursuit approaches to government formation and duration are helpful in explaining European governments, but only to a certain extent. We will see that this tension between general theories and country specific circumstances recurs when we now take the next step to examine welfare state theories in the European context.

Appendix 7.1   *Governments in office in Europe between 1990 and 1995*

Country	In	Out	NO MO	SU RA	NO PA	PA SU	PO OR	TY MA	MI WI	TY CA
Albania:										
Carcani	01.82	02.91								
Nano	02.91	06.91	4		1					
Bufi	06.91	12.91	6	12.5	6	98	L	GR	NO	MU
Ahmet	12.91	04.92	4	8.3			CA			
Meksi	04.92	12.94	32	66.7	3	71	B	GR	NO	MU
Meksi	12.94				1	66	R	GR	MW	SI
Austria:										
Vranitsky	01.87	12.90	47	97.9	2	86	B	GR	MW	MU
Vranitsky	12.90	11.94	47	97.9	2	77	B	GR	MW	MU
Vranitsky	11.94	12.95	13	27.1	2	65	B	GR	MW	MU
Belgium:										
Martens	06.88	09.91	39	81.3	5	71	B	GR	NO	MU
Martens	09.91	11.91	2	4.2	4	63	B	GR	NO	MU
Martens	11.91	03.92	4	8.3	4	57	B	SM	MW	MU
Dehaene	03.92	06.95	39	81.3	4	57	B	SM	MW	MU
Dehaene	06.95				4	55	B	SM	MW	MU

Appendix 7.1 *Continued*

Bulgaria:

Atanasov	03.86	02.90							
Lukanov	02.90	09.90	8		1		L		
Lukanov	09.90	12.90	3	6.3	1	53	L	SM	MW	SI
Popov	12.90	11.91	11	22.9	3	93	B	GR	NO	MU
Dimitrov	11.91	12.92	13	27.1	1	46	B	MI	NO	SI
Berov	12.92	09.94	22	45.8	2	54	B	SM	MW	MU
Indzhova	09.94	12.94	3	6.3			CA		
Videnov	12.94				2	52	L	SM	MW	MU

Croatia:

Mesić	05.90	08.90	3						
Manolić	08.90	07.91	11						
Gregurić	07.91	08.92	13						
Šarinić	08.92	04.93	8	16.7	1	63	R	GR	MW	SI
Valentić	04.93	11.95	32	66.7	1	63	R	GR	MW	SI
Matesa	11.95				1	53	R	SM	MW	SI

Czech Republic:

Pitra	10.88	02.90							
Pithart	02.90	06.90							
Pithart	06.90	07.92	25	52.1	3	75	B	GR	NO	MU
Klaus	07.92	01.93	6	12.5	4	56	R	SM	MW	MU
Klaus	01.93		37	77.1	4	56	R	SM	MW	MU

Denmark:

Schlüter	12.89	12.90	12	25.0	2	33	R	MI	NO	MU
Schlüter	12.90	01.93	25	52.1	2	34	R	MI	NO	MU
Rasmussen	01.93	09.94	20	41.7	4	51	B	SM	MW	MU
Rasmussen	09.94				3	43	B	NO	NO	MU

Estonia:

Savisaar	04.90	01.92							
Vähi	01.92	10.92							
Laar	10.92	10.94	24	50.0	2	41	B	MI	NO	MU
Tarand	10.94	03.95	6	12.5			CA		
Vähi	04.95	11.95	7	14.6	2	56	R	SM	MW	MU
Vähi	11.95				2	59	R	SM	MW	MU

Finland:

Holkeri	04.87	08.90	40	83.3	4	66	B	GR	NO	MU
Holkeri	08.90	04.91	8	16.7	3	61	B	GR	NO	MU
Aho	04.91	04.95	48	100.0	4	58	R	SM	NO	MU
Lipponen	04.95				5	72	B	GR	NO	MU

France:

Rocard	06.88	05.91	35	58.3	2	48	L	MI	NO	MU
Cresson	05.91	04.92	11	18.3	2	48	L	MI	NO	MU
Bérégovoy	04.92	03.93	11	18.3	2	48	L	MI	NO	MU
Balladur	03.93	05.95	26	54.2	2	80	R	GR	MW	MU
Juppé	05.95				2	80	R	GR	MW	MU

Appendix 7.1   *Continued*

Germany:

Kohl	03.87	10.90	42	87.5	2	54	R	SM	MW	MU
Kohl	10.90	01.91	3	6.3	2	54	R	SM	MW	MU
Kohl	01.91	10.94	45	93.7	2	54	R	SM	MW	MU
Kohl	10.94				2	51	R	SM	MW	MU

Greece:

Zolotas	11.89	04.90	5	10.4	3	99	B	GR	NO	MU
Mitsotakis	04.90	10.93	42	87.5	1	51	R	SM	MW	SI
Papandreou	10.93	01.96	27	56.3	1	57	L	SM	MW	SI

Hungary:

Nemeth	11.88	05.90								
Antall	05.90	12.93	42	87.5	3	60	R	SM	NO	MU
Boross	12.93	06.94	6	12.5	3	51	R	SM	MW	MU
Horn	06.94				2	72	B	GR	NO	MU

Iceland:

Hermannsson	09.89	04.91	19	39.6	4	57	B	SM	MW	MU
Oddsson	04.91	04.95	48	100.0	2	57	B	SM	MW	MU
Oddsson	04.95				2	63	R	GR	MW	MU

Ireland:

Haughey	07.89	02.92	31	51.7	2	50	R	MI	NO	MU
Reynolds	02.92	10.92	8	13.3	2	50	R	MI	NO	MU
Reynolds	10.92	01.93	3	5.0	1	46	R	MI	NO	SI
Reynolds	01.93	12.94	23	38.3	2	61	B	GR	MW	MU
Bruton	12.94				3	47	B	MI	NO	MU

Italy:

Andreotti	07.89	04.91	19	31.7	5	60	B	SM	NO	MU
Andreotti	04.91	07.92	15	25.0	4	56	B	SM	NO	MU
Amato	07.92	04.93	9	15.0	4	53	B	SM	MW	MU
Ciampi	04.93	04.94	12	20.0	4	53	B	SM	MW	MU
Berlusconi	04.94	01.95	9	15.0	3	58	R	SM	MW	MU
Dini	01.95	01.96	12	20.0			CA			

Latvia:

Godmanis	05.90	11.91	18							
Godmanis	11.91	08.93	21							
Birkavs	08.93	09.94	13	27.1	2	48	R	MI	NO	MU
Gailis	09.94	12.95	15	31.3	2	40	R	MI	NO	MU

Lithuania:

Prunskiene	03.90	01.91	10							
Vagnorius	01.91	07.92	6							
Abišala	07.92	12.92	5							
Lubys	12.92	03.93	3	6.3	1	52	L	SM	MW	SI
Slezevicius	03.93		36	75.0	1	52	L	SM	MW	SI

Appendix 7.1   *Continued*

Luxembourg:

Santer	07.89	06.94	59	100.0	2	59	B	SM	MW	MU
Santer	06.94	12.94	6	10.0	2	63	B	GR	MW	MU
Juncker	01.95				2	63	B	GR	MW	MU

Netherlands:

| Lubbers | 11.89 | 08.94 | 57 | 100.0 | 2 | 69 | B | GR | MW | MU |
| Kok | 08.94 | | | | 3 | 61 | B | GR | MW | MU |

Norway:

Syse	10.89	11.90	13	27.1	3	38	R	MI	NO	MU
Brundtland	11.90	09.93	34	70.8	1	38	L	MI	NO	SI
Brundtland	09.93	09.97	48	100.0	1	41	L	MI	NO	SI

Poland:

Mazowiecki	08.89	01.91	16							
Bielecki	01.91	12.91	11							
Olszewski	12.91	06.92	6	12.5	3	26	R	MI	NO	MU
Pawlak	06.92	07.92	1	2.1	5	49	B	MI	NO	MU
Suchocka	07.92	10.93	15	31.3	7	42	R	MI	NO	MU
Pawlak	10.93	03.95	16	33.3	2	66	B	GR	MW	MU
Oleksy	03.95				2	66	B	GR	MW	MU

Portugal:

Silva	08.87	10.91	50	100.0	2	61	R	GR	NO	MU
Silva	10.91	10.95	48	100.0	1	58	R	SM	MW	MU
Gueterres	10.95				1	49	L	MI	NO	SI

Romania:

Roman	12.89	06.90	6							
Roman	06.90	10.91	16	33.3	1	66	L	GR	MW	SI
Stolojan	10.91	11.92	13	27.1	4	77	B	GR	NO	MU
Vacaroiu	11.92	09.96	46	95.8	2	34	B	MI	NO	MU

Slovakia:

Čič	12.89	06.90								
Mečiar	06.90	03.91	9	18.8	3	57	B	SM	MW	MU
Carnogursky	03.91	06.92	15	31.3	3	43	B	MI	NO	MU
Mečiar	06.92	03.94	21	43.8	2	59	R	SM	MW	MU
Moravčik	03.94	12.94	9	18.8	5	35	B	MI	NO	MU
Mečiar	12.94				3	55	B	SM	MW	MU

Slovenia:

Peterle	05.90	04.92	23							
Drnovsek	04.92	01.93	9							
Drnovsek	01.93	03.94	14	29.2	5	68	B	GR	NO	MU
Drnovsek	03.94	01.96	20	41.7	3	68	B	GR	NO	MU

Appendix 7.1 *Continued*

Spain:										
Gonzales	11.89	06.93	43	89.6	1	51	L	SM	MW	SI
Gonzales	06.93	03.96	33	68.8	1	45	L	MI	NO	SI

Sweden:										
Carlsson	09.88	10.91	37	100.0	1	45	L	MI	NO	SI
Bildt	10.91	10.94	36	100.0	4	49	R	MI	NO	MU
Carlsson	10.94	03.96	17	35.4	1	46	L	MI	NO	SI

Switzerland:										
Hurliman	10.87	10.91	48	100.0	4	72	B	GR	NO	MU
Felber	10.91	10.95	48	100.0	4	73	B	GR	NO	MU
Villiger	10.95				4	81	B	GR	NO	MU

United Kingdom:										
Thatcher	06.87	11.90	41	68.3	1	58	R	SM	MW	SI
Major	11.90	04.92	17	28.3	1	57	R	SM	MW	SI
Major	04.92		50	83.3	1	57	R	SM	MW	SI

Yugoslavia:										
Marković	03.89	07.92								
Panić	07.92	12.92	4	8.3	2	60	L	GR	NO	MU
Kontić	12.92	03.93	3	4.1	2	60	L	GR	NO	MU
Kontić	03.93		36	75.0	2	60	L	GR	NO	MU

Notes:

IN =	month of formation of government
OUT =	month of resignation of government
NO MO =	duration of government in number of months
SU RA =	survival rate of government, i.e. real duration of government in relation to expected duration expressed as a percentage of time
NO PA =	number of parties in government
PO OR =	political orientation of government: CA = caretaker; L = left-wing; R = right-wing; B = balanced
TY MA =	type of majority: MI = minority government; SM = small majority; GR = grand majority
MI WI =	minimum-winning cabinet: MW = minimum-winning; NO = no minimum-winning
TY CA =	type of cabinet: MU = multi-party government, SI = single-party government.

8

The Public Sector

Politics includes more than the constitution (Chapter 5), the party system (Chapter 6) and the government (Chapter 7). In this chapter we broaden the analysis by looking at public policies, which in the European context are much focused on the welfare state. What kinds of public expenditures are there in the European public sector and how do they vary from one country to another?

Measuring the public sector in a country presents several problems about reliable and valid indicators. We employ money measures exclusively. The Communist legacy in Eastern Europe makes the public–private sector distinction ambiguous there, as many people still work in state enterprises that would normally be private in Western Europe, although the various privatization strategies reduce public employment.

The purpose of this chapter is to look at the size and structure of public policies in European countries by means of an enquiry into two well-known welfare state models that attempt to explain how the public sector is structured in a society with an advanced economy. The first emphasizes public sector convergence or similarities between the public sector in various countries (Wilensky, 1975), whereas the second underlines public sector differences or divergence among countries (Esping-Andersen, 1990). These two models comprise in reality two different theories about the mechanisms or forces that enhance welfare state expenditures, the convergence model focusing on affluence and the divergence model on political traditions, including corporatist practices. First we look at data about the public sector in order to establish how public expenditures vary in terms of overall size and composition.

Overall Public Sector Size

The public sector is an aggregate concept at a very high level of summation. One may decompose it in various ways. First, the public sector as the totality of activities of governments at various levels in the political system may be identified by either of its three characteristic entities (Rose, 1984): money, employees as well as laws and by-laws. Since we restrict our analysis to the first category, we deal with income and expenditure items of the public sector.

Second, once one has decided to focus on money as the method for

Table 8.1   *Overall size of the public sector: current expenditures*

Country set	Current expenditure/GDP		
	1989	1991	1993
CORE EC	48.0 (5)	50.1 (5)	52.1 (5)
OTHER EC	42.1 (6)	44.8 (6)	47.8 (6)
OUTSIDE EC	41.7 (6)	44.8 (6)	49.9 (6)
CORE EAST	57.1 (6)	50.8 (6)	48.1 (6)
EAST PERIPHERY	48.0 (5)	40.6 (6)	37.5 (6)
All	47.3 (28)	46.1 (29)	46.9 (29)

Note: Current expenditures: public consumption expenditures, interest on the public debt, subsidies and social security transfers to households. What the EBRD calls 'general government expenditure' is roughly equal to what the OECD labels 'current disbursements'.

Sources: EBRD (1994, 1995); OECD (1994d, 1995a).

measuring the public sector one faces another choice, namely, the institutional method of unpacking the public sector versus the functional one. The first looks at the income and expenditures of various levels of government: the central or national government versus the regional or local governments in order to describe how public sector money is raised and spent by different governments including the possibility that money is moved internally in the public sector from one level of government to another.

On the other hand, there is the functional way of classifying income items and expenditure categories. Here one typically starts by distinguishing between allocation and transfer payments (social security) and then goes on to identify various types of allocative expenditures (public consumption). One also separates between the three standard income sources such as taxation involving different types of taxes, user fees and public borrowing. Below we concentrate upon the *functional* division of public sector expenditures. It should be underlined that the data for East European countries is less reliable than those for Western Europe.

One standard indicator on the overall size of the public sector is the total amount of money channelled through the budgetary system. Either one looks at data about the income side or at the expenditure side of the public sector. Table 8.1 presents expenditure data about the total size of the public sector.

As we see from Table 8.1, the size of the public sector has already been reduced considerably in the former Communist states. Whereas public expenditures go down in Eastern Europe, they continue to go up in Western Europe. Actually, there is little difference between the country sets with the exception of EAST PERIPHERY where public sector reduction has been dramatic. The averages for the other four country sets are very close to each other somewhere around 48–50 per cent of GDP. Thus, one may

Table 8.2　*Overall size of the public sector: total revenues*

Country set	Total revenues/GDP		
	1989	1991	1993
CORE EC	46.7　(5)	47.6　(5)	48.8　(5)
OTHER EC	41.0　(6)	42.2　(6)	43.4　(6)
OUTSIDE EC	47.4　(6)	47.6　(6)	47.9　(6)
CORE EAST	55.9　(6)	47.6　(6)	44.1　(6)
EAST PERIPHERY	45.2　(5)	36.1　(6)	34.3　(6)
All	47.3 (28)	44.1 (29)	43.5 (29)

Note: Total revenues: direct and indirect taxes, social security contributions. What the IMF names 'general government revenue' roughly equals 'current receipts of government' in the OECD; data from the EBRD have been used for interpolation.

Sources: IMF (1994), EBRD (1995), OECD (1995a).

establish that the mixed economy is the typical feature all over Europe, although a few countries are so-called outliers, that is, they display either much higher or much lower scores. Which are they in the 1993 data?

Among the countries with a public sector above 55 per cent of the GDP we find: Sweden, Hungary, Denmark, Finland, the Netherlands and Belgium. At the other opposite pole there are the following countries where public expenditures are around 35 per cent of GDP: Latvia, Estonia, Lithuania, Iceland, Croatia and Switzerland. It is interesting to observe that some East European countries now have a lower level of public expenditure than several West European countries. Yet, one must recall that these numbers are relative figures. In absolute measures public expenditures are considerably larger in Western Europe than in Eastern Europe, while the GDP is much larger in the former than in the latter.

What we observe in Table 8.1 is the continued advance in Western Europe in the early 1990s of what J. Schumpeter already after the First World War called the Tax State (Schumpeter, 1954). With the demise of the planned economy all states in Europe have accepted a mixture of capitalism and socialism, according to which blend the institutions of the market economy coexist with state intervention (Chapter 2), which may be more or less extensive in different countries. Perhaps the most startling finding is not the overall convergence towards a mixed economy all over Europe, but that the tax state has maintained its overall size in Western Europe in the early 1990s despite the strong market drive in many countries including large-scale privatization plans. Table 8.2 contains information about general government revenues where the difference between expenditures and revenues is made up of public sector borrowing.

The variation on the income side mirrors the variation on the output side, the difference being variations in deficit spending. The two East European sets display a sharp downward trend in total revenues as a percentage of GDP over only a couple of years, whereas in the West

European sets there is a steady but slow advance. The tax state is largest in the Scandinavian countries and the Netherlands, whereas it is lowest in the Baltic states.

Let us turn to a closer examination of what the tax state does. Enquiring into what causes big government promotes one should look at the functional division of public expenditures remembering that they refer to information about so-called government outputs and not outcomes. Big government in Europe attempts to realize a welfare state, but it is always an open question whether large governmental effort as measured by huge public expenditures brings about better outcomes for society in the form of individual well-being.

Big government in the European form of a welfare state comprises two different types of expenditures: public resource allocation and income redistribution. Welfare state differences between countries reflect on the one hand various overall welfare state ambitions and on the other hand different orientations of the welfare state towards either allocative tasks – that is, provision of goods and services – or redistributive tasks – namely, transfer payments.

The concept of a welfare state in Europe involves three kinds of commitments, which may be delivered by means of alternative institutional arrangements: (1) public provision of certain services such as education, health and services for the elderly virtually without user fees; (2) income maintenance programmes through which the public sector guarantees a certain percentage of the income when a person suffers adversity in the form of sickness or unemployment and has the right to receive a pension; and (3) active labour market policies in order to promote full employment. What, more specifically, is public resource allocation?

Allocative Expenditures

Functionally, one distinguishes between final government consumption, which is the cost for public resource allocation, and transfer payments to either households or firms as well as interest payments on the state debt. Table 8.3 gives data about the total costs for allocation, which stands for the provision of goods and services by government at any level in the political system which are provided more or less without any user fees.

Here, we have higher scores for OTHER EC and OUTSIDE EC but lower ones for CORE EC, CORE EAST and EAST PERIPHERY. The allocative expenditures are high in the following countries: Sweden, Denmark, Finland, Norway, the United Kingdom, Greece and Poland, where final government consumption is above 20 per cent of the GDP. Note that the size of the productive state in Europe is fairly constant in the early 1990s

Next we will examine the variation in a few key allocative items of expenditures. Here, the basic separation is between welfare state tasks, such as education and health on the one hand, and the classical functions of

Table 8.3   *Government final consumption in percentage of GDP*

Country set	1991	1992	1993
CORE EC (5)	16.4	16.5	16.6
OTHER EC (5)	19.6	19.6	19.7
OUTSIDE EC (5)	20.8	21.3	21.3
CORE EAST (4)	15.0	19.2	18.3
EAST PERIPHERY (3)	12.0	20.2	19.5
All (22)	17.3	19.2	19.0

Note: Government final consumption consists of expenditures on goods and services for public administration, defence, health and education. What the IMF calls 'goods and services' is roughly comparable with what the OECD names 'government final consumption expenditure'.

Sources: IMF (1994), OECD (1995a).

Table 8.4   *Health expenditures in percentage of GDP, around 1990–1*

Country set	Total health	Public health
CORE EC	8.3 (6)	6.0 (5)
INSIDE EC	6.5 (6)	5.0 (6)
OUTSIDE EC	8.5 (6)	6.3 (5)
CORE EAST	5.3 (5)	4.2 (5)
EAST PERIPHERY	3.8 (2)	3.3 (3)
All	7.0 (25)	5.1 (24)

Sources: Total health: UNDP (1994); Public health: World Bank (1993).

the state, namely maintaining internal and external order, on the other hand. The costs for various allocative purposes vary from one country to another depending on how the programmes have been framed as well as how strong the ambitions behind the various programmes are. Table 8.4 shows the share of GDP that is allocated to health services in general and to public health care in particular.

The East–West divide appears in these data, as West European countries spend more on health. However, there is also a North–South divide as North European countries spend more than South European ones. Much of health care is socialized all over Europe, but there are a few countries with much private health care, such as France, Italy and Switzerland. In the Nordic countries almost all health care is publicly provided. The huge difference between CORE EC and OUTSIDE EC on the one hand, CORE EAST and EAST PERIPHERY on the other hand reflects not only policy preferences but also simply resources.

The highest public health expenditures are to be found in Sweden, Norway, France, Belgium and Finland, whereas the lowest occur among

Table 8.5   *Education and labour market expenditures in percentage of GDP, around 1990–1*

Country set	Public education	Labour market
CORE EC	5.1 (6)	2.8 (6)
INSIDE EC	5.4 (5)	3.2 (6)
OUTSIDE EC	6.0 (6)	3.4 (5)
CORE EAST	4.8 (5)	1.8 (5)
EAST PERIPHERY	– (0)	– (0)
All	5.3 (22)	2.8 (22)

Sources: OECD (1994a); UNDP (1994).

the following countries: Romania, Lithuania, Albania, Yugoslavia, Poland and Greece. The British public health care system is cost efficient, meaning that the expenditures are not low simply because the level of ambition is meagre, which is the case in Eastern Europe.

Table 8.5 examines the costs for education and labour market policies. The former includes all kinds of public education – primary, secondary and tertiary – for which data are available for only four country sets.

The country differences are not that striking with regard to public expenditures on education, as the averages for each country set come close to the overall average. But some countries are different. Thus, a few countries have high public expenditures on education such as Norway, Sweden, Hungary, Finland, Denmark, Iceland, Luxembourg and the Netherlands where the country scores range from a high 6.8 per cent to a medium 5.6 per cent. At the same time much the same group of countries have high labour market policy costs: Denmark, Sweden, Finland, Ireland, Belgium, Spain, Germany and the Netherlands in the range between 6.5 per cent and 3.3 per cent of GDP. The costs for labour market policies differ considerably as some countries allocate less than 1 per cent of GDP to this item, for example Switzerland.

The expenditures for health, education and labour market policies make up by far the largest portion of the costs for general government consumption. In Europe public sector activities in these areas are considered as citizen rights, which are often entrenched in constitutional documents. The obligation of the state towards its citizens to provide them with access to health care, with educational opportunities as well as with protection against unemployment is acknowledged by almost all political parties. What varies is the capacity of the state to deliver upon its promises, where the gulf between ideal and reality is large in Eastern Europe especially.

Besides these welfare state costs general government consumption also includes the expenditures for internal and external security as well as the costs for infrastructure insofar as it is not financed by user fees. Typically, these items of public resource allocation are less costly than the core welfare state functions.

Table 8.6   *Military expenditures in percentage of GDP*

Country set	1990	1993
CORE EC	2.4 (6)	2.3 (5)
OTHER EC	3.0 (6)	2.8 (6)
OUTSIDE EC	1.6 (6)	2.1 (4)
CORE EAST	2.1 (5)	2.8 (5)
EAST PERIPHERY	4.8 (1)	4.6 (2)
All	2.4 (24)	2.7 (22)

Sources: 1990: UNDP (1994); 1993: EB (1993: 232).

Table 8.6 presents an estimation of the costs for one of the classical state functions, the provision of external safety. The costs for military programmes may though go very high in certain cases, especially when a country is at war.

On average, countries in Europe devote 2.5 per cent of their GDP to military spending. The figure for EAST PERIPHERY is considerably higher, but it represents only one or two countries, such as Albania. Had data been available for the countries that are involved in the civil war in former Yugoslavia, then the figures would have been much higher. In OUTSIDE EC military spending is less, as here we have countries that are not members of any military alliance. The countries that have large military expenditures are the NATO members such as the United Kingdom (4.2 per cent), France (3.5 per cent) and Germany (2.8 per cent). However, the country with the highest recorded level of military spending is Greece with 5.5 per cent. Also surprisingly, Norway is stated to have higher military expenditures (3.1 per cent) than either Poland (2.7 per cent) and Romania (1.4 per cent) have admitted publicly.

Thus far, the major finding is that on each single item of allocative expenditures there are not extensive differences between the West European and the East European country sets. This reflects less the continued existence of a communist welfare state than the fact that the GDP is much lower in East European countries, meaning that rather small actual public expenditures make up a large part of the GDP. Although there are remnants of what was once a model of the communist welfare state covering various kinds of welfare expenditures, the large relative shares of public expenditures in Eastern Europe more probably reflect their weak economic bases.

Any analysis of public expenditures is incomplete while it does not include redistribution or the transfer of money from government to different groups, including households. The issuing of pay cheques constitutes a formidable part of the costs for the welfare state. One should remind oneself that the concept of a welfare state covers allocative expenditures for education, health and social care and include considerable transfer payments. The welfare state includes both allocation and income redistribution. Now we turn to the latter.

Table 8.7   *Social security payments as a percentage of GDP*

Country set	1985–90		1992		1993	
CORE EC (6)	23.0	(6)	21.3	(5)	22.0	(5)
OTHER EC (6)	16.7	(6)	15.8	(6)	16.2	(6)
OUTSIDE EC (5)	21.9	(5)	18.4	(6)	19.5	(6)
CORE EAST (4)	15.9	(4)	15.8	(6)	15.6	(6)
EAST PERIPHERY (1)	17.2	(1)	12.5	(3)	11.9	(3)
All (22)	19.5	(22)	17.1	(26)	17.5	(26)

Note: Social security transfers comprise social security benefits, social assistance grants, unfunded employee pension and welfare benefits, and transfers to private non-profit institutions serving households.

Sources: 1985–90: UNDP (1994); 1992 and 1993: IMF (1994), OECD (1995a).

Social Security

Income redistribution in the form of transfer payments looms large in the welfare state, accounting for a considerable portion of big government in Europe. Social security expenditures include a number of different items of income maintenance. Most countries have some sort of public pension schemes, not only for their government employees but also for the general public. Unemployment benefits are paid out in most European countries, although the level of compensation differs. Sickness benefits exist in some countries, which is also true of more specific transfer programmes such as maternity leave and child allowances.

Table 8.7 illustrates what all these items add up to in terms of transfer payments or public expenditures for redistributive purposes measured as a percentage of GDP. We see that transfer payments as a percentage of GDP constitute huge items of expenditure in the public sector in almost all European countries. In a few countries it constitutes 50 per cent of the total public expenditures. On average, about 18–20 per cent of GDP is redistributed from various tax groups to different recipients of money cheques.

The income maintenance programmes include various insurance schemes such as pensions, sickness, unemployment and maternity. And they comprise programmes for social assistance and family support, for example in the form of child allowances. Countries differ institutionally both with regard to how generous these programmes are in terms of cash payments as well as concerning whether various client groups are treated in the same way or differently, and finally in terms of funding schemes. But most countries in Europe have social security programmes of some sort (Council of Europe, 1993; GVG, 1994; CEC, 1995b).

In Europe the countries mainly fund their transfer programmes by means of pay-as-you-go schemes, which places tremendous pressure on the state coffers as the age structure of the European populations changes towards a higher proportion of elderly people. At the same time, there is little growth in the total number of those employed, even when there is moderate economic growth, meaning that the burden on those occupationally active must be raised or transfer payments will have to be cut back.

The redistributive ambition is especially high in CORE EC and OUTSIDE EC, but considerably lower in OTHER EC and EAST PERIPHERY. The impression that the redistributive effort is less all over Eastern Europe is supported in the data. But transfer payments are not non-existent in the former Communist countries, although these countries have cut back substantially on the ambitions of the so-called Communist welfare state (Castles, 1986; Rys, 1993; Götting, 1994). Again, the small differences in relative expenditures between West European and East European countries may reflect differences in the base, the GDP.

The countries with huge transfer payments of around 25–30 per cent of GDP include both countries with a long-term Social Democratic regime and countries where Christian Democracy has been dominant in politics. At the other end of the scale we find the following countries with small transfer payments: Portugal, Poland, Greece, Switzerland and Spain with between 10 and 13 per cent. As is readily seen, these countries are either poor relatively speaking or they constitute so-called market regimes.

It is undeniable that the country differences in terms of transfer payments are large both absolutely and relatively speaking, but the overall trend is that all countries increasingly take on various kinds of redistributive tasks. Income redistribution has been on the rise in terms of both costs and political saliency for several decades now, as more people grow older and demand an acceptable pension to which the state increasingly contributes.

Having given an overview of the public sector in Europe, examining allocative and redistributive expenditures, we now turn to two well-known models which attempt to explain the country variation that the information above indicates. The models which we focus on here enter the rather extensive literature on the welfare state.

Theorizing the European Welfare State

Theories about the welfare state deal with several themes, ranging from the historical analysis of the origins of the welfare state to the contemporary assessment of the relevance of welfare state reform strategies. One much debated issue has been to identify the factors behind the country variation in welfare state expenditures. There are two chief competing models, one underlining convergence and the other divergence.

The convergence model argues that the European welfare state will grow increasingly alike from one country to another as the level of affluence increases in all of them. A higher income allows more possibilities for public spending on other items than those necessary for survival such as food. Moreover, a higher level of affluence is generated by industrialization and urbanization which create a need for more public spending on infrastructure or research and development for example. A modern statement of the convergence model of the welfare state is to be found in Wilensky (1975). He states:

> My guiding hypotheses are that variations in both welfare-state practice and ideology can be explained by variations in (1) political centralization as it relates to (2) social heterogeneity and internal cleavages, (3) stratification and mobility (especially the position of middle strata), (4) the size of the working class and the nature of its organization, and (5) the influence of the military. I suggest that if rich countries become more alike in these attributes of structure, they will develop similar welfare-state practices and ideologies. (Wilensky, 1975: 50)

One factor of tremendous weight in enhancing more of similarity in the attributes of structure, which Wilensky mentions, is affluence and its social correlates (see Chapters 2 and 3).

The divergence model claims contrarily that the European welfare state harbours quite different welfare state regimes. Either a country adopts the one or the other, but these regimes are truly distinct. Esping-Andersen (1990) argues to the effect that there is little evidence of convergence between the three basic welfare regimes he identified.

The divergence model claims that there is no such thing as one welfare state. Welfare regimes differ fundamentally with regard to both the quantity and quality of welfare state spending. Esping-Andersen's model comprises three distinct welfare regimes: (1) Neo-liberal welfare regimes; (2) Universal Welfare Regimes; and (3) Conservative welfare regimes. The labelling of these different welfare state regimes varies as (2) is sometimes called the 'Social Democratic Model' or the 'Corporatist welfare state', while (1) is often referred to as the 'Conservative model' and (3) is often called the 'Christian Democratic Model' or 'Social Catholicism'. This is actually rather confusing, because the non-socialist parties in the Nordic countries supported the Scandinavian model and corporatism has been prominent in countries with a so-called conservative welfare regime at the same time as the neo-liberal regime has been backed by real conservative parties.

It is true that one may distinguish theoretically between various aspects of a welfare regime. One important dimension is whether the programmes involve comprehensive rights or whether they are means tested hand-outs from government to targeted weak groups. Another dimension is whether the programmes are universal in the sense that each and everyone is treated equally under the various schemes or whether there are status distinctions built into the programmes in the form of different rights for different groups. But it is not a straightforward task to classify the public sectors in Europe on the basis of combinations between degree of universality and comprehensiveness in a general sense.

A neo-liberal welfare regime would be based on means tested mechanisms. The Scandinavian or Nordic model of a welfare state may be singled out as universal and comprehensive. Finally, there is a mixed welfare regime which combines comprehensiveness with status distinctions, as in

Germany and Austria.) But all these three types are really pure types or ideal-types meaning that in reality the welfare state of a country is more or less close to such an ideal-type. How does one classify Belgium and the Netherlands or France and Italy, not to mention Eastern Europe with remnants of the Communist welfare state?

In fact, the welfare state in a country may mix features from each model in its separate parts meaning that we have to recognize that pure welfare state regimes do not exist. One also has to take into account that countries may make changes in their welfare states over time pulling their public sector away from one ideal-type towards another. Such changes may occur in a rapid fashion as in the United Kingdom in the 1980s and in Sweden in the 1990s.

To pin down which country operates which type of welfare regime is beset with difficulties. One would assume that countries with a neo-liberal welfare regime have lower welfare state expenditures than a country that adheres to the Nordic model, which is universal and comprehensive. But are there any neo-liberal regimes in Europe? What about the so-called conservative welfare state regimes? How large are welfare expenditures that they typically have? It is difficult to distinguish practically between these regimes and the so-called social democratic welfare regimes, as both use status distinctions of some sort in at least some programmes.

We suggest that one employs a distinction between two kinds of welfare states along somewhat different lines than those pursued in the literature. Some countries concentrate on redistribution, that is, their transfer payments are high as a percentage of GDP including pensions, unemployment and sickness benefits, educational allowances, and so on. Other countries have large allocative welfare states where government provides services virtually without user fees, mainly health care and education.

We thus arrive at Table 8.8 where three measures of the welfare state in Europe are presented, based upon Tables 8.4, 8.5 and 8.7. Allocative welfare state expenditures cover the costs for public education and health care as well as for labour market policies. The redistributive welfare state comprises the costs for social security payments. Finally, Table 8.8 includes a third category summarizing the earlier two categories into an overall measure of the size of welfare state expenditures.

Table 8.8 shows two things. On the one hand, there is a European welfare state, as all countries devote substantial amounts of their GDP to both allocative and redistributive items of expenditure. Also in Eastern Europe there are welfare state expenditures amounting to more than 25 per cent of GDP.

On the other hand, there exists a considerable country variation in the size of the European welfare state, especially when one adds up both allocative and redistributive items of expenditure as in the overall measure. Total welfare state expenditures are clearly higher in CORE EC and OUTSIDE EC than in OTHER EC and CORE EAST. Yet, the overall measure hides an interesting variation between the allocative and redistributive welfare state

Table 8.8 *Welfare state expenditures as a percentage of GDP*

Country set	Allocative welfare state	Redistributive welfare state	Total welfare state
CORE EC	14.1 (5)	21.3 (5)	35.4 (5)
OTHER EC	14.1 (5)	15.8 (6)	30.0 (5)
OUTSIDE EC	15.7 (5)	18.4 (6)	36.5 (5)
CORE EAST	11.5 (4)	15.8 (6)	28.3 (4)
EAST PERIPHERY	–	12.5 (3)	–
All	14.0 (19)	17.1 (26)	32.7 (19)

Sources: Tables 8.4, 8.5 and 8.7 (1992).

which does not coincide with the distinction between different welfare state regimes.

The allocative welfare states are the following countries: the Nordic countries, the United Kingdom and Spain, with some 15 per cent or more of GDP allocated to government provision of goods and services. But the redistributive welfare states include besides Sweden and Denmark also the Netherlands, France, Germany, Austria and Italy with over 20 per cent of GDP going to income redistribution. Although there is some overlap between the two sets of welfare states, it is astonishingly small.

Some of the redistributive welfare states are rather low on allocative expenditures, such as Austria and Italy. And some of the countries with rather large allocative expenditures, such as Spain and the United Kingdom, display fairly low levels of redistributive expenditures. Switzerland is consistently low on both allocative and redistributive expenditures. The distinction between the allocative and the redistributive welfare state blurs the established separation between welfare regimes.

Now, one may interpret the Wilensky and Esping-Andersen models as alternative theories about the mechanisms behind welfare state expenditures. Whereas the convergence model assumes a simple mechanism linking affluence with the state provision of welfare services, the divergence model takes more factors into account such as political parties and trade unions. We must now proceed to enquire into which factors lie behind the variation portrayed in Table 8.8. Does politics matter? Or are economic factors more important? The divergence model launched by Esping-Andersen underlines political factors including the position of the trade unions, whereas the convergence model by Wilensky focuses upon affluence. One key political factor in theories about the welfare is corporatism. What is 'corporatism'?

Corporatism

The labelling of welfare regimes is often an implicit statement of a causal hypothesis. When one speaks of the 'Social Democratic Model' or the 'Christian Democratic Model', then one commits oneself to an assumption about causality, which should be brought out into the open and tested by means of empirical analysis. Is it really the case that the strength of the Social Democratic movement explains the build up of the Scandinavian model or that the large electoral support for Christian Democracy is the key factor behind the Conservative welfare state? Could not Christian parties or other non-socialist parties support a universal and comprehensive welfare regime? Do conservative parties tend to support a Conservative or Liberal welfare regime?

When a welfare state is given different labels such as 'Social Democratic' or 'Christian Democratic' or 'Corporatist', then the intention is that these labels not only identify distinct welfare regimes but that they also name the mechanism behind the regime. Thus, we have a few key hypotheses which entail that large welfare expenditures are driven by either Social Democratic or Christian Democratic governments or that they are connected with corporatist institutions. Let us examine the corporatist models more closely. The corporatist theme looks at the variation in strength of interest organizations, either in society or in access to public policy-making and policy implementation.

Firstly, 'corporatism' may stand for strong centralization of industrial relations. Thus, the extent of hierarchy in the structure of interest organizations is examined, both on the labour side and among the employers' associations (Crouch, 1993; Bean, 1994).

Second, 'corporatism' may refer more specifically to a strong trade union movement as measured by trade union participation of the rank and file in the labour force, that is trade union density. This aspect refers to how encompassing the unions are in terms of membership (Armingeon, 1989; Visser, 1991, 1993; Western, 1993, 1995). Correspondingly, one may examine how firms organize themselves into branch organizations or employers' associations.

Third, 'corporatism' denotes a special pattern of relationships between government, the business community and trade unions, including élite cooperation in various forms between these three kinds of partners. Here, 'corporatism' stands for a distinct mode of governing the economy based on interaction and reciprocities between politicians, employers or firms and the trade unions (Hollingsworth et al., 1994). Corporatist patterns of decision-making involve interest consultation on matters concerning, for example wages as well as interest consultation in relation to policy and implementation (Lehmbruch and Schmitter, 1982). Thus, the well-known tripartite model used to offer institutions for the interaction between business, labour and government in some West European countries, but its relevance at the macro level has decreased although it may still be employed at the meso level or micro level.

A number of scales of corporatism have been suggested, classifying countries in Western Europe and other OECD countries (Schmitter, 1981; Cameron, 1984; Bruno and Sachs, 1985; Calmfors and Driffill, 1988; Lijphart and Crepatz, 1991; Alvarez et al., 1991; Keman and Pennings,

1995). The difficulty with these scales is that scholars are not in agreement about how to identify several countries such as Switzerland, the Netherlands, Germany, the United Kingdom, Italy and France, reflecting uncertainty about what the core meaning of 'corporatism' is. These scales of corporatism seem to be based on different deliberations on trade union density, the amount of centralization of industrial relations and the occurrence of institutionalized interaction between government, business and labour including policy-making and policy implementation.

One strand in corporatist thought connects with the concept of *Konkordanzdemokratie*, which underlines the contribution of institutions of power-sharing to democratic stability (Schmidt, 1995). It is sometimes argued that so-called consociational devices and corporatist patterns of policy-making are basically one and the same thing. However, *Konkordanzdemokratie* entails a special kind of government formation – oversized coalitions, which need not be typical in countries which are said to practise corporatism (Lehmbruch, 1992; Abromeit, 1993).

Another strand in corporatist theory underlines the structure of the trade union movement, in particular how encompassing trade union participation is (union density) or how centralized the trade union movement tends to be. It is, then, believed that corporatism as trade union density and corporatism as interlocking networks of policy-making go together, but this is not necesarily so. Take for example the Netherlands or Switzerland, which some claim have corporatist institutions, but their trade union movements are not encompassing. Or compare Germany and the United Kingdom, where the trade union density is actually higher in the latter than in the former, although the former was considered corporatist (Streeck, 1992). As Ebbinghaus underlines, the trade union movement in Western Europe is multifaceted, where membership ratio is only one aspect to be taken into account (Ebbinghaus, 1995). For Eastern Europe the key problem concerns what will happen to the large trade unions once they are no longer integrated into the state (Ost, 1993; Reutter, 1994).

The corporatist model about public expenditures may be tested empirically by either measuring the strength of the trade unions or by developing an index measuring the institutionalization of a set of rules for interest *intermediation* and policy *concertation* between all kinds of organized interests. The first approach is easier to handle than the second one, because scholars are not in agreement about the existence of corporatist institutions in various countries. Every country in Europe seems to have its special institutions for interrelating government, business and the unions. Actually, corporatist institutions for interest intermediation and policy concertation are not easily identified in a straightforward manner, and their influence in a country tends to fluctuate over time. If the Nordic countries and Austria have corporatist institutions, then what about Germany, the BeNeLux countries and Switzerland? What level does 'corporatism' refer to: macro, meso or micro?

When corporatism is singled out as a critical determinant for welfare

Table 8.9 *Trade union membership*

Country set	Unionization rate 1: 1988–92		Unionization rate 2: 1990		Unionization rate 3: 1990–2	
CORE EC	45.5	(6)	35.7	(6)	34.7	(6)
OTHER EC	43.5	(6)	39.7	(6)	39.5	(6)
OUTSIDE EC	70.0	(6)	60.2	(6)	60.3	(6)
CORE EAST	50.0	(5)	50.0	(1)	50.0	(3)
EAST PERIPHERY	53.3	(3)	–		53.3	(3)
All	52.5	(26)	45.2	(19)	46.8	(26)

Sources: Unionization rate 1: ILO (1992, 1993a); Visser (1993); Waller and Myant (1993); unionization rate 2: UNDP (1994); unionization rate 3: ILO (1992, 1993a), Waller and Myant (1993), OECD (1994a).

state expenditures, then one may ask whether corporatism is a necessary or sufficient condition for welfare state ambitions. Corporatist institutions are virtually non-existent in France and Italy, but the welfare state effort is heavy in these countries, particularly the redistributive welfare state. The welfare state has expanded in Southern Europe in the last decade, but corporatist institutions have not been put in place (Castles, 1995). Switzerland would also be an anomaly in this perspective, since its welfare state ambitions are low but it has corporatist institutions, at least according to some interpretations, although that is a contested matter.

For the first version of the corporatist model trade union membership is the critical factor. Table 8.9 provides the information about trade union density, or the ability of trade unions to mobilize a certain percentage of the workforce.

Although the data on trade unions in Eastern Europe represent rough estimates, Table 8.9 indicates that trade unions are weak mainly in certain parts of Western Europe (Cook, 1995; Héthy, 1995; Western, 1995). The countries where trade union density is low, that is, 30 per cent or lower, include: France, Spain, Switzerland, Greece and the Netherlands. And the countries where trade union membership is the normal routine include the Nordic Countries and Belgium, while in a few countries those organized constitute about half of the total workforce, such as in Ireland and the United Kingdom.

Data on trade union density referring to actual membership as indicated by the payment of dues may be complemented by survey data, which records whether the respondent considers himself/herself a union member. Table 8.10 gives data on participation in trade unions. The figures are lower than those in Table 8.9 because the set of respondents includes all adults.

The information about trade union participation contained in survey data complements the picture drawn above, as it shows that the country variation is very wide, but that Eastern Europe hardly differs from Western Europe. One set of countries scores about 50 per cent or more:

Table 8.10   *Participation in trade unions, around 1990–1*

Country set	Belong to trade unions (%)
CORE EC (5)	13.7
OTHER EC (5)	16.0
OUTSIDE EC (6)	36.9
CORE EAST (3)	25.7
EAST PERIPHERY (5)	40.6
All (24)	27.1

Sources: Inglehart (1993: V22); see Appendix 9.1.

Iceland, Estonia, Sweden, Lithuania, Latvia and Denmark; while in another set less than 10 per cent respond that they participate in trade unions: Spain, Portugal, France, Italy, Switzerland and Ireland. Admitting that there is no perfect match between these two measures on trade union membership, we will still use trade union density data in order to test the corporatism model about welfare state expenditures. It is, however, only one among several political factors that may be relevant for the explanation of welfare state effort.

Affluence or Trade Union Density?

The convergence model explaining the welfare state adduces affluence as the one and key factor behind the country variation in welfare state expenditures. Yet, economic affluence seems to offer only a necessary and not a sufficient condition for welfare state spending. A rich country need not have a large public sector, but if it for various reasons chooses to build up one, then it certainly needs an affluent economy to provide the necessary tax resources. If affluence is only a necessary condition, then which other factors matter for the critical choice between a welfare state and a welfare society? Another relevant economic factor is the openness of the economy, as it has been argued that countries where imports and exports constitute a large portion of the GDP (IMPEX-indicator) need welfare state expenditures to soften the uncertainties stemming from the international economy (Cameron, 1978).

The divergence model for interpreting the welfare state points at political factors as being decisive for the welfare regime that a country adopts. Among the political factors the power position of the labour movement, that is the strength of Social Democracy in the electorate as well as governments, has been mentioned as one determinant besides corporatism and trade union density. What also needs to be taken into account is the power of conservative parties among the non-socialist parties, as conservative parties tend to lean towards neo-liberalism favouring privatization and a reduction of the welfare state (Castles, 1982). A corollary to this argument would be that the welfare state is maintained at a

Table 8.11 *Determinants of welfare state expenditures*

Factors	Total welfare expenditures	Allocative welfare expenditure	Redistribution welfare expenditure
SOCDP	.29	.47	.31
LEFTP	−.30	−.34	−.32
CONSP	.23	.28	−.09
RELP	−.00	−.10	.34
LEFTGOV	.12	.17	.15
RIGHTGOV	−.25	.05	−.08
UNION1	.50	.63	.11
UNION3	.38	.56	−.10
IMPEX93	.13	.11	.18
LNGNPC	.51	.55	.36
LNPPP	.43	.46	.44

Note: SOCDP = electoral strength of Social Democratic Party 1990–95; LEFTP = Communist and Left-Socialist Party strength; CONSP = Conservative Party strength; RELP = Religious Party strength; LEFTGOV = Left-Wing Governments; RIGHTGOV = Right-Wing Governments; UNION1 = Unionization Rate 1; UNION3 = Unionization Rate 3; IMPEX93 = Imports and Exports/GPD; LNGNPC = Nat. log. of Gross National Product per Capita 1992; LNPPP = Nat. log. of Purchasing Power Parity per Capita 1992.

high level where Christian Democratic parties are strong or where balanced governments including both the right and the left are in power.

Table 8.11 presents some correlations between welfare state expenditures items and economic and political factors. A strict test of welfare state models would require much more analysis going deeper into how large welfare state expenditures emerged in the post-war period on the one hand, and how they have been changed recently on the other hand. Here, we simply note that both the convergence model as well as the divergence model receives some support.

Thus, affluence does indeed go together with welfare state effort, as Wilensky emphasized. The richer a country is, the larger its welfare state ambitions tend to be – with the significant exception of Switzerland. However, there is little support for the hypothesis that the more open the economy of a country, the larger its welfare state ambitions (Cameron, 1978).

Trade union density also varies in accordance with welfare state effort. Countries where trade union membership is encompassing as a percentage of the workforce tend to have huge welfare state expenditures, especially for allocative purposes. Again, there are exceptions, for example the Netherlands, France and Italy. There is only a weak connection between the strength of the Social Democrats and overall welfare state effort, as the association mainly refers to the allocative welfare state. The strength of the Christian Democrats has only one implication for the welfare state, and that is a considerable redistributional effort.

Again, one may point out the relevance of the distinction between the allocative and the redistributive welfare states, as they have somewhat different conditions that sustain them. Whereas the allocative welfare state is enhanced by Social Democracy and strong trade unions, the redistributive welfare state is mainly driven by higher levels of affluence. In fact, a higher level of affluence is the only factor that drives up both types of welfare state ambitions.

Concerning the party support for the welfare state, one must recall not only that religious parties have suffered a decline in voter support recently but also that the West European welfare state has been supported by other parties than the Social Democrats and the Christian Democrats including Liberal, former Agrarian and Conservative parties as well. Interestingly, there is a negative connection between support for former Communist parties and welfare state effort, which expresses the realities in Eastern Europe, namely the dismantling of the Communist welfare state, which the former Communist parties can only delay if they attempt to halt the public sector retrenchement in Eastern Europe.

The hypothesis that encompassing trade union movements succesfully call for high welfare state expenditures applies to the Nordic countries and Austria. But it fails elsewhere in Europe, for example in France, the Netherlands and Italy, where the trade union movement is weakly organized. In relation to these countries the hypothesis that affluence is the key factor behind welfare state effort seems more applicable, but then why is Switzerland the only welfare society in Europe? What matters in Eastern Europe would be affluence, as these countries cannot afford to maintain a strong welfare state, despite the fact that some of these countries have encompassing trade unions.

Conclusion

The public sector in European countries is founded in one way or another on large-scale welfare state expenditures, where one should distinguish clearly between allocative or redistributive. In Eastern Europe public expenditures have rapidly been reduced as a percentage of GDP in several countries since the fall of the Communist systems. Perhaps Estonia and the Czech Republic would today qualify as a welfare society together with Switzerland which never developed a welfare state.

The West European welfare state has been much researched in the literature on policy outputs and outcomes. The convergence tradition links welfare state expenditures with affluence, whereas the divergence tradition claims that there are different types of welfare states – distinct welfare state regimes.

Almost all European countries adhere to the model of a mixed economy, meaning that public expenditures amount to somewhere between 40 and 60 per cent of GDP except for a few outliers on both sides of this scale. The bulk of the public expenditures are made up of costs in relation to welfare state policies. Looking at various types of public expenditures included in the public sector concept one may establish that there are many similarities among the European countries. All countries in Europe have both allocative and redistributive policies, as there is convergence in Europe towards the predicament that the state is responsible for the provision of certain goods and services, such as health care and education, as well as being obliged to guarantee the maintenance of a certain level of income. Welfare policies have become citizen rights.

On the other hand, among the conspicuous country differences one may point out that the overall welfare state effort is more extensive in Northern Europe than in Southern Europe, as well as that some East European countries have cut back their public expenditures more drastically than countries in Western Europe that attempted large-scale privatization. One should make a distinction between allocative and redistributive welfare regimes, because there are several countries besides the Nordic countries that have very high redistributive expenditures such as the Netherlands, France and Italy, which at the same time are low on allocative welfare expenditures.

In the convergence approach to the differences in welfare state effort as measured by the ratio of overall welfare expenditures to the GDP the focus is upon affluence. Economic resources make possible welfare expenditures: the higher the GDP the larger the ratio. In the divergence framework, country differences in welfare policies reflect political factors, including both the strength of political parties and the organization of interest groups. One critical factor is corporatism, which would enhance welfare state effort.

But it is not clear what 'corporatism' stands for. On the one hand, it refers to hierarchical and encompassing interest organizations, especially in the trade union movement. On the other hand, it denotes specific institutions for the interaction between government, business and trade unions. Since it is not easy to identify the occurrence of corporatist interest intermediation and policy concertation in European countries, we focused on trade union strength as measured by trade union density.

Examining the impact of affluence, trade unions and political parties, the finding in this chapter is that the first two factors are more important than the last one in determining welfare state expenditures. However, neither affluence nor trade union strength explain all the variation. Clearly, the level of affluence, as the convergene model predicts, is one major condition for overall welfare state effort, but trade union density also matters, especially for allocative welfare state expenditures. Social Democracy mainly impacts upon allocation whereas Christian Democracy is chiefly supportive of redistribution.

Paradoxically, the welfare state is expanding in Western Europe despite all the talk about privatization, but the welfare state is being sharply cut back in some East European countries. As things now stand, most countries in Europe have a mixed economy, but it is not easy to predict future trends. It is a real possibility that there will be more welfare societies in Eastern Europe than in Western Europe around 2000, but we must remember that increasing affluence in the East may also push up welfare state ambitions. We now turn to the analysis of political culture, and we will observe the same phenomenon, namely that one cannot take for granted that Western Europe is always a few steps ahead of Eastern Europe in development. When it comes to political culture, the test is post-modernization. What does this concept mean?

9

Political Culture

In the early 1990s the countries of Europe are all multi-party democracies. They all cherish the institutions of representative democracy as the proper mechanisms for governing the public sector and the institutions of the competitive market economy have spread into Eastern Europe after being harmonized among West European countries through the EC activities. Yet, getting the institutions right may not be enough to guarantee the viability of the democratic regime. The way institutions actually work depends on social capital, or the beliefs, values, attitudes of the individuals participating in various forms in democratic choice processes (Putnam, 1993). Democracies tend to have a special political culture of trust in and common understanding of the rules of the political game, as suggested early on by Tingsten (1965).

The Introductory Chapter warned against reductionism or the temptation to look on one social dimension as a reflection of another more basic one. Although the economic differences between countries in Europe are huge, the possibility of extensive similarities in political institutions and actual behaviour patterns among them cannot be ruled out, and we have found ample evidence for the existence of many similarities between European countries with regard to state structure, party systems and government formation. Now when we look at political attitudes we must again allow for the possibility of the autonomy of culture.

Political attitudes can be studied from several different angles. The five volumes published in 1995 within the framework of the project *Beliefs in Government*, use the now existing large data bases comprising information about people's political beliefs and values for analysing numerous questions about politics, from local action groups over national government issues to international questions (Borre and Scarbrough, 1995; Niedermayer and Sinnott, 1995; van Deth and Scarbrough, 1995). Here, the focus is on the foundation of democratic politics in the political culture. The democratic regime in European countries will have a higher likelihood of surviving or flourishing, if it is supported by a political culture that is secular, non-extremist and activist at the same time as there is a developed civil society. Is there such a political culture all over Europe now?

Studying Political Culture

The concept of political culture refers to attitudes that individuals hold in relation to politics broadly conceived. In the literature on political culture one often sees a distinction between cognitive attitudes, or beliefs in how things are, and values, or attitudes towards how things ought to be. It is a matter of dispute whether the political attitudes of citizens tend to make up a consistent system of attitudes, or whether political attitudes are held on a more ad hoc basis. Certain political attitudes seem to be more resistant to change, often singled out as 'fundamental beliefs and values'. The study of political culture has developed much recently due to the immense increase in the availability of surveys of various kinds.

Frame of Reference

The examination of data about political attitudes among the inhabitants in European countries tends to be guided by concepts connected with the theme of modernity or post-modernization (Klingemann and Fuchs, 1995; van Deth and Scarbrough, 1995). Although this is not the place to enter a debate about post-modernization theory, as it is after all the target of much contestation among scholars, the post-modernization theories seem to offer a broad perspective on attitudes and the changes in beliefs and values that have accompanied the coming of the post-industrial society (Bell, 1976a, 1976b).

The concept of modernity refers to the 'current state of modern societies' (Bourricaud, 1987: 14), and the post-modernization theories attempt to interpret the current predicament of the advanced capitalist societies by identifying a few key themes which dominate the discourse or culture. One finds in this literature ideas to the effect that the process of modernization has reached a new stage in Europe (Bourdieu, 1990).

We came across the notion of a post-industrial society in Chapter 3, which concept is derived from the social structure and its adaptation towards the needs of a service economy. Bell writes:

> Broadly speaking, if industrial society is based on machine technology, post-industrial society is shaped by an intellectual technology. And if capital and labor are the major structural features of industrial society, information and knowledge are those of the post-industrial society. (Bell, 1976a: xiii)

And he concludes that the 'information society' or the 'knowledge society' has a social organization that is vastly different. This is a highly relevant theme in relation to European trends, but here the question concerns an entity Bell does not mention, namely values. Do political values have a distinct configuration in the post-industrial society? If one may observe the coming of a post-industrial society all over Europe, then can we conclude that also a post-industrial culture is in the making? Lash states:

> It is these newer, post-industrial middle classes, with their bases in the media, higher education, finance, advertising, merchandising, and international exchanges, that provide an audience for postmodern culture. (Lash, 1990: 20)

There is little doubt about the argument that the post-industrial social stratification is different from that of the industrial society. What one wishes to know is how to identify postmodern culture. What are the basic political beliefs and values of the post-industrial society?

One post-modernization theory focuses on the spreading of a post-materialist ideology. Post-materialism is a hypothesis about changes in beliefs and values in recent years (Inglehart, 1977, 1990; Abramson and Inglehart, 1995), which argues that post-materialism is a new set of attitudes that have emerged alongside the coming of a post-industrial economy. The post-materialist theory seems to be highly relevant to European politics, as it claims both that post-materialism has its stronghold in Europe after the Second World War and that it comprises a set of attitudes with clear political implications.

Post-materialism is one post-modernization theory which has aroused much attention. Three things are problematic in the concept of a post-materialist culture. First, it is not clear what is distinctive of post-materialist values (Flanagan, 1982). Second, one has researched how widespread such post-materialist values are in the population and whether they still receive increased acceptance. Third, there is the question of what the effects of these values are on politics, for example on electoral behaviour and party identification (Knutsen, 1995b).

It should be pointed out that the post-materialism theme only touches certain political beliefs or values, namely those attitudes that are related to the tension between economic growth and quality of life. It adds a new dimension to the left–right one, which while dealing with divisive redistributional issues is about materialistic concerns. Post-materialism covers concerns about other aspects of life than those deriving from economic growth such as the environment, well-being as well as personality development. Yet, how does one identify post-materialist values? Environmental values are one expression of post-materialism but there are also libertarian values and hedonistic values. And these attitudes do not go together, implying that post-materialism is a complex phenomenon that needs to be unpacked.

Although post-materialism has a limited focus on political attitudes, it makes strong claims about explaining political change. Thus, the transition from a predominantly materialist political culture to one where post-materialist values are well represented, especially among younger generations, is said to be the process behind dealignment and realignment in the electoral behaviour of European voters. Yet, one may argue that political culture and changes in political attitudes in Europe involve more than simply materialism versus post-materialism.

Other post-modernization theories deal more generally with individual modernization, which refers to an increase in personal skills as well as changes in values along both moral and hedonistic dimensions (Inkeles, 1983; van Deth, 1995). For us the critical question is whether the post-industrial society is connected with a political culture that supports democratic politics. It has been argued in some post-modernization theories that the post-industrial society harbours a political legitimacy crisis (Klingemann and Fuchs, 1995). Let us examine data from survey research on political culture in order to see whether there are attitudes in various

European countries which could undermine the democratic regimes in these countries (Kaase and Newton, 1995).

Data

In the European context survey research has benefited from the publication of the Euro-barometer survey, which was initiated by the European Community in 1973. The Euro-barometer surveys are published regularly on the basis of two annual surveys which makes longitudinal analysis of attitudinal change feasible.

In 1981 a European Values Survey was introduced covering 10 countries (Stoetzel, 1983), to which were added eight countries in the form of a World Values Survey (Inglehart, 1990). This survey was repeated in 1990–1 (Inglehart, 1993). The European Union also conducts a Central and Eastern Euro-barometer (CEEB; Reif and Cunningham, 1992–5). In addition there are other sources of information about attitudes among East European inhabitants such as United States Information Agency's Office of Research, Paul Lazarsfeld Society, Vienna and the New Democracies Barometer.

Below we employ mainly data from the 1990–1 World Values Survey (Inglehart, 1993). The information has been gathered from the respondents' replies to specific questions, which we have identified by stating the number of these variables (questions) in the data files and codebooks from which the information has been taken (Appendix 9.4). The scores reported on in the tables below are based on country averages for a sample responding to the survey questions. The data for DDR and BRD have been combined into one score for Germany. The same has been done with Northern Ireland and Great Britain resulting in a score for the United Kingdom. On the other hand, the information about the CSSR has been divided into scores for the Czech and Slovak Republics, respectively. In some cases we have also relied on Euro-barometer data as well as information from the Central and Eastern Euro-barometer.

We start with the post-materialism theme and then proceed to look at life satisfaction. We include attitudes about religion and politics. Finally, we examine data about political interest and civil society.

Post-materialism

Post-materialism claims that there has been a profound change in values during the postwar period (Inglehart, 1990). The generation born after the Second World War has different attitudes towards economic values and their place in relation to other human values. Key concepts in the so-called post-materialist orientation are quality of life and environmental protection, which values take precedence over economic growth and consumerism. Inglehart has substantiated his model by empirical research into

Table 9.1 *Materialist and post-materialist values*

Country set	Materialist orientation	Post-materialist orientation
CORE EC (5)	18.3	27.0
OTHER EC (5)	24.4	17.0
OUTSIDE EC (6)	17.2	20.8
CORE EAST (5)	32.5	8.8
EAST PERIPHERY (4)	28.4	8.7
All (25)	23.7	16.9

Source: Inglehart (1993: V259, V260).

political attitudes, which has been developed by other researchers (Knutsen, 1995a).

In order to identify the post-materialist value orientations a specific scale has been constructed that measures the extent of materialism and post-materialism in attitudes. Table 9.1 gives the scores for two such scales, where respondents were asked about their priority for the following items: (1) maintaining order in the nation; (2) fighting rising prices; (3) giving people more to say in important government decisions; and (4) protecting freedom of speech. People who favour items (1) and (2) have a materialist orientation whereas people who underline (3) and (4) display a post-materialist one. People with other priorities are said to have a mixed value orientation.

One can observe a clear difference between Western and Eastern Europe, as materialist values have a much stronger position in the East than in the West and correspondingly lower with regard to post-materialist values. At the same time one detects an interesting similarity between residents within CORE EC and OUTSIDE EC on the one hand and OTHER EC on the other, as the latter set is more committed to materialism than the former sets of countries. In Hungary 48 per cent of the respondents express a materialist orientation, in Portugal 38 per cent and in Estonia and Poland 31 per cent, whereas in Finland and the Netherlands the scores are much lower, at 7 and 11 per cent respectively.

The Inglehart hypothesis amounts to a convergence model, as it predicts that higher levels of affluence in Europe will be conducive to the acceptance of post-materialist attitudes everywhere. Abramson and Inglehart (1995) state in relation to evidence that there is a clear trend towards more and more support for post-materialist attitudes in seven out of eight West European societies:

> The pattern of change over the past two decades results from a variety of factors, although, as we shall see, the main long-term factor pushing Post-materialism upward is generational replacement. (Abramson and Inglehart, 1995: 13)

Actually, only in Belgium did this shift in the ratio of materialists to post-materialists fail to take place. A note of caution should be added here, as there is in many countries a fluctuation over time in the support for post-

Table 9.2 *Satisfaction measures (1–10) (average scores)*

Country set	Financial satisfaction	Overall satisfaction
CORE EC	6.8 (5)	7.3 (5)
OTHER EC	6.5 (5)	7.6 (5)
OUTSIDE EC	6.9 (6)	7.7 (6)
CORE EAST	4.9 (5)	6.0 (5)
EAST PERIPHERY	4.6 (3)	6.0 (4)
All	6.1 (24)	7.0 (25)

Source: Inglehart (1993: V132, V96).

materialist attitudes. When the economy moves into depression, then post-materialism is also down.

Satisfaction with Life

Now, one may continue this analysis by probing data that shed light on how people in Europe view their predicament at the moment, measured in terms of satisfaction. First, one may look at financial satisfaction in particular or overall satisfaction in general (Table 9.2), which follows the overall ranking of countries in terms of affluence data, at least so with regard to Switzerland, which ranks highest on both satisfaction scores.

Life is more difficult in Eastern Europe than in Western Europe, Table 9.2 indicates. Interestingly, the average satisfaction scores are almost similar for all the West European sets of countries, despite the considerable differences in affluence between Northern and Southern Europe. The average scores for Spain and Portugal are marginally different from those for Germany and Austria.

Let us look at other aspects of well-being such as health and feeling of happiness (Table 9.3). The average measures for CORE EAST and EAST PERIPHERY are so low that quality of life in these parts of Europe must be rather different from that in Western Europe – at least it is perceived in that way by the residents themselves. The low score on health state for CORE EC is surprising, but CORE EC also comes a little further down on the happiness scale. High scores on the question about happiness are to be found in the Netherlands (46 per cent), Ireland (44 per cent) and Denmark (43 per cent). On the state of health question Ireland (49 per cent), Denmark (48 per cent) and Sweden (45 per cent) report very high scores on satisfaction or well-being.

Let us proceed the enquiry into political attitudes by complementing the analysis of satisfaction looking at two other aspects, which one would assume not to be closely connected with the satisfaction measures above.

The picture that one may derive from Table 9.4 is not the same one that is forthcoming in the other tables. It is actually quite astonishing that the differences between the country sets are not more pronounced when it

Table 9.3   *Well-being: happiness and health (percentages in agreement)*

Country set	Happiness	State of health
CORE EC (5)	28.4	22.0
OTHER EC (5)	31.1	32.2
OUTSIDE EC (6)	33.0	36.2
CORE EAST (5)	7.4	9.0
EAST PERIPHERY (4)	4.4	6.1
All (25)	22.0	22.3

Source: Inglehart (1993: V18, V83).

Table 9.4   *Individual autonomy and home life satisfaction (1–10) (average scores)*

Country set	Individual autonomy	Home life satisfaction
CORE EC (5)	6.5	7.8
OTHER EC (5)	7.1	8.2
OUTSIDE EC (6)	7.1	7.9
CORE EAST (5)	6.0	7.4
EAST PERIPHERY (3)	6.4	6.4
All (25)	6.7	7.6

Source: Inglehart (1993: V95, V180).

comes to the attitude towards individual autonomy. One might have expected that the East–West or North–South divisions would have surfaced again, but this is not so. The general experience of individual autonomy is as high in Eastern Europe as in the set of CORE EC countries. Spain reports the highest score which turns out to be considerably above that of both the Netherlands and France. Things are different again with regard to home life satisfaction, which is a function of many other things besides affluence and the political system with the Danish score as the highest one, well above both Austria and Latvia.

Finally, Table 9.5 looks at how strong localism is in the belief-systems of Europeans. One may separate between universalistic and particularistic values depending on whether a person identifies with a special locality or region. In a universalistic value orientation an individual would not be strongly attached to a local community or a region. One may expect that a local or regional orientation is inversely related to feelings of national identity as well as how far the nation-building process has proceeded. Universalism may express a sort of political satisfaction, namely the acceptance of the country as a united whole.

From the information in Table 9.5 it seems to be the case that a local orientation need not carry with it a regional orientation. The high average

Table 9.5   *Particularism: identification with locality or region*
(percentages in agreement)

Country set	Local identification	Regional identification
CORE EC (5)	41.2	15.1
OTHER EC (5)	44.3	19.2
OUTSIDE EC (6)	47.4	15.9
CORE EAST (5)	40.7	15.5
EAST PERIPHERY (3)	34.0	46.4
All (25)	42.0	21.2

Source: Inglehart (1993: V320).

score for EAST PERIPHERY on regional identification depends on very high values in the following countries: Lithuania, Estonia, Latvia and the Slovak Republic, which when the survey was conducted in 1990–1 were still not nation-states. On the other hand, low scores on regional identification are to be found in Hungary, Iceland, the Netherlands, Slovenia and Bulgaria. The countries where regionalism attract some attention among people include Germany, Switzerland, the United Kingdom and Spain, that is countries where there has been a debate about national identity and regional autonomy.

On average, a much smaller portion of the population carries with itself a regional identification than a local orientation. A very strong local identification is to be found in a variety of countries such as: Norway, Hungary, Sweden, Denmark, Switzerland, Bulgaria and Belgium. Localism occurs mainly in unitary states or homogeneous nation-states whereas regionalism is to be found in federal states. Evidently, localism is another kind of phenomenon than regionalism.

To summarize, human satisfaction may be described by asking people a number of questions pertaining to their life situation as they themselves perceive and evaluate it. In the debate, much attention has focused on the emergence of post-materialistic values. However, one may wish to broaden the focus and include quality of life, happiness, health, autonomy and regionalism. There is a clear East–West divide in the average scores for the countries included in the data reported on here. But do the country scores covary in the same fashion over all indicators?

Appendix 9.1 shows that only some of the average country scores on the measures stated above tend to go together. This is true of the happiness and overall satisfaction which are high in countries where post-materialism is strong. The autonomy scores tend to be high in countries with high measures for overall satisfaction and happiness, but autonomy has little to do with post-materialism. Localism and regionalism, with a negative correlation between the two, are altogether independent of the materialism–post-materialism dimension. Thus, one may conclude that there are more aspects of political attitudes than the dimension of materialism versus post-materialism. The emergence of post-materialist

Table 9.6 *Relevance of religion: percentages who agree*

Country set	Importance of religion	Is respondent religious?	Belief in God
CORE EC	46.6 (5)	64.9 (5)	71.3 (5)
OTHER EC	54.8 (5)	68.8 (5)	83.3 (5)
OUTSIDE EC	45.3 (6)	61.1 (6)	71.6 (5)
CORE EAST	38.9 (5)	57.9 (5)	67.4 (3)
EAST PERIPHERY	30.9 (4)	51.0 (4)	60.5 (2)
All	43.9 (25)	61.1 (25)	72.7 (20)

Source: Inglehart (1993: V9, V151, V166).

attitudes may be interpreted as one aspect of modernity in the closing of this century. But what about religion and politics?

Religious Attitudes

Materialist value orientations have a ring of down-to-earth attitudes. They position a person with regard to overall satisfaction with life as well as more specifically in terms of financial satisfaction. Yet, there is more to human belief-systems than materialism. One such additional dimension is religion, or the attitudes that people form about the meaning of life besides economic achievement.

Post-modernization theories entail that people form more and more sophisticated belief-systems about the meaning of life. A consequence would be a reduction in the strength and attraction of religious practices, as the search for essences in life would be channelled along more secularistic routes. What is the status of religious belief among Europeans? Let us tap the other worldly values by looking at data about religious attitudes (Table 9.6).

It appears from Table 9.6 that religious beliefs are only considered to be important by a majority of the people in OTHER EC, where we have two countries with a strong position for Catholicism: Ireland and Portugal. In this country set we also find the percentages with the highest positive response rates to the more specific questions about religiosity and belief in God. The former Communist countries are more secular than Western Europe. Among the Protestant countries only Iceland displays high scores on all three questions. There is a systematic pattern though in the data in Table 9.6 as the countries tend to score the same on all three indicators.

Religious attitude is one thing and religious behaviour another matter. Table 9.7 contains data about actual religious practices. The pattern concerning religious practices as revealed in Table 9.7 is not a consistent one, because there is a variety of religious behaviours. The indicators on religious organizations and denominations do not go together with those on church attendance.

Interestingly, the countries with the most intense religious practices as measured by actual attendance in church are to be found in OTHER EC and

Table 9.7 *Religious practice: church adherence and attendance (percentages)*

Country set	Belongs to religious organization	Belongs to religious denomination	Attends services	
			once/week	once/month
CORE EC	15.6 (5)	69.0 (5)	22.4 (5)	32.7 (5)
OTHER EC	10.5 (5)	81.9 (5)	33.4 (5)	42.3 (6)
OUTSIDE EC	19.2 (6)	81.3 (6)	10.9 (6)	21.7 (6)
CORE EAST	6.7 (2)	54.0 (4)	24.6 (6)	35.8 (5)
EAST PERIPHERY	3.3 (4)	46.6 (4)	12.3 (5)	21.9 (2)
All	12.4 (22)	70.5 (24)	20.5 (27)	31.7 (23)

Sources: Inglehart (1993: V20, V143, V147). Concerning data about weekly attendance additional information has been taken from CEEB (1991).

CORE EAST. Here, we have very high scores in relation to weekly attendance for Ireland (81 per cent) and Poland (65 per cent) as well as high scores for Portugal (39 per cent), Italy (38 per cent), Slovakia (33 per cent), Austria (26 per cent) and Switzerland (24 per cent).

Church attendance is reported to be below 10 per cent in the following countries: the Nordic countries, Latvia and Estonia as well as Bulgaria and the Czech Republic. Yet, on the other two indicators on religious behaviour, namely, belonging to a religious organization or denomination, some of these countries score high. What matters here is whether a country has a state church institution or not. Thus, the Netherlands score high on membership in a religious organization whereas the Nordic countries score very high on membership in a religious denomination, meaning in this case automatic entrance into the state church by birth.

Despite these differences in types of religious behaviour, the picture that emerges from Table 9.7 substantiates the basic observation that religion has become a formal organization in Europe, where only a minority of about 20 per cent of the population really follow church practices. In a country such as France where the state has been separated from the church, people tend to belong to some religious denomination (62 per cent) but few are members of a religious organization (6 per cent), and church attendance is not frequent, only some 10 (weekly data) or about 16 (monthly data) per cent saying that they attend church regularly.

Another way to get at the practical significance of religion is to focus on the political implications of religious attitudes. Table 9.8 presents a few indicators on this. The divorce rates comprising also those separated are high in Latvia, Estonia, Sweden and the Czech Republic, and very low in Ireland, Spain, Portugal and Slovenia as well as Italy. A rather substantial group of about 20 per cent in several of the West European countries such as France, Belgium, Portugal, the Netherlands, the United Kingdom and Denmark consider marriage as outdated, although the actual number of divorced tends to be slightly higher in the East European sets.

Table 9.8 *Political issues with religious implications*

Country set	Divorced	Marriage outdated	Approve abortion	Importance of God in life
	(Percentages in agreement)			(Average scores)
CORE EC	4.9 (5)	20.5 (5)	93.2 (5)	5.3 (5)
OTHER EC	4.1 (5)	16.8 (5)	85.1 (5)	6.1 (5)
OUTSIDE EC	5.7 (6)	11.4 (6)	95.5 (5)	5.3 (6)
CORE EAST	5.0 (5)	9.7 (5)	91.1 (3)	5.9 (3)
EAST PERIPHERY	7.7 (4)	11.6 (4)	91.9 (4)	4.6 (2)
All	5.4 (25)	14.0 (25)	91.4 (22)	5.5 (21)

Note: The abortion question contains the qualification that the health of the mother is in danger. The scale measuring the attitude towards the importance of God in life ranges from 1 to 10.

Source: Inglehart (1993: V181, V216, V237, V176).

The two other indicators on the implications of religion for practical policy strongly corroborate the securalization theme inherent in the modernity debate. The huge percentages all over Europe amounting to 90 per cent who accept abortion when necessary show that religious fanaticism has little support. And the rather lukewarm figure of an average score of 5 on a scale between 1 and 10 measuring how important God is considered to be in real life makes one ask whether the formal organization of all the churches in Europe rests on clay feet in the post-industrial society.

Europe is, the evidence from surveys shows, very much a place on earth where each and every individual has a strong worldly orientation. Appendix 9.2, containing a correlation analysis of the indicators on religious attitudes, confirms the observation that only in countries where there is frequent church attendance does religion play a major political role according to people's attitudes. Secularized attitudes is certainly one aspect of a post-modern culture, but cannot post-modernization come into conflict with an interest in politics too?

Interest in Politics

One may see signs that political involvement declines in Europe. There is a weariness about political élites and the electorate shows increasing signs of disloyalty. Can we find systematic data about how political attitudes vary from one country to another in Europe? Let us first look at the survey information about the level of interest in politics in general. One may wish to distinguish between various dimensions in political value orientations. First, there is the interest in politics. Table 9.9 has a few indicators on this aspect.

There are two findings in Table 9.9. On the one hand one may establish

Table 9.9   *Interest in politics (percentages)*

Country set	Importance of politics	Discuss politics	Interested in politics
CORE EC (5)	36.9 (5)	15.7 (5)	12.3 (5)
OTHER EC (5)	30.5 (5)	13.5 (5)	9.6 (5)
OUTSIDE EC (5)	36.9 (6)	16.9 (6)	15.7 (6)
CORE EAST (5)	35.7 (5)	28.4 (6)	32.6 (5)
EAST PERIPHERY (3)	43.8 (4)	40.1 (5)	16.1 (4)
All	35.7 (25)	22.9 (27)	17.2 (25)

Sources: Inglehart (1993: V8, V10, V241). Additions have been made from CEEB (1991) concerning 'Discuss politics'.

that there is a general feeling of political apathy all over Europe. In some European countries political interest is even so low that less than 10 per cent claim an interest, as for instance in Spain, Italy, Portugal, Belgium, France, Poland and Ireland. On an average, less than 40 per cent of the population in the various countries say that they find politics important. Only in the Netherlands, Lithuania and Norway are 50 per cent of the respondents of the opinion that politics is important.

On the other hand, one also finds that political apathy is more widespread in Western Europe than in Eastern Europe. In whatever manner questions about interest in politics is phrased, the average country scores for Eastern Europe are higher than those for West European countries. Political apathy is most widespread in OTHER EC countries. Two feasible interpretations are: either post-modernization in Western Europe reduces political involvement, or political involvement in Eastern Europe was exceptional at the time of measurement, that is, the years of system transition. Political apathy is not a constant phenomenon. Strong latent political values may become activated if there is an event that calls forth political mobilization, as happened in Europe in 1968 for instance.

Second, one may enquire into which political values people in Europe adhere to, although they are not at the moment prone to organize in voluntary political organizations such as the political party. Table 9.10 ends our report on political value orientations by including a few indicators on the adherence to political ideologies.

What appears from these two questions about ideological attitudes among European residents is moderation. There is more of political disillusionment in Eastern Europe, but at the same time equality is given precedence to freedom among respondents in CORE EAST, which is not the case in any other country set. About 70 per cent state that freedom is more important than equality in Finland, Lithuania, Estonia, Sweden and Norway. In Slovakia, Portugal, Slovenia, Iceland, the Czech Republic and Italy equality is preferred to freedom by a majority.

It seems to be the case that the median voter attitudes in Europe links an emphasis on liberty with a belief that society may be reformed by government actions, which amounts to a combination that both the

Table 9.10   *Adherence to political ideologies (percentages in agreement)*

Country set	Freedom more important than equality	Society may be improved by reforms
CORE EC	53.9 (5)	75.4 (5)
OTHER EC	51.7 (5)	81.1 (5)
OUTSIDE EC	62.1 (6)	80.0 (5)
CORE EAST	47.3 (5)	57.5 (5)
EAST PERIPHERY	67.0 (4)	62.9 (4)
All	55.2 (25)	71.1 (24)

Source: Inglehart (1993: V247, V249).

Table 9.11   *Left–right scale (1–10)*

Country set	Average scores
CORE EC	5.2 (5)
OTHER EC	5.5 (5)
OUTSIDE EC	5.9 (6)
CORE EAST	5.5 (6)
EAST PERIPHERY	5.7 (5)
All	5.7 (27)

Sources: Inglehart (1993: V248). Additions have been made from CEEB (1991).

extreme left and the extreme right tends to negate. Table 9.11 shows that political man in the European context is located in the centre of the left–right continuum.

The averages for the five country sets are almost identical. A few countries tend towards the left whereas a few others lean towards the right. Among the former we have Spain, Italy, France and Slovenia and to the latter belong Austria, Finland, Ireland, Lithuania and Estonia. There is little support all over Europe in mass beliefs and values for extremist ideologies.

Civil Society

A political culture that is supportive of democratic institutions for politics would have to be based on a thriving civil society. The concept of civil society derives from the opposition between state and society, or the public and private sectors. Democratic viability or longevity requires that there is a system of organizations that are independent of government. Such a civil society with its own institutions fosters an open compromise culture where people have trust in each other and can accept a temporary loss in an election without questioning the regime (Fukuyama, 1995).

Table 9.12 contains information about one aspect of the so-called civil society, meaning whether people are members of voluntary organizations,

Table 9.12   *Participation in voluntary organizations (percentages)*

Country set	Political parties	No voluntary organization
CORE EC	6.2 (5)	42.1 (5)
OTHER EC	4.2 (5)	50.2 (5)
OUTSIDE EC	12.3 (6)	23.0 (4)
CORE EAST	6.9 (2)	43.3 (2)
EAST PERIPHERY	9.3 (4)	40.0 (4)
All	8.0 (22)	40.0 (20)

Source: Inglehart (1993: V23, V35).

including political parties. Given widespread political apathy, may we also expect a low degree of actual participation in voluntary organizations, especially those with an explicit political orientation?

Civil society is strongly institutionalized in OUTSIDE EC countries, mainly due to the extensive participation in trade unions in the countries that make up this set (see Table 8.10). At the same time civil society thrives not so much upon participation in political parties. Less than 10 per cent of the respondents belongs formally to a political party on an average. In a few countries political party membership attracts more than that: Latvia, Iceland, Norway, Finland, Austria, Bulgaria and Sweden.

The rather high scores on membership in voluntary organizations for Eastern Europe relates mainly to trade union membership. Yet, the high scores for some East European countries with regard to trade union membership may still reflect a historical legacy of obligatory participation. The figures for Hungary and Romania are on a par with those for Finland and Germany, that is, slightly lower but not as low as those for the Netherlands and the United Kingdom. Civil society need not be made up of political parties and trade unions, but these organizations make up a sizeable part of it.

As a consequence the countries where a majority of the respondents answer that they are not members of any voluntary organizations are the following: Spain, Portugal, Italy, Slovenia, France and Ireland. This is certainly contrary to the established image of Eastern Europe as that part of Europe where civil society is least developed due to the legacy of Communism.

What is truly perplexing is that one of the West European sets, OTHER EC, is often as different as the East European sets. This applies to both religious attitudes, political apathy and participation in voluntary organizations. The legacy of Catholicism in Southern Europe is no doubt reflected here, but can one really conclude that civil society is weaker in this part of Europe than in Eastern Europe? Table 9.13 gives information about the level of trust in European societies, their *social capital* as it were.

The level of distrust in society is clearly higher in Eastern Europe than in Western Europe. This is a different indicator on the vitality of civil society and it expresses how people look on each other in reciprocal interaction.

Table 9.13   *Trust: percentages who agree that most people can be trusted*

Country set	Percentages
CORE EC (5)	36.1
OTHER EC (5)	40.9
OUTSIDE EC (6)	52.0
CORE EAST (5)	28.5
EAST PERIPHERY (4)	23.7
All (25)	37.4

Source: Inglehart (1993: V94).

More than half of the respondents in the Nordic countries and the Netherlands state that they have trust in their fellow citizens whereas the corresponding figure is down to about 20 per cent for Slovenia, Latvia, Portugal, the Slovak Republic and Hungary. It is surprising though that trust is not higher in CORE EC countries with France at only 23 per cent agreeing, and Germany and Italy at 35 per cent.

It remains to examine whether countries that score high on one indicator on political interest and civil society also score high on the others. Appendix 9.3 has the correlation matrix. There is a tendency to the effect that countries where the average scores for participation in political parties or trade unions are higher also report a higher level of citizen interest in politics. The positive associations are not striking though, as interest in politics need not be channelled through formal participation in parties or trade unions. There is a clear negative association between lack of participation in civil society and party membership and union membership, which corroborates the general notion that parties and unions are important organizations in civil society. What does this mean for the specific trust in the democratic regime?

Satisfaction with Democracy

The probabiltiy of successfully building a democratic regime depends not only upon social and institutional matters. The attitudes of citizens towards the viability of democratic politics affect not so much the transition stage but certainly the consolidation phase.

In the survey data there is available information about the present level of satisfaction with democracy (Table 9.14). Are there significant differences between the established democracies in the West and the emerging democracies in Southern and Eastern Europe?

The differences in opinion between West and East European democracies about the satisfaction with the democratic regime are substantial. The low scores of satisfaction in CORE EAST are surprising, considering that some of these countries have managed quite a radical institutional transformation in a few years. Less than half the respondents in East European

Table 9.14   *Percentages who state they are satisfied with democracy*

Country set	1991		1992		1993		1994	
CORE EC	52.8	(6)	51.5	(6)	49.5	(6)	58.0	(6)
OTHER EC	59.3	(6)	55.3	(6)	52.7	(6)	52.3	(6)
OUTSIDE EC	–		59.7	(3)	–		66.0	(4)
CORE EAST	31.2	(6)	30.2	(6)	29.5	(6)	24.0	(6)
EAST PERIPHERY	40.5	(4)	36.6	(5)	35.6	(5)	32.0	(5)
All	46.5	(22)	45.5	(26)	42.1	(23)	45.6	(27)

Sources: CORE EAST and EAST PERIPHERY: CEEB (1991–5); CORE EC and OTHER EC: *Eurobarometer: Trends 1974–1993* and *Eurobarometer 42*; OUTSIDE EC: *Eftabarometer*, 1992 and *Eurobarometer 42* and *43*.

democracies state that they are satisfied with democracy whereas in Western Europe the corresponding figures are above the 50 per cent mark.

One may interpret these differences in two ways. First, satisfaction with democracy could reflect experience with democracy. A high level of satisfaction is found in the countries with a long time span of uninterrupted democratic regime. Second, a low level of satisfaction with democracy may reflect disappointment with party politics and social conditions as these happened to turn out after the introduction of a democratic regime, although there may be no wish to return to an authoritarian regime. We suggest the second interpretation is the most plausible one in relation to Table 9.14. At the same time, the low figures for satisfaction with democracy in Eastern Europe indicate that a democratic regime not only has an intrinsic value but must also be effective in raising living conditions for people, that is, possess an extrinsic value.

Conclusion

In this chapter we have examined a number of aspects of political attitudes, all relating to how beliefs and values foster the acceptance of the legitimacy of democratic politics. In the short-run the stability of a democratic regime may be more affected by the actions of élites or the identification of the right institutions. In the long-run democratic stability needs a political culture that endorses the kind of politics that democracies harbour.

The major finding in this chapter is the low figures for trust in democracy in Eastern Europe. Only about 30 per cent of the respondents in these new democracies state that they are satisfied with the regime. This is such a low figure that if things do not change the political cultures in these countries may not present democracy with a much needed legitimacy. Yet, these low scores may simply reflect a disappointment that the introduction of democracy did not raise living standards more quickly. When one looks at other aspects of political culture than the satisfaction scores, then there is more cause for optimism.

The post-modernization theme is dominant in the study of political beliefs and values, attempting to explicate the culture of a post-industrial society. One may tap the notion of modernity – 'the current state of societies' – by surveying political attitudes in European countries. Is the post-industrial society characterized by a specific political culture, expressed in for example post-materialist values?

The assessment of post-modernization theory underlines complexity in the sense that political attitudes are made up of different dimensions which cannot be reduced to one common core of values (van Deth and Scarbrough, 1995). In relation to the data about European political attitudes assembled by means of the World Values Survey 1990–1 (Inglehart, 1993) we make the same observation.

Post-materialist beliefs and values are only one of many components in the European political culture. It reflects the economic dimension of a country as it is connected with the overall level of affluence. Thus, post-materialist values have a strong backing in CORE EC and OUTSIDE EC countries. However, other kinds of political attitudes do not reflect economic conditions. Thus, we note that a different aspect of modernity, namely secularization, is as widespread in Eastern as in Western Europe.

European political attitudes are a combination of political apathy and moderation. Political extremism has little support but the focus on the middle range of the left–right scale is attended by an overall scepticism towards political activism. The European electorate is lukewarm in relation to politics, not only with regard to formal participation in parties but also in terms of general interest in political matters, especially in Western Europe. In fact, political apathy is more extensive in CORE EC and OTHER EC countries than in CORE EAST and EAST PERIPHERY countries.

The overall generalization that one may dare to make in relation to information about political attitudes collected through surveys is that European citizens do not differ much in terms of beliefs or values as long as the attitudes are not closely connected with economic issues. In terms of happiness and state of health there is a vast gulf between Western Europe and Eastern Europe. But with regard to participation in voluntary organizations and overall trust, then the differences are smaller.

Yet, social capital is more abundant in Northern and Central Europe – the OUTSIDE EC countries. There is a risk for divergence between the political cultures of the European democracies, if satisfaction with democracy does not go up in Eastern Europe and civil society is not strengthened in Southern Europe. If such a divergence process takes place, then it will certainly affect democratic stability.

Appendix 9.1　*Correlation matrix over satisfaction values*

	M	S	H	A	L
Materialism (M)	–				
Satisfaction (S)	−.56	–			
Happiness (H)	−.55	.85	–		
Autonomy (A)	−.35	.75	.48	–	
Localism (L)	.10	.36	.48	.24	–
Regionalism (R)	.08	−.42	−.47	−.13	−.54

Sources: The data have been taken from Tables 9.1–9.5.

Appendix 9.2　*Correlation matrix for religious values*

Church attendance once/week	
Importance of religion	.79
Importance of God in life	.84
Is respondent religious	.63

Sources: Tables 9.7–9.9

Appendix 9.3　*Correlation matrix for political values*

	Participation in political parties	Participation in trade unions
Importance of politics	.40	.38
Discuss politics	.39	.49
Interested in politics	.53	.19
Freedom versus equality	.41	.52
Left–right scale	.45	.40

Sources: Tables 9.11–9.13.

Appendix 9.4　*Questions linked to variables used in Chapter 9 (and 8) from the World Values Survey*

Table 8.10: V22
Please look carefully at the following list of voluntary organizations and activities and say which, if any, do you belong to?
Trade unions. (Agree)

Table 9.1: V259 and V260
If you had to choose which one of the things on this card would you say is most important? And which would be the next most important?

- Maintaining order in the nation
- Giving people more to say in important government decisions
- Fighting rising prices
- Protecting freedom of speech
- Don't know

Table 9.2: V132 and V96
How satisfied are you with the financial situation of your household? All things considered, how satisfied are you with your life as a whole these days?

　　1　2　3　4　5　6　7　8　9　10

Dissatisfied　　　　　　　　　　Satisfied

Appendix 9.4 *Continued*

Table 9.3: V18 and V83
Taking all things together, would you say you are very happy? (agree) All in all, how would you describe your state of health these days? Would you say it is very good? (agree)

Table 9.4: V95 and V180
Some people feel they have completely free choice and control over their lives, and other people feel that what they do has no real effect on what happens to them. Please use the scale to indicate how much freedom of choice and control you feel you have over the way your life turns out.

   1 2 3 4 5 6 7 8 9 10
None at all   A great deal

Overall, how satisfied or dissatisfied are you with your home life?

   1 2 3 4 5 6 7 8 9 10
Dissatisfied   Satisfied

Table 9.5: V320
Which of these geographical groups would you say you belong to first of all?
Locality or town where you live (=local identification)
State or region of country where you live (=regional identification)

Table 9.6: V9, V151 and V166
Please say, for each of the following, how important it is in your life. Religion: very important or quite important (agree)

Independently of whether you go to church or not, would you say you are a religious person? (agree)

Which, if any, of the following do you believe in? God? (yes)

Table 9.7: V20, V143 and V147
Please look carefully at the following list of voluntary organizations and activities and say which, if any, do you belong to?
Religious or church organizations. (Agree)

Do you belong to a religious denomination? (Yes)

Apart from weddings, funerals and christenings, about how often do you attend religious services these days?
More than once a week or once a week (=weekly)
More than once a week or once a week or once a month (=monthly)

[In CEEB 3: Frequency of church attendance:
Several times/week or once a week (=weekly)]

Table 9.8: V181, V216, V237 and V176
Are you currently divorced or separated? (agree)

Do you agree or disagree with the following statement?
Marriage is an out-dated institution. (Yes)

Do you approve or disapprove of abortion under the following circumstances?
Where the mother's health is at risk by the pregnancy. (Approve)

And how important is God in your life? Please use this card to indicate. 10 means very important and 1 means not at all important.

   1 2 3 4 5 6 7 8 9 10
Not at all   Very

Appendix 9.4   *Continued*

Table 9.9: V8, V10 and V241
Please say, for each of the following, how important it is in your life. Politics: very important or quite important (agree)

When you get together with your friends, would you say you discuss political matters frequently, occasionally or never?
Frequently. (Agree)

[In CEEB 3: Does R(espondent) discuss political matters?
Frequently. (Agree)]

How interested would you say you are in politics?
Very interested. (Agree)

Table 9.10: V247 and V249
Which of these two statements comes closest to your own opinion?
A. I find that both freedom and equality are important. But if I were to choose one or the other, I would consider personal freedom more important, that is, everyone can live in freedom and develop without hindrance.
B. Certainly both freedom and equality are important. But if I were to choose one or the other, I would consider equality more important, that is, that nobody is underprivileged and that social class differences are not so strong.
Agree with statement A.

On this card are three basic kinds of attitudes concerning the society we live in. Please choose the one which best describes your own opinion.
Our society must be gradually improved by reform. (Agree)

Table 9.11: V248
In political matters, people talk of 'the left' and 'the right'. How would you place your views on this scale, generally speaking?

       1 2 3 4 5 6 7 8 9 10
Left   Right

[In CEEB 3: Left-right-selfplacement:
Left = 1, Right = 10.]

Table 9.12: V23 and V35
Please look carefully at the following list of voluntary organizations and activities and say which, if any, do you belong to?
Political parties or groups. (Agree)
None. (Agree)

Table 9.13: V94
Generally speaking, would you say that most people can be trusted or that you can't be too careful in dealing with people?
Most people can be trusted. (Agree)

Table 9.14: Satisfaction with democracy in own country
Euro-barometer:
On the whole, are you very satisfied, not very satisfied or not at all satisfied with the way democracy works in (our country)?
Would you say you are very satisfied or fairly satisfied? (Agree)

[CEEB: On the whole, are you very satisfied, fairly satisfied, not very satisfied or not at all satisfied with the way democracy is developing in (our country)?
Very satisfied or fairly satisfied. (Agree)]

[EFTABAROMETER 92: On the whole, are you very satisfied, not very satisfied or not at all satisfied with the way democracy works in (your country)? Would you say you are very satisfied or fairly satisfied? (Agree)]

Sources:

EOS Gallup Europe (1992) *Eftabarometer Autumn 92*. s.1.: EOS Gallup Europe
[Computer File] [EFTABAROMETER]
CEC (1994) *Eurobarometer: Trends 1974–1993*. Brussels: European Commission.
[EUROBAROMETER]
CEC (1995c) *Eurobarometer 42*. Brussels: European Commission. [EUROBAROMETER]
CEC (1996) *Eurobarometer 43*. Brussels: European Commission. [EUROBAROMETER]
Inglehart, R. (1993) *World Values Survey 1990–91*. Ann Arbor, MI: Institute for Social
Research, University of Michigan [Computer File] [WVS]
Reif, K. and Cunningham, G. (1992) *Central and Eastern Euro-Barometer 2*. Autumn 1991
[Computer File]. Köln: Zentralarchiv für empirische Sozialforschung [producer].
[CEEB]
Reif, K. and Cunningham, G. (1994) *Central and Eastern Euro-Barometer 3*. Autumn 1992
[Computer File]. Köln: Zentralarchiv für empirische Sozialforschung [producer].
[CEEB]
Reif, K. and Cunningham, G. (1994) *Central and Eastern Euro-Barometer 4*. Autumn 1993
[Computer File]. Köln. Zentralarchiv für empirische Sozialforschung [producer].
[CEEB]
Reif, K. and Cunningham, G. (1995) *Central and Eastern Euro-Barometer 5*. Autumn 1995
[Computer File]. Köln. Zentralarchiv für empirische Sozialforschung [producer].
[CEEB]

Concluding Chapter: Party Governance

In the earlier chapters we have reported on a large number of findings concerning European politics as it appears in the early 1990s. What sense can be made of these often isolated observations concerning state institutions (Chapter 5), the party systems (Chapter 6), the formation and duration of governments (Chapter 7), the public sector (Chapter 8) and political culture (Chapter 9)?

Looking at politics in various countries one may either focus on the differences or one may bring forward the similarities. No two countries are entirely different or completely similar for that matter. In the postwar research on European politics the prevailing approaches have been of the divergence kind, not only in relation to the implications of the existence of the Iron Curtain but also in relation to West European political realities. We suggest that time is now ripe for trying to model politics within the framework of the convergence perspective.

Is convergence in European politics driven by economic and social forces or does it result from the political forces themselves. We suggest that it is the latter that holds for Europe, one of the chief reasons being the evidence for the autonomy of politics. The purpose of this final chapter is to outline an interpretation with which one may account for several of the characteristic features of European politics, as they were identified in Chapters 5 to 9.

We outline an argument to the effect that convergence in European politics may be understood in terms of the institutionalization of the basic mechanisms of party governance in the post-industrial society. Democratic politics all over Europe adhere more or less to the basic principles of party governance, which may work themselves out somewhat differently in various countries, reflecting different historical legacies.

Autonomy of Politics

If one takes a reductionist approach to country politics and underlines the importance of the economy for political behaviour, then there is much to be said in favour of a divergence perspective on European politics. The substantial differences in affluence between Western and Eastern Europe would, according to this perspective, create formidable forces that would make politics entirely different in the West compared with the East. But, as many scholars have pointed out in relation to Marxist analyses, politics

Table 10.1 *Analysis of variance of economic and social factors*

	Five sets 2		Two sets 2	
	Eta	Sign	Eta	Sign
Economic modernization	.57	.00	.33	.00
GNP 1925	.56	.00	.45	.00
Agricultural employment 1930	.59	.00	.53	.00
GNPC 1993	.82	.00	.70	.00
PPP 1993	.81	.00	.68	.00
Agricultural employment 1990	.45	.00	.38	.00
Service employment 1990	.75	.00	.72	.00
Human development index 1995	.65	.00	.63	.00
Gender development index	.43	.03	.11	.11

Note: Five country sets: CORE EC, OTHER EC, OUTSIDE EC, CORE EAST, EAST PERIPHERY; Two country sets: Western Europe, Eastern Europe.

possesses a certain amount of autonomy in relation to economic forces. A reductionist approach to European politics like in economic determinism would fail to recognize the many similarities in political institutions as well as in behaviour.

In Chapter 2 we observed that the economies of Europe differ in terms of total output, mainly along the West–East division but also to some extent along a North–South division. Chapter Three examined the consequences of these differences in affluence for the social structure. And one may indeed observe several ways in which modernity or the post-industrial society has developed furthest in Northern Europe. Yet, there are at the same time many striking similarities between the societies in Europe, whether they are located in the North, South, West or East, because the tertiary sector is increasing everywhere. What limits the implications of the differences in wealth is that economic growth tends to be higher in the less affluent countries than in the more affluent ones in Western Europe, all other things being equal, which is conducive to economic convergence.

An analysis of variance may be employed to probe how extensive the differences in economic and social factors are between a few sets of European countries (see Table 10.1). We divide the European countries into five sets on the one hand and two sets on the other hand. The five set classification is the same as the one used in all the earlier chapters: three West European sets and two East European sets, whereas the two set classification is the separation of West European and East European countries. The eta-squared statistic measuring the amount of variation between the sets in relation to all the country variation indicates how much similarity there is between the sets. The eta-squared statistic ranges from 0 to 1, high scores indicating much difference between the sets.

The major finding in Table 10.1 is that of vast differences in socio-economic structure within Europe. The eta-squared scores are consistently high and significant both for the two set separation and the five set separation meaning that these categories really explain much of the country variation. One may note that the eta-squared scores are consistently higher for the five set division than for the simple West–East separation, which is evidence that socio-economic structure in Europe varies not only along the Western–Eastern Europe separation but also between West European countries, namely along the North–South divide. Given such strong socio-economic differences in Europe, what are the consequences for political behaviour and political institutions? If it is true that politics mirror economic and social factors, then politics in Eastern Europe should be altogether different from politics in Western Europe. But that is clearly not the case, given the evidence in Chapters 5–9.

One way to probe into the extent of autonomy of politics in relation to economic and social structure is to examine the variation in political behaviour, political institutions and political culture and compare it with the variation in economic and social factors (Table 10.1). Let us look systematically at the eta-squared coefficients in relation to the aspects of politics that were covered in Chapters 5 to 9 (Table 10.2).

Our categories refer to five sets on the one hand and two sets on the other hand, that is, Western versus Eastern Europe. We now enquire into whether the country variation on key political aspects is larger between these five categories or sets or whether the variation within each category or set is larger. Taking the determinism perspective starting from the vast socio-economic differences between these categories we expect high eta-squared values for politics also. What is the validity of economic determinism?

The finding here in relation to the scores of the eta coefficient in Table 10.2 is the confirmation of the autonomy of politics from economic forces and the social structure. Only when we come to political culture do we find a few eta-squared scores higher than .5. For most other aspects of political institutions and behaviour, in the state or in the party systems or in government the eta-squared values are below .5, meaning that the variation within the categories is larger than the variation between the categories. Interestingly, one may note that the only cases with significant eta-squared scores are to be found among the political culture items, which tend to reflect more the vast economic differences between countries (Gundelach, 1994). Yet, even here we note the occurrence of the autonomy of politics, as the more directly politically relevant cultural items display low eta-squared values.

What enhances the autonomy of politics? Well, before we point out a few factors that directly enhance political convergence among countries with different economic and social structures, it is worth pointing out that historical legacies could lessen the consequences of socio-economic causality. What we are referring to is the cleavage patterns that countries tend to bring with them from the past. Consider again an analysis of variance in Table 10.3.

Table 10.2   *Analysis of variance of politics: institutions, behaviour and culture*

	Five sets 2		Two sets 2	
	Eta	Sign	Eta	Sign
Political institutions:				
State format	.16	.32	.04	.29
Monarchy	.27	.08	.25	.00
Election system	.14	.40	.01	.64
Presidentialism	.15	.37	.11	.07
The judiciary	.31	.04	.19	.02
Democracy 1994	.53	.00	.43	.00
The party systems:				
Electoral participation	.08	.71	.00	.78
Fractionalization	.21	.19	.05	.23
Polarization	.20	.40	.00	.93
Volatility in votes	.66	.00	.57	.00
Governments:				
Survival rate	.45	.00	.35	.00
Number of parties in governments	.24	.12	.00	.82
Single-party governments	.22	.16	.00	.81
Multi-party governments	.21	.17	.00	.87
Minority goverments	.06	.79	.00	.99
Grand majority governments	.15	.34	.04	.29
Minimum winning coalition	.19	.23	.05	.21
Balanced governments	.17	.28	.00	.79
Public sector:				
General government expenditures	.28	.09	.13	.05
General government revenues	.33	.04	.17	.03
Allocative welfare expenditure	.28	.16	.22	.04
Redistributive welfare expenditure	.28	.13	.12	.09
Total welfare expenditure	.32	.11	.15	.11
Political culture				
Post-materialism	.67	.00	.53	.00
Overall satisfaction	.72	.00	.70	.00
Interest in politics	.29	.13	.16	.05
Left–right orientation	.31	.07	.00	.96
Freedom before equality	.29	.12	.02	.51
Participation in parties	.47	.02	.00	.79
Participation in voluntary organizations	.26	.30	.00	.87
Trust on other people	.50	.01	.34	.00
Satisfaction with democracy	.56	.00	.51	.00

Source: The analysis of variance is based on the same data set that has been used in the Tables in Chapters 5–9.

Comparing the eta-squared scores in Table 10.3 with those stated in Table 10.1, one can draw the conclusion that the variation in cleavages among European countries does not coincide with the variation in socio-economic structure. The various ethnic and religious cleavages, which have

Table 10.3   *Analysis of variance of cleavages, 1900–90*

	Five sets 2		Two sets 2	
	Eta	Sign	Eta	Sign
Ethno-linguistic fragmentation 1920	.29	.05	.23	.00
Ethno-linguistic structure 1920	.24	.11	.17	.02
Religious fragmentation 1900	.26	.08	.24	.00
Religious structure	.17	.27	.13	.04
Protestantism 1900	.35	.02	.12	.06
Catholicism 1900	.19	.23	.00	.86
Orthodox 1900	.19	.23	.14	.04
Muslim 1900	.12	.48	.07	.15
Jews 1900	.49	.00	.19	.01
Other 1900	.24	.12	.06	.19
Ethno-linguistic fragmentation 1990	.23	.14	.07	.14
Ethno-linguistic structure 1990	.23	.14	.07	.15
Religious fragmentation 1990	.21	.18	.07	.14
Religious structure 1990	.17	.27	.03	.36
Protestantism 1990	.39	.00	.09	.11
Catholicism 1990	.16	.33	.01	.70
Orthodox 1990	.15	.35	.09	.10
Other 1990	.16	.31	.01	.63
Family structure	.53	.00	.43	.00

Source: The analysis of variance is based on data reported on in the corresponding tables in Chapter 1.

played a major role in country politics, have a variation among countries that is to a considerable extent independent of the country differences in economic and social structure.

Besides, the autonomy of politics in Europe from economic and social forces is enhanced by two factors. First, widespread institutional diffusion in the form of constitutional transplantation after the fall of the Iron Curtain in 1989, replacing the Communist institutions with West-European ones. Second, harmonization of legal rules and policies within the framework of the European Community since 1958, covering more and more countries in Europe.

There is not only large-scale constitutional copying at work, but the institutions of the European Union are being implemented in increasing numbers of countries. Chapter 4 examined the profound process of institutional innovation and harmonization that has taken place since the Treaty of Rome in 1957, creating the EC in 1958. In addition to inherited cleavages from the past and the ongoing processes of institutional diffusion, we wish to underline the contribution to political convergence by the operation of party government itself. We wish to argue that the basic source of convergence in terms of actual behaviour is the institutionalization of the principles of party government in a setting of media politics, the 'political game' so to speak.

Logic of Party Government

Assume that we start from a set of naïve and unrealistic assumptions about the players and the institutions that regulate their actions. We wish to keep the assumptions down to a minimum in order to arrive at a simple and parsimonious model with a few interesting implications which are related to the interpretation of the various chapter findings. Of our four assumptions, the first two refer to motivation in political behaviour and the last two deal with the institutional environment of political action.

Assumptions

We have two assumptions about the motivation of political parties and voters:

1 Political parties are critically dependent on the probability of winning electoral support and playing a role in government formation.
2 The electorate tends to be myopic rewarding political parties who favour their interests and punishing those that do not.

Although these two assumptions about motivation in politics are in line with standard notions about rationality in politics, they are far from innocuous. What they rule out is that political action by élites is entirely of an ideological nature, where commitments to long-term goals completely override short-term tactics and strategy. They furthermore rule out that the electorate is stalled behind deep-seated cleavages which generation after generation become socialized into as well as mobilize behind.

The two assumptions about the institutional setting in which political motivation is carried out focus on the one hand on the immense importance that the political party has been able to attract to itself in Europe. In no other part of the world is the political party the key institution to the same extent as in Europe. On the other, the institutional assumptions underline the media as the new all-important set of vehicles for political campaining. Thus, we have two further assumptions:

3 Multi-party systems offer the organizational setting for competition among political parties.
4 The mass media offer the main interaction and communication channels between political parties and the electorate.

Also these second two assumptions are in line with a look at European politics, but they are hardly self-evident in any sense. The mass media become players having an importance of their own only when certain institutions are in place, such as the freedom of the media and when the media have access to large-scale resources of their own.

There has been much discussion in the social sciences recently concerning the status of assumptions about motivation. It concerns both the interpretation of the nature of interests or so-called 'utility', whether the latter involves only self-interests or can be broadened to cover also solidarity or altruism. The debate about motivation also focuses on the notion of interest maximization, as it has often been pointed out that it requires too much of individuals. People, let alone those in élite positions, do not behave according to the postulates of rationality, possessing complete information about available alternatives of actions and their consequences as well as being able to rank these consistently according to their utility. Political action tends to be incremental or marginalist, if not simply irrational or symbolic.

Making generalizations about the institutional setting for political behaviour in Europe today is not a straightforward task. One scholar may place the emphasis differently from another and the characteristic features may come and go quickly. Developmental trends surface and perish as the examples of the system transition in Eastern Europe, predicted by few and fully understood by none, show.

A number of commentators on recent European politics have focused on the arrival at a total support for one kind of political regime, representative democracy, and one set of economic institutions, the market economy. The withdrawal of support for extremist alternatives has been described as the end of history. We will take these two institutions, democracy and the market economy, for granted. They structure the relationship between élites and the population. Yet, in order to understand the logic of the interaction between politicians and the electorate in Europe, we need these two additional assumptions which are more specifically descriptive of the European scene.

Political parties play a role in European politics that is not matched in other countries which adhere to the same basic institutions of democracy and the market economy. Although individual politicians may dominate their parties at times, party discipline looms larger than entrepreneurial politics in Europe. The political élites channel their efforts through party machines, which have been integrated into the state in various ways. European politics has been party government since the introduction of mass polities around the time of the First World War. It is true that party membership has declined in the last decade, but party organization has not lost its dominating position in representative democracy in Europe (Aarts, 1995; Biorcio and Mannheimer, 1995; Schmitt and Holmberg, 1995; Widfeldt, 1995).

The immense role that the mass media play in politics is, however, a more recent phenomenon. The revolution in communication technologies since the end of the Second World War began to impact on mass politics in the late 1960s and its influence has only increased in the last decades. Elections may be decided by the media and the monitoring by the media of political processes structures the entire interaction between politicians and the electorate.

Mass medias develop skills in the search for and publication of spectacular news, which attract much attention for a short time. The revelation of such news in relation to political matters creates opportunities as well as resulting in risks for politicians in their interaction with the electorate. Extensive media coverage of political campaigns can both score the victor and bring forward a looser.

Political parties have to pay ever more attention to how they get their message across in the media. It may take a long time to build up a favourable media image, but it may take only a few minutes to become infamous by committing a mistake that is relayed by the media. Media politics fosters political symbolism. Political parties that master the language of politics and can correctly time their usage of key expressions have a clear advantage over politicians who cling to a more traditional style of conducting politics.

The electorate is also much affected by media politics. It breaks up traditional loyalties between the voter and the party, as it forces the voter to focus on the issues, which may shift from one election to another. Favourable or unfavourable media attention on one party may induce the voter to vote in a different manner than he/she used to do. Evidently, a substantial portion of the electorate does not make up its mind how to vote until the very last day of the campaign, meaning that there are ample opportunities for affecting their choices by last minute favourable or unfavourable news.

The revolution in information technologies has during the last years begun to have an impact on the political parties, not only when they are in government but also when they act outside of the government arena. This applies not only to television and the spectacular increase in the number of new channels that provide millions of viewers with information about politics on an almost continuous basis. The attention by the newspapers on party politics has shifted in tone, as there is no limit to how deep journalists are prepared to dig once they spot peculiar practices.

Now, taking the assumptions together they allow us to derive a few interesting implications, which are relevant to the findings in the various chapters in our volume.

Implications

If, generally speaking, the electorate is basically myopic, and the political parties act tactically and strategically, then if the institutional setting is one of several political parties which are monitored instantly by an independent mass media, then profound electoral volatility is likely to occur.

In pursuing their interests, the voters will favour political parties who make credible promises and punish parties who fail to deliver. The multi-party setting entails that there are always a stream of alternatives to choose between, both at one election and between one election and another. The mass media will see to it that the electorate is provided with another stream of information about what politicians offer and actually accomplish. If this is the logic of party governance, then voter instability must be the outcome. Only if one adds another assumption to the framework is it possible to derive voter loyalty. The well-known party frozen hypothesis by

Lipset and Rokkan did just that, although it was presented not as an assumption about West European politics but as a finding from extensive research on party outcomes at elections since the formation of mass polities.

The Lipset and Rokkan model established that stability by arguing first that voters were deeply committed to long-term party loyalty in accordance with inherited cleavages along ethnic, religious and class divisions in society and, second, that party outcomes at the aggregate level could hover from one election to another but that micro losses and gains would even out at the aggregate level.

The behavioural research on European politics since the mid-1970s has not confirmed the first part of the argument about stability. Profound processes of electoral dealignment and realignment have been discovered. Gross voter volatility has shot up in country after country. New dimensions in belief-systems have been unravelled. And class voting has declined sharply. There is little evidence today of substantial voter loyalty to the political parties. New social groups have emerged.

The second part of the argument runs against the phenomena described in Chapter 6: the occurrence of earthquake elections, the emergence of flash parties, the transformation of the extreme wing parties. The increase in net volatility entails that the lack of voter loyalty begins to surface in electoral instability.

Party uncertainty can only increase as a result of electoral instability. The political parties increasingly face a sceptic electorate, well informed by the media about the accomplishments of political parties as well as their private lives. In such a world of voter myopia, media monitoring and fierce competition between political parties, issue politics must be the outcome.

Political parties can only respond to voter disloyalty and electoral myopia by focusing on specific issues on which they may communicate to the media where they stand. This sets up a kind of quid pro quo interaction between parties and the voters, which may be monitored by the media. Political parties that deliver on their promises on the issues stand a better chance of electoral success than political parties that either promise the wrong things or fail to deliver. They will be punished at the next election, even to the extreme of complete rejection of the entire party.

Now, party governance focusing on issue politics in a media driven environment where the electorate is myopic and politicians self-centered, is more driven by the generation of legitimacy through concrete actions and actual accomplishments than legitimacy deriving from ideological commitments. And the key for political parties to accomplish anything is access to government power and the resources of the bureaucracy. Thus, party governance in a multi-party setting will involve the politics of coalition building.

Electoral instability as the foundation for a multi-party system means that few parties can hope for a majority position for themselves, at least not over several elections, because the electorate will punish incumbent cabinets in the hope that change will result in anything better. There will thus be a drive for the making and maintenance of coalitions.

Finally, the focus on issues means that policy-making will be orientated towards results and the myopia of the electorate entails that promises of favours will be promoted whereas predictions about losses from the operation of policies will be counteracted in electoral behaviour. Thus, political parties will increasingly use public expenditures as tools for enhancing their probability of electoral successes. Welfare state policies offer the political parties the means for the conduct of this type of politics, because they cover a set of broad programmes which when combined with taxation policies give parties a wide range of options for coalition building. Welfare state expenditures will not be reduced in Europe despite all talk about privatization.

Party governance is the politics of electoral volatility, issue politics, the politics of coalition building and the politics of the welfare state. The logic of party governance will work itself out differently in various countries, reflecting historical legacies and institutional variation. Yet, the basic logic of governance is the same, from Iceland and Portugal in the West to Estonia and Bulgaria in the East, from Norway and Finland in the North to Italy and Greece in the South.

The model may also be broadened to account for the rise of new social movements. No doubt there has been increasing support for groups that focus on so-called 'new' issues. Sometimes these new social movements employ a non-parliamentary strategy, orientating themselves towards the grassroots level, trying to mobilize the support of ordinary citizens and inhabitants through personal interaction.

In other examples of new social movements the parliamentary arena has been regarded as an important one in order to get the message across and also to be able to influence the making of policies. Often new social movements employ both strategies but we find examples where the parliamentary and non-parliamentary strategies run into conflict.

Opportunities for the enhancement of new social movements derive from the very forces that have been identified in the model, that is, increasing voter volatility and intensified media attention, particularly in relation to 'newness'. Yet, at the same time these same forces limit the scope of manoeuvring for these new social movements. Also they can suffer from voter disloyalty and the failure to launch an election tactics that is conveyed in a positive manner by the media.

Thus, it is no surprise that new social movements have been successful from the early 1980s and onwards, such as environmental groups in Germany, Sweden, Switzerland and Austria. But it is also understandable that there are limits to how large these social movements can become, because the other parties may take countermeasures and the new social groups may themselves experience the effects of increasing voter volatility. Again the media and their both extensive and intensive coverage of the issues is the filter through which the communication about new social groups is basically handled, despite the emphasis of some of these movements on grassroots activities.

The media play a crucial role in party governance of the European type. The way they operate is conducive to myopia and uncertainty on the part of both political parties and the electorate. News comes in the form of specific items which attract the attention of people for a short time, the more so the more conspicuous or shocking the news is.

Media politics breaks up cleavage politics. It supports the introduction and maintenance of a game of politics characterized by symbolism and opportunism. Party governance is a political game in which parties put up politicians as candidates in elections in order to enhance the prospects of the party to play a key role in government formation, thereby having a say in the making of public policies. This kind of politics makes ethnicity, religion and class less relevant for the structuring of the electorate and the issues. Class voting declines. Once in place this game tends to receive its own momentum, rendering it a certain amount of autonomy in relation to other forces such as economic ones.

The emergence of media politics in Europe has still to be researched in depth. What seems to be in operation here is a combination of the new high-level technology in the information sector and the tendency for political parties and single politicians to engage in opportunistic behaviour, that is, self-interest seeking with guile. Incidentally, one may also stretch the assumption about behaviour opportunism to the mass media people themselves, as news is not a commodity that advertises itself. The media sector itself involves competition between various groups about attention, time and resources. Monitoring political events may constitute a vital opportunity for the media to present its case. In a political game where communication is handled by powerful mass media, what is the relationship between economic structure and political behaviour?

The political parties have less and less to offer their voters in terms of public programmes. Instead they have to pay increasing attention to cut back management problems. And they are under closer and closer scrutiny from the mass media.

The growth in the resources for the mass media as well as the turn to a more aggressive investigative reporting style puts pressure on the political parties. Not only have the number of press conferences gone up, as party leaders must allocate more time simply to be available to the press. But the general increase in the attention paid to party practices leaves little room for the political parties to act without the risk of public scrutiny and its consequences. Simply the anticipation of what could happen if things get out of hand when negative news begins coming from the mass media constrains the political parties to an unprecedented degree.

Adapting in mass media politics is a new phenomenon that calls for skills of a special kind besides endurance and shrewdness in general. Formal responsibility is sharply up, as the party leader may at any time be called on to answer questions about the party platform or party practices. However, real responsibility may be sharply down, because politicians need to come up with answers to problems they know not how to solve. The life time of politicians goes down as a function of the increased mass media attention. It is becoming more frequent that party leaders have to step down due to failures in responding well to the media challenge.

Continued Relevance of Divergence Models

The prevailing perspective on European politics has been that of divergence. This is true not only with regard to the whole of Europe where the confrontation between Western and Eastern institutions of the polity and the economy made this perfectly natural – the Iron Curtain, but it also holds with regard to Western Europe.

The kind of politics that the so-called people's democracies harboured must quite naturally be different from the politics of a regime based on parliamentary democracy and the market economy. There is no problem with divergence up to the sudden collapse of Communism. From Leninism Eastern Europe inherited the institutions of the dictatorship of the proletariat, involving the rule of the revolutionary avant-garde and the principle of democratic centralism. Stalinism added to this institutional fabric the principles of the command economy. The East European countries have moved away from these institutions, all definitely in relation to the hegemony of the Communist Party and some more than others with regard to the command economy.

Also in relation to Western Europe the divergence approach seemed to offer the most insights, at least for the interpretation of the politics of the decades following the end of the Second World War. Thus, Duverger early on underlined the difference between a majoritarian and a proportional election system in terms of the overall consequences for political stability. Sartori identified the polarized multi-party systems as harbouring a special kind of highly unstable politics. Elazar launched a model of a federal state claiming that this format was more conducive to stability than the unitary framework. And Lijphart presented a synopsis by suggesting a sharp distinction between two types of political systems in Western Europe, the Westminster model and the Continental/Consociational/Consensus model. In the analysis of the public sector similar divergence models were proposed contrasting market regimes with comprehensive welfare states, sometimes labelled 'corporatist' regimes (Crouch, 1993).

We do certainly not argue that these divergence models are now irrelevant or cannot be applied to data about European politics. There are interesting differences between the countries in Europe, which these divergence models identify and interpret in a systematic fashion. Our argument is only that these divergence models are not as relevant as they used to be. The politics of European countries have more in common in the early 1990s than ever before. Our volume has attempted to identify these communalities in Chapters 5–9 as well as suggested a simple model in this chapter that may account for the growth of similarities among European countries insofar as politics is concerned.

It will remain an important task to research the differences between the European countries. In that future research the major divergence models will play a major role. However, they need to be applied in a fresh manner to all the countries in Europe, among which – as we claim – there are seminal processes of convergence taking place.

Major Convergence Processes

In this final chapter we have on the one hand shown that the evidence from the European scene in the early 1990s supports the idea of the autonomy of politics, meaning that the vast economic differences between many countries in Europe do not shape country politics. On the other hand, we have introduced a model of party government which accounts for the many political similarities between the countries in Europe.

In European politics the political parties are key players. The states within the European Union as well as the few states that are outside the EU adhere to the principles of party government, meaning that political parties play a decisive role in elections recruiting the national assemblies, in forming the government and in making policies. Yet, party government is in a flux, not only in the democracies in Eastern Europe but also in West European countries.

The overall development trend for political parties in the post-industrial society is, however, a reduction in power, prestige and membership. It is becoming increasingly difficult for the political parties to maintain themselves, facing challenges from an electorate that is less and less loyal to the parties and increasingly disrespectful. The revelations of corrupt practices in a few countries have hardly enhanced the reputation of politicians. Here we will take a closer look at the change processes that the political parties find it difficult to cope with and we also pinpoint a few of the key responses of the political parties.

Since the 1970s West European politics has been transformed by the occurrence of a few major change processes. They all affect the conditions for party government, having an impact on the basic circumstances under which political parties act and call for an adaptation or determinate responses from the political parties. We are talking about the following long-term change processes in each country. First, internally in the electorate, in the distinction between the public and the private sector and in the operations of the mass media. Second, externally in the environment of the nation-state, that is, the trend towards European integration. Since 1990 East European politics have been transformed radically by the institutional transformation. Although West European and East European countries come from very different paths of development, the outcomes in the 1990s show many similarities.

The Electorate

What has happened in the early 1990s is that more or less the carpet has been pulled away from underneath the political parties. The ties between the electorate and the political parties have changed dramatically, as voters display less and less loyalty to the parties. In several countries net volatility is sharply up in the period since 1980. In most countries the average net change is now above 10 per cent, and in a few countries almost 20 per cent or more. The increase in net volatitily hides an even more substantial increase in gross voter volatility. In countries where data are available about gross voter volatility one may find high scores of around 30–50 per cent. The data indicate the occurrence of the earthquake election. Earthquake elections are the most manifest signs of profound processes of dealignment, during which new parties may arise due to realignment processes. Volatility in votes and seats is very high in the new democracies in Eastern Europe.

The political parties in both Western and Eastern Europe face an increasingly volatile electorate, where no political party can be safe in an electoral niche. The sharp increase in voter volatility refers to the demand side of the public household. At the same time major forces on the supply side of the public household put additional strain on the political parties, namely the public sector problems.

Public Sector

Already around 1980 the growth of government in Western Europe had reached such proportions that many spoke about government overload. There was a realization of the increasing problems of governance and coordination in an ever expanding public sector. These difficulties have been aggravated in the last decade when the welfare state has matured around an overall measure of about 50 per cent of the total resources in society. A number of countries score above 50 per cent at the moment whereas only a few are down below 40 per cent of the GDP.

In Eastern Europe, civil society is reemerging as the size of the public sector is scaled down towards the levels found in Western Europe. Countries that used to have a small public sector such as Spain, Portugal and Greece have rapidly expanded their welfare state up towards the average measures for Western Europe. The United Kingdom tried aggressively to cut back on the size of its public sector, but did not really accomplish that much in terms of a reduction of overall public expenditures.

The maturing of the welfare state creates problems for the political parties. They can no longer use promises of new programmes or additional spending in their relations with the electorate. More and more attention has to be paid to devising strategies to cope with the malfunctioning of the public sector: deficit spending, inefficiencies and the call for privatization. The public sector is today more of a burden than an asset to the political parties. To expand the public programmes or invent new ones is easy, but to cut expenditures or enhance productivity and efficiency in government is problematic. Increasingly, the governments of Europe have resorted to deficit spending at the same time as unemployment figures have soared. Most governments are in the red in the early 1990s, struggling with the enormous costs of the sharp increase in unemployment. The change in unemployment is such a major one that it needs to be repeatedly emphasized. The levels of unemployment are substantially higher also in Eastern Europe following the demise of the command economy and the development of a mixed economy of some sort in these countries too.

European Integration

The mass medias have no doubt grown in power in relation to the political parties. There is no way that even the strong party leaders for the big European political parties can emerge successful from a confrontation with the mass media. At the same time another major development has also weakened the political parties, namely, European political integration.

The strong position of the political parties in Europe rests on the institutions of party government. As long as the political parties offer the key mechanisms for representing the population in the political arena and constitute the vehicles of democratic government, they can be assured of influence. However, the relevance of the national arena has been reduced by the emergence of the new supranational bodies within the EU. Increasingly, policies are being framed within the EU institutions.

Thus far, the political parties have not been able to come up with a response to the consequences for party government of the European integration. The attempts to strengthen their influence at the top of the new supranational structures have met with only limited success, as the European Parliament where the political parties participate remains weak in relation to the other main EU institutions, although it has improved its position. In the late 1980s and early 1990s the Commission and the Council of Ministers expanded EU legislation considerably in various directions and ways. Simultaneously, the EU Court has increasingly underlined the federal implications of the existence of a bulk of EU law, namely that EU directives and regulations have to be implemented in the member states, even when they contradict municipal legislation.

However, it is not only EU directives and regulation that tend to drive out national legislation. It is increasingly popular to employ EU recommendations as policy guidelines, even though they are not strictly speaking law. Policy objectives, technologies and norms are taken over from Brussels and introduced into the making and implementation of national policies, also in countries that are only associated with the EU, such as a few East European countries. What space is there left over for the political parties in innovating or reforming public policies?

The consequences of the major change processes depicted above depend to some extent also on the way the political parties react. Here we focus on three main responses: (1) the emergence of new political parties reflecting partly new belief-systems; (2) the reorientation of the old established parties towards a more adaptive style of politics; and (3) the resort to symbolic policy-making attempting to solve public sector problems by moving them from one place to another.

New Politics

The increasing instability in the electorate has opened up possibilities for the introduction of new political parties. A new phenomenon is the flash party, which suddenly breaks through, receives a not insignificant voter support but fades away in the next elections. The rise and decline of populist parties fits this pattern well, but such a process may also characterize the election fortunes of the green parties and the ethnic parties. Involvement with new social movements is up.

The number of parties has increased in the last decade. This is true of the left wing as well as of the right wing. At the same time as the support for the traditional Communist parties has dwindled in the West, other left-wing parties have done better, including the Greens. On the right side there are not only populist parties but also new regionally-based parties or nationalist parties. In the centre, a couple of new parties have been formed, linked to specific issues. In Eastern Europe party system fractionalization has replaced the hegemony of the Communist parties, which have been transformed into democratic left-wing parties. More and more, the European party systems have become fractionalized, which certainly does not make the formation of stable governments any easier.

Entrepreneurial Politics

The established political parties can hardly just sit by looking at what goes on as their competitors try to snatch voters away from them. The response of the major European parties has been to resort to politics based on issues and images channelled through the mass media. Not all of them have succeeded. Perhaps the most extreme case of unsuccessful adaptation is the large Italian Christian Democratic Party, which almost totally tumbled.

Responding to the increasing volatility in the electorate the major political parties in Europe attempt to stabilize their environment by resorting to issue politics. As it is no longer feasible to appeal to traditional loyalties, the political parties have to look at each issue on its own terms, trying to predict which standpoint will bring most votes or result in the least loss of votes. Ideological strategies are less and less relevant, as parties find that they may have to take contradictory standpoints on issues in order to raise the probability that they can score some additional votes on each separate issue. Each election calls for a special tactical approach, depending on which issues tend to occur.

Responding to the large influence of the mass media, the large political parties engage in media politics, that is, they target television and newspapers for strategic and tactical manoeuvres. Press conferences are becoming more frequent. Party leaders are called on to comment on this or that event. Often the initiative to press conferences is taken by the party itself, when it feels it has something new to say.

Symbolic Policy-making

Responding to the public sector problems, political parties increasingly employ symbols instead of taking real action. The complexity of social problems is so large and the difficulties in getting public programmes to operate effectively so great that political parties can only promise, not deliver.

The huge public deficits set sharp limits to the introduction of new public programmes. What one can hope for is to make government more efficient with the available resources. However, improving productivity in government is a difficult task. If bureaucracy is not the solution to improving the quality of life but part of the problem of government, then what can the political parties provide their voters with in exchange for their votes?

Government overload and deficit spending call for actions by the political parties to reduce government spending. But cut back management is hardly popular with the electorate, neither in the West nor in the East. Faced by cross-pressure from the electorate demanding favours and from the public purse requiring spending reductions political parties employ symbols to create images of a reality that does not exit. Parties make promises of a 'new future', 'responsible government', 'major public sector reforms' and 'decentralization of power', although it is far from clear what is actually meant.

The politics of promises is short-sighted. It results in disappointments where the electorate starts to engage in negative voting, punishing the political parties which promise the most but deliver the least. Negative voting is on the increase as incumbent governments find it increasingly difficult to stay in power after one election period. Since political parties use so much jargon promising so many great new things but delivering so little, the voter can at least express his/her dissatisfaction by not supporting the parties in power. Opportunism spreads.

Conclusion

At the same time as the political parties are the main actors in the democracies in the European countries, they are operating in a less and less secure post-industrial society. Increasing electoral volatility, mass media pressure, the welfare state crisis and European integration have changed the environment for the political parties. The political parties attempt to adapt to the post-industrial society, but far from all are successful. The party systems in Western Europe experience one after the other earthquake elections when established parties tumble. Flash parties have begun to appear and traditional parties engage in issue politics in order to safeguard themselves against major losses in the election arena. And the party systems in Eastern Europe are only partly down the road to some degree of stability.

In European politics as it evolves in the 1990s convergence factors meet divergence conditions. And the political appearance in some 30 European countries results from this contestation between convergence and divergence. The European game of politics shows more and more similarities despite economic and social differences as well as lingering historical legacies. If this analysis of the mechanisms operating behind party government has something to say, then we may expect more convergence in European politics in the future. *Eller något i den stilen.*

Bibliography

Aarts, K. (1995) 'Intermediate organizations and interest representation', in H.-D. Klingemann and D. Fuchs (eds), *Citizens and the State*. Oxford: Oxford University Press. pp. 227–57.

Abramson, P. and Inglehart, R. (1995) *Value Change in Global Perspective*. Ann Arbor: The University of Michigan Press.

Abromeit, H. (1993) *Interessenvermittlung zwischen Konkurrenz und Konkordanz*. Opladen: Leske and Budrich.

Agh, A. (1994) 'The Hungarian party system and party theory in the transition of Central Europe', *Journal of Theoretical Politics*, 6, 217–38.

Agh, A. (1995) 'Parliaments as policy-making bodies in East Central Europe: The case of Hungary', *Budapest Papers on Democratic Transition*, no. 142.

Allum, P. (1995) *State and Society in Western Europe*. Cambridge: Polity Press.

Alton, T.P. (1989) 'Comparison of overall economic performance in the East European countries', in R. Weichardt (ed.), *Les économies d'Europe de l'Est sous l'influence de M. Gorbatchev: Colloque 23–25 mars 1988 Bruxelles*. Bruxelles: NATO, pp. 26–50.

Alvarez, M., Garrett, G. and Lange, P. (1991) 'Government partisanship, labor organization, and macroeconomic performance', *American Political Science Review*, 85, 539–56.

Andersen, S.S. and Eliassen, K. (1993) *Making Policy in Europe: The Europeification of National Policy-Making*. London: Sage.

Anderson, P. and Camiller, P. (eds) (1994) *Mapping the West European Left*. London: Verso.

Andeweg, R.B. and Irwin, G.A. (1993) *Dutch Government and Politics*. Basingstoke: Macmillan.

Archer, M.S. and Giner, S. (eds) (1971) *Contemporary Europe: Class, Status and Power*. London: Weidenfeld and Nicolson.

Armingeon, K. (1989) 'Arbeitsbeziehungen und Gewerkschaftsentwicklung in den achtziger Jahren: Ein Vergleich den OECD-Ländern', *Politische Vierteljahresschrift*, 30, 603–28.

Arter, D. (1995) 'Estonia after the March 1995 Riigikogu election: Still an anti-party system', *The Journal of Communist Studies and Transition Politics*, 11, 249–71.

Åslund, A. (1995) *How Russia became a Market Economy*. Washington, DC: Brookings.

Atkinson, A.B. and Micklewright, J. (1992) *Economic Transformation in Eastern Europe and the Distribution of Income*. Cambridge: Cambridge University Press.

Atkinson, A.B., Rainwater, L. and Smeeding, T.M. (1995) *Income Distribution in OECD Countries: Evidence from the Luxembourg Income Study*. Paris: OECD.

Aylott, N. (1995) 'Back to the future: The 1994 Swedish election', *Party Politics*, 1, 419–29.

Bairoch, P. (1976) 'Europe's Gross National Product 1800–1975', *Journal of European Economic History*, 5, 273–340.

Baldwin-Edwards, M. and Schain, M.A. (eds) (1994) 'The politics of immigration in Western Europe', *West European Politics*, 17, 2.

Banac, I. (ed.) (1992) *Eastern Europe in Revolution*. Ithaca: Cornell University Press.

Banks, A.S. (1971) *Cross-Polity Time-Series Data*. Cambridge, MA: MIT Press.

Banks, A.S. (1994) *Cross-National Time-Series Data Archive*. Binghamton, NY: Center for Social Analysis, State University of New York at Binghampton.

Barany, Z. and Volgyes, I. (eds) (1995) *The Legacies of Communism in Eastern Europe*. Baltimore: Johns Hopkins University Press.

Barrett, D.B. (ed.) (1982) *World Christian Encyclopedia: A Comparative Study of Churches and Religions in the Modern World AD 1900–2000*. Nairobi: Oxford University Press.

Barro, R.J. (1991) 'Economic growth in a cross section of countries', *Quarterly Journal of Economics*, 106, May, 407–43.

Barro, R.J. and Sala-i-Martin, X. (1992) 'Convergence', *Journal of Political Economy*, 100, 223–51.

Bartolini, S. and Mair, P. (1990) *Identity, Competition, and Electoral Availability: The Stability of European Electorates 1885–1985*. Cambridge: Cambridge University Press.

Batley, R. and Stoker, G. (eds) (1991) *Local government in Europe: Trends and Developments*. Basingstoke: Macmillan.

Baylis, T.A. (1996) 'Presidents versus prime ministers: Shaping executive authority in Eastern Europe', *World Politics*, 48, 297–323.

Bean, R. (1994) *Comparative Industrial Relations: An Introduction to Cross-national Perspectives*. 2nd edn. London: Routledge.

Bell, D. (1976a) *The Coming of Post-Industrial Society*. New York: Basic Books.

Bell, D. (1976b) *The Cultural Contradictions of Capitalism*. New York: Basic Books.

Benderly, J. and Kraft, E. (eds) (1994) *Independent Slovenia: Origins, Movements, Prospects*. New York: St. Martin's Press.

Bennett, C.J. (1991) 'What is policy convergence and what causes it?', *British Journal of Political Science*, 21, 215–33.

Berglund, S. and Dellenbrant, J.Å. (eds) (1994) *The New Democracies in Eastern Europe: Party Systems and Political Cleavages*. Aldershot: Edward Elgar.

Beyme, K. von (ed.) (1988) 'Right-wing extremism in Western Europe', *West European Politics*, 11, 2.

Beyme, K. von (1994) *Systemwechsel in Osteuropa*. Frankfurt: Suhrkamp.

Bibic, A. (1993) 'The emergence of pluralism in Slovenia', *Communist and Post-Communist Studies*, 26, 367–86.

Biorcio, R. and Mannheimer, R. (1995) 'Relationships between citizens and political parties', in H.-D. Klingemann and D. Fuchs (eds) *Citizens and the State*. Oxford: Oxford University Press. pp. 206–26.

Bird, R.M. and Wallich, C. (1994) 'Local finance and economic reform in Eastern Europe', *Environment and Planning C: Government and Policy*, 12, 263–76.

Black, C. (1966) *The Dynamics of Modernization*. New York: Harper and Row.

Blais, A. and Carty, R.K. (1990) 'Does proportional representation foster voter turnout?', *European Journal of Political Research*, 18, 167–81.

Blaustein, A.P. and Flanz, G. (1972–) *Constitutions of the Countries of the World*. New York: Oceana Publications.

Blondel, J. (1968) 'Party systems and patterns of government in Western democracies', *Canadian Journal of Political Science*, 1, 180–203.

Blondel, J. (1995) 'Toward a systematic analysis of government–party relationships', *International Political Science Review*, 16, 127–43.

Bloomfield, J. (1979) *Passive Revolution: Politics and the Czechoslovak Working Class 1945–1948*. London: Allison and Busby.

Bogdanor, V. (ed.) (1983) *Coalition Government in Western Europe*. London: Heinemann.

Bourdieu, P. (1990) *The Logic of Practice*. Cambridge: Polity Press.

Borre, O. and Scarbrough, E. (eds) (1995) *The Scope of Government*. Oxford: Oxford University Press.

Bourricaud, F. (1987) 'Modernity, "universal reference" and the process of modernization', in S.N. Eisenstadt (ed.), *Patterns of Modernity: Volume I: The West*. New York: New York University Press. pp. 12–21.

Brady, H.E. and Kaplan, C.S. (1994) 'Eastern Europe and the former Soviet Union', in D. Butler and A. Ranney (eds), *Referendums around the World: The Growing Use of Direct Democracy*. Basingstoke: Macmillan. pp. 174–217.

Brokl, L. and Mansfeldova, Z. (1993) 'Czechoslovakia', in R. Koole and P. Mair (eds), *Political Data Yearbook, 1993. European Journal of Political Research*, 24, 397–410.

Browne, E.C. and Dreijmanis, J. (eds) (1982) *Government Coalitions in Western Democracies*. New York: Longman.

Bruno, M. and Sachs, J. (1985) *The Economics of Worldwide Stagflation*. Cambridge, MA: Harvard University Press.

Bueno de Mesquita, B. and Stokman, F.N. (eds) (1994) *European Community Decision Making: Models, Applications, and Comparisons*. New Haven, CT: Yale University Press.

Budge, I. and Keman, H. (1990) *Parties and Democracy: Coalition Formation and Government Functioning in Twenty States*. Oxford: Oxford University Press.

Bull, M.J. and Heywood, P. (eds) (1994) *West European Communist Parties after the Revolutions of 1989*. Basingstoke: Macmillan.

Bungs, D. (1993) 'Moderates win parliamentary elections in Latvia', *RFE/RL Research Report*, 2, 28, 1–6.

Burgess, M. and Gagnon, A.G. (eds) (1993) *Comparative Federalism and Federation*. New York: Harvester Wheatsheaf.

Butler, D. and Ranney, A. (eds) (1994) *Referendums around the World: The Growing Use of Direct Democracy*. Basingstoke: Macmillan.

Butler, D. and Särlvik, B. (eds) (1990) 'Special issue: Elections in Eastern Europe', *Electoral Studies*, 9, 4.

Calic, M.-J. (1995) *Der Krieg in Bosnien-Hercegovina: Ursachen, Konfliktstrukturen, Internationalen Lösungsversuche*. Frankfurt: Suhrkamp.

Calmfors, L. and Driffill, J. (1988) 'Centralization of wage bargaining', *Economic Policy*, 6, 13–61.

Cameron, D.R. (1978) 'The expansion of the public economy: A comparative analysis', *American Political Science Review*, 72, 1243–61.

Cameron, D.R. (1984) 'Social democracy, corporatism, labour quiescence, and the representation of economic interests in advanced capitalist society', in J.H. Goldthorpe (ed.), *Order and Conflict in Contemporary Capitalism: Studies in the Political Economy of Western European Nations*. Oxford: Clarendon Press. pp. 143–78.

Castillo, P. del and Lopez Nieto, L. (1994) 'Spain', in R. Koole and P. Mair (eds), *Political Data Yearbook, 1994. European Journal of Political Research*, 26, 423–9.

Castles, F.G. (ed.) (1982) *The Impact of Parties: Politics and Policies in Democratic Capitalist States*. London: Sage.

Castles, F.G. (1986) 'Whatever happened to the communist welfare state?', *Studies in Comparative Communism*, 19, 213–26.

Castles, F.G. (1995) 'Welfare state development in Southern Europe', *West European Politics*, 18, 2, 291–313.

Castles, F.G. and Mair, P. (1984) 'Left–right political scales: Some "expert" judgments', *European Journal of Political Research*, 12, 73–88.

CDLR (Committee on Local and Regional Authorities) (1995) *The Size of Municipalities, Efficiency and Citizen Participation*. Strasbourg: Council of Europe Press.

CEC (Commission of the European Communities) (1994) *Eurobarometer: Trends 1974–1993*. Brussels: European Commission.

CEC (Commission of the European Communities) (1995a) *Official Journal of the European Communities*. 14 November 1995.

CEC (Commission of the European Communities) (1995b) *MISSOC: Social Protection in the Member States of the Community*. Brussels: Commission of the European Communities.

CEC (Commission of the European Communities) (1995c) *Eurobarometer 42*. Brussels: European Commision.

CEC (Commission of the European Communities) (1996) *Eurobarometer 43*. Brussels: European Commission.

Central Intelligence Agency (1994) *The World Factbook 1994–95*. Washington, DC: Brassey.

Chandler, J.A. (ed.) (1993) *Local Government in Liberal Democracies: An Introductory Survey*. London: Routledge.

Cheles, L., Ferguson, R. and Vaughan, M. (eds) (1991) *Neo-Fascism in Europe*. London: Longman.

Chirot, D. (1994) *How Societies Change*. Thousand Oaks, CA: Pine Forge Press.

Clark, J. and Wildavsky, A. (1990) *The Moral Collapse of Communism: Poland as a Cautionary Tale*. San Francisco: ICS Press.

Clark, T.N. (1993) 'Local democracy and innovation in Eastern Europe', *Environment and Planning C: Government and Policy*, 11, 171–98.

Coakley, J. (ed.) (1992) *The Social Origins of Nationalist Movements: The Contemporary West European Experience*. London: Sage.

Cohen, L.J. (1993) *Broken Bonds: The Disintegration of Yugoslavia*. Boulder, CO: Westview Press.

Cole, A. (1993) 'The presidential party and the Fifth Republic', *West European Politics*, 16, 2, 49–66.

Collier, D. (1991) 'The comparative method: Two decades of change', in D. Rustow and K.P. Erickson (eds), *Comparative Political Dynamics: Global Research Perspectives*. New York: HarperCollins. pp. 7–31.

Cook, L.J. (1995) 'Labor unions in post-communist countries', *Problems of Post-Communism*, 42, 2, 13–18.

Coughlin, R.M. (1992) 'Convergence theories', in E.F. Borgatta and M.L. Borgatta (eds), *Encyclopedia of Sociology*. Vol. 1. New York: Macmillan. pp. 295–303.

Coulson, A. (ed.) (1995) *Local Government in Eastern Europe: Establishing Democracy at the Grassroots*. Aldershot: Edward Elgar.

Council of Europe (1993) *Comparative Tables of Social Security Schemes in Council of Europe Member States not Members of the European Communities, in Australia and in Canada*. Strasbourg: Council of Europe Press.

Crawford, B. and Lijphart, A. (1995) 'Explaining political and economic change in post-communist Eastern Europe: Old legacies, new institutions, hegemonic norms, and international pressures', *Comparative Political Studies*, 28, 171–99.

Crepatz, M.L. (1990) 'The impact of party polarization and postmaterialism on voter turnout', *European Journal of Political Research*, 18, 183–205.

Crouch, C. (1993) *Industrial Relations and European State Traditions*. Oxford: Clarendon Press.

Daalder, H. (1984) 'In search of the centre of European parties systems', *American Political Science Review*, 78, 92–109.

Daalder, H. (1992) 'A crisis of party?', *Scandinavian Political Studies*, 15, 269–88.

Daalder, H. and Irwin, G.A. (eds) (1989) 'Politics in the Netherlands: How much change?', *West European Politics*, 12, 1.

De Swaan, A. (1973) *Coalition Theories and Cabinet Formation*. Amsterdam: Elsevier.

Deppe, R., Dubiel, H. and Rödel, U. (eds) (1991) *Demokratischer Umbruch in Osteuropa*. Frankfurt: Suhrkamp.

Deruette, S. and Loeb-Mayer, N. (1992) 'Belgium', in R. Koole and P. Mair (eds), *Political Data Yearbook, 1992. European Journal of Political Research*, 22, 363–72.

Deutsch, K. (1963) *The Nerves of Government: Models of Political Communication and Control*. New York: Free Press.

Donovan, M. (1994) 'The 1994 election in Italy: Normalisation or continuing exceptionalism?' *West European Politics*, 17, 4, 193–201.

Döring, H. (ed.) (1995) *Parliaments and Majority Rule in Western Europe*. Frankfurt: Campus Verlag.

Downs, A. (1957) *An Economic Theory of Democracy*. New York: Harper and Brothers.

Dreyfus, M. (1991) *L'Europe des socialistes*. Brussels: Editions Complexe.

Duhamel, O. and Mény, Y. (eds) (1992) *Dictionnaire Constitutionnel*. Paris: PUF.

Durand, J.-D. (1995) *L'Europe de la démocratie chrétienne*. Brussels: Editions Complexe.

Duranton-Crabol, A.-M. (1991) *L'Europe de l'extreme droite*. Brussels: Editions Complexe.

Durkheim, E. ([1893] 1964) *The Division of Labor in Society*. New York: Free Press.

Durkheim, E. ([1897] 1970) *Suicide: A Study in Sociology*. London: Routledge and Kegan Paul.

Duverger, M. ([1951] 1964) *Political Parties: Their Organization and Activity in the Modern State*. London: Methuen.

Duverger, M. (1986) 'Duverger's law: Forty years later', in B. Grofman and A. Lijphart (eds), *Electoral Laws and Their Political Consequences*. New York. Agathon Press. pp. 69–84.

EB (Encyclopaedia Britannica) (1993–95) *Britannica Book of the Year: Britannica World Data*. Chicago: Encyclopaedia Britannica.

Ebbinghaus, B. (1995) 'The development of trade unions in Western Europe: Global convergence or cross-national diversity?', *Eurodata Newsletter*, 1, 2, 1–8.

EBRD (European Bank for Reconstruction and Development) (1994) *Transition Report October 1994*. London: EBRD.

EBRD (European Bank for Reconstruction and Development) (1995) *Transition Report 1995*. London: EBRD.

Eberstadt, N. (1994) 'Health and mortality in Central and Eastern Europe: Retrospect and prospect', in J. Millar and S. Wolchik (eds), *The Social Legacy of Communism*. Cambridge: Cambridge University Press. pp. 196–225.

ECE (Economic Commission for Europe) (1995a) *Annual Bulletin of Housing and Building Statistics for Europe and North America*. New York: United Nations: Vol. 37 1993.

ECE (Economic Commission for Europe) (1995b) *Economic Survey of Europe in 1994–1995*. New York: United Nations.

The Economist (1995) 'A survey of the internet', 1–7 July.

El-Agraa, A.M. (1990) *The Economics of the European Community*. 3rd edn. Hemel Hempstead: Philip Allan.

Elazar, D.J. (1987) *Exploring Federalism*. Tuscaloosa, AL: University of Alabama Press.

Elazar, D.J. (1995) 'Federalism', in S.M. Lipset (ed.), *The Encyclopedia of Democracy*. Vol. 2. pp. 474–82.

Electoral Studies (1990–5) Exeter: Elsevier Science.

EOS Gallup Europe (1992) *Eftabarometer Autumn 92*. s.1.: EOS Gallup Europe [Computer File].

Esping-Andersen, G. (1990) *The Three Worlds of Welfare Capitalism*. Cambridge: Polity Press.

The Europa World Yearbook (1995) London: Europa Publications.

European Commission (1990–5) *Central and Eastern Eurobarometer*, nos 1–5. Cologne: Zentralarchiv.

Evans, G. and Whitefield, S. (1993) 'Identifying the bases of party competition in Eastern Europe', *British Journal of Political Science*, 23, 521–48.

Fassmann, H. and Münz, R. (1992) 'Patterns and trends of international migration in Western Europe', *Population and Development Review*, 18, 457–80.

Fassmann, H. and Münz, R. (1994) 'European east–west migration 1945–1992', *International Migration Review*, 27, 520–38.

Der Fischer Welt Almanach (yearly: 1959–) Frankfurt: Fischer Taschenbuchverlag.

Fisher, S. (1995) 'Prime minister and president grapple for power' [Slovakia], *Transition*, 1, 11, 38–42.

Fitzmaurice, J. (1993) 'The Estonian elections of 1992', *Electoral Studies*, 12, 168–73.

Fitzmaurice, J. (1995) 'The Danish general election of September 1994', *West European Politics*, 18, 2, 418–21.

Flanagan, S.C. (1982) 'Changing values in advanced industrial societies: Inglehart's Silent Revolution from the perspective of Japanese findings', *Comparative Political Studies*, 14, 403–44.

Flere, S. (1991) 'Denominational affiliation in Yugoslavia, 1931–1987', *East European Quarterly*, 25, 145–65.

Fowkes, B. (1993) *The Rise and Fall of Communism in Eastern Europe*. Basingstoke: Macmillan.

Frankland, E.G. (1995) 'Green revolutions: The role of Green parties in eastern-Europe transition, 1989–1994', *East European Quarterly*, 29, 315–45.

Freedom House (1990) *Freedom in the World: Political Rights and Civil Liberties 1989–1990*. New York: Freedom House.

Freedom House (1991) *Freedom in the World: Political Rights and Civil Liberties 1990–1991*. New York: Freedom House.

Freedom House (1993) *Freedom in the World: The Annual Survey of Political Rights and Civil Liberties 1992–1993*. New York: Freedom House.

Freedom House (1995) *Freedom in the World: The Annual Survey of Political Rights and Civil Liberties 1994–1995*. New York: Freedom House.

Freedom House (1996) *Freedom Review*. Vol. 27, no. 1.

Fries, F. (1995) Les Grands Debats Européens. Paris: Seuil.

Fuchs, D. and Klingemann, H.-D. (1995) 'Citizens and the state: A relationship transformed', in H.-D. Klingemann and D. Fuchs (eds), *Citizens and the State*. Oxford: Oxford University Press. pp. 419–43.

Fukuyama, F. (1995) *Trust: The Social Virtues and the Creation of Prosperity*. New York: Free Press.

Furlong, P. (1994) *Modern Italy: Representation and Reform*. London: Routledge.

Furtak, R.K. (ed.) (1990) *Elections in Socialist States*. Hemel Hempstead: Harvester Wheatsheaf.

Galbraith, J.K. (1967) *The New Industrial State*. Boston, MA: Houghton Mifflin.

Gallagher, M., Laver, M. and Mair, P. (1995) *Representative Government in Modern Europe*. 2nd edn. New York: McGraw-Hill.

Gallagher, T. (1995a) *Romania after Ceaușescu*. Edinburgh: Edinburgh University Press.

Gallagher, T. (1995b) 'Democratization in the Balkans: Challenges and prospects', *Democratization*, 2, 337–61.

Gamson, W. (1961) 'A theory of coalition formation', *American Sociological Review*, 26, 373–82.

Gärtner, H. (1995) 'Rechtsextremismus und neue Rechte', *Österreichisches Zeitschrift für Politikwissenschaft*, 24, 253–61.

George, S. (1991) *Politics and Policy in the European Community*. 2nd edn. Oxford: Oxford University Press.

Gerlich, P. (1973) 'The institutionalization of European parliaments', in A. Kornberg (ed.), *Legislatures in Comparative Perspective*. New York: David McKay. pp. 94–113.

Gilbert, M. (1995) *The Italian Revolution: The End of Politics, Italian Style?* Boulder, CO: Westview Press.

Gillespie, R. and Paterson, W.E. (eds) (1993) 'Rethinking social democracy in Western Europe', *West European Politics*, 16, 1.

Giner, S. and Archer, M.S. (eds) (1978) *Contemporary Europe: Social Structures and Cultural Patterns*. London: Routledge and Kegan Paul.

Girnius, S. (1992) 'The parliamentary elections in Lithuania', *RFE/RL Research Report*, 1, 48, 6–12.

Glaessner, G.-J. (1994) *Demokratie nach dem Ende des Kommunismus: Regimewechsel, Transition und Demokratisierung im Postkommunismus*. Opladen: Westdeutscher Verlag.

Goldthorpe, J.H. (1984) 'The end of convergence: Corporatist and dualist tendencies in modern Western societies', in J.H. Goldthorpe (ed.), *Order and Conflict in Contemporary Capitalism: Studies in the Political Economy of Western European Nations*. Cambridge: Cambridge University Press. pp. 315–43.

Gonzales Enriques, C. (1995) 'Electoral systems and political stability in Central and Eastern Europe', *Budapest Papers on Democratic Transition*, no. 132.

Götting, U. (1994) 'Destruction, adjustment and innovation: Social policy transformation in Eastern and Central Europe', *Journal of European Social Policy*, 4, 181–200.

Good, D.F. (1994) 'The economic lag of Central and Eastern Europe: Income estimates for the Habsburg successor states, 1870–1910', *The Journal of Economic History*, 54, 869–91.

Gotovitch, J., Delwit, P. and De Waele, J.M. (1992) *L'Europe des communistes*. Brussels: Editions Complexe.

Gowan, P. (1995) 'Neo-liberal theory and practice for Eastern Europe', *New Left Review*, 213, 3–60.

Goyder, D.G. (1992) *EC Competition Law*. 2nd edn. Oxford: Clarendon Press.

Grofman, B. and Lijphart, A. (eds) (1986) *Electoral Laws and Their Political Consequences*. New York: Agathon Press.

Guchet, Y. (ed.) (1994) *Les systèmes politiques des pays de l'Union Européenne*. Paris: Armand Colin.

Gundelach, P. (1994) 'National value differences: Modernization or institutionalization?', *International Journal of Comparative Sociology*, 35, 37–58.

Gurr, T.R. (1990) *Polity II: Political Structures and Regime Change, 1800–1986*. Boulder, CO: Center for Comparative Politics [computer file].

GVG (Gesellschaft für Versicherungswissenschaft und -gestaltung) (eds) (1994) *Soziale Sicherung in West-, Mittel- und Osteuropa*. Baden-Baden: Nomos.

Gwartney, J., Lawson, R. and Block, W. (1996) *Economic Freedom of the World 1975–1995*. Vancouver: Fraser Institute.

Hall, D. (1994) *Albania and the Albanians*. London: Pinter.

Haller, M. and Schachner-Blazizek, P. (eds) (1994) *Europa – wohin?: Wirtschaftliche Integration, soziale Gerechtigkeit und Demokratie*. Graz: Leykam Verlag.

Hanley, D. (ed.) (1994) *Christian Democracy in Europe*. London: Pinter.

Hardarson, O.T. (1992) 'Iceland', in R. Koole and P. Mair (eds), *Political Data Yearbook, 1992. European Journal of Political Research*, 22, 429–35.

Hayward, J. and Page, E.C. (eds) (1995) *Governing the New Europe*. Cambridge: Polity Press.

Hearl, D. (1994) 'Luxembourg', *Electoral Studies*, 13, 349–57.

Heidar, K. (1994) 'Norway', in R. Koole and P. Mair (eds), *Political Data Yearbook, 1994. European Journal of Political Research*, 26, 389–95.

Held, J. (ed.) (1993) *Democracy and Right-Wing Politics in Eastern Europe in the 1990s*. New York: Columbia University Press.

Hesse, J.J. (ed.) (1978) *Politikverflechtung im föderativen Staat*. Baden-Baden: Nomos.

Hesse, J.J. and Johnson, N. (eds) (1995) *Constitutional Policy and Change in Europe*. Oxford: Oxford University Press.

Héthy, L. (1995) 'Anatomy of a tripartite experiment: Attempted social and economic agreement in Hungary', *International Labour Review*, 134, 361–76.

Hewitt, C. (1977) 'The effect of political democracy and social democracy on equality in industrial societies: A cross-national comparison', *American Sociological Review*, 42, 450–64.

Heywood, P. (1995) *The Government and Politics of Spain*. Basingstoke: Macmillan.

Hibbing, J.R. and Patterson, S.C (1994) 'The emergence of democratic parliaments in Central and Eastern Europe', in G.W. Copeland and S.C. Patterson (eds), *Parliaments in the Modern World: Changing Institutions*. Ann Arbor: The University of Michigan Press. pp. 129–50.

Hine, D. (1993) *Governing Italy: The Politics of Bargained Pluralism*. Oxford: Oxford University Press.

Hollingsworth, J.R., Schmitter, P.C. and Streeck, W. (eds) (1994) *Governing Capitalist Economies*. Oxford: Oxford University Press.

Howard, A.E.D. (ed.) (1993) *Constitution Making in Eastern Europe*. Baltimore: Johns Hopkins University Press.

Huber, J. and Inglehart, R. (1995) 'Expert interpretations of party space and party locations in 42 societies', *Party Politics*, 1, 73–111.

Huber, E., Ragin, C. and Stephens, J.D. (1993) 'Social democracy, christian democracy, constitutional structure, and the welfare state', *American Journal of Sociology*, 99, 711–49.

Ignazi, P. (1992) 'The silent counter-revolution: Hypotheses on the emergence of extreme right-wing parties in Europe', *European Journal of Political Research*, 22, 3–34.

Ignazi, P. (1993) 'Italy', in R. Koole and P. Mair (eds), *Political Data Yearbook, 1993. European Journal of Political Research*, 24, 475–83.

International Institute for Democracy (1995) *The Rebirth of Democracy: 12 Constitutions of Central and Eastern Europe*. Strasbourg: Council of Europe Press.

ILO (International Labour Organization) (1992) *World Labour Report 1992*. Geneva: ILO.

ILO (International Labour Organization) (1993a) *World Labour Report 1993*. Geneva: ILO.

ILO (International Labour Organization) (1993b) *Yearbook of Labour Statistics 1993*. Geneva: ILO.

ILO (International Labour Organization) (1994) *Yearbook of Labour Statistics 1994*. Geneva: ILO.

ILO (International Labour Organization) (1995) *Yearbook of Labour Statistics 1995*. Geneva: ILO.

IMF (International Monetary Fund) (1993) *Government Finance Statistics Yearbook*. Washington, DC: IMF.

IMF (International Monetary Fund) (1994) *World Economic Outlook: October 1994*. Washington, DC: IMF.

IMF (International Monetary Fund) (1995) *World Economic Outlook: October 1995*. Washington, DC: IMF.

Immerfall, S. (1994) *Einführung in den Europäischen Gesellschaftsvergleich: Ansätze, Problemstellungen, Befunde*. Passau: Wissenschaftsverlag Rothe.

Inglehart, R. (1977) *The Silent Revolution: Changing Values and Political Styles among Western Publics*. Princeton: Princeton University Press.

Inglehart, R. (1990) *Culture Shift in Advanced Industrial Society*. Princeton: Princeton University Press.

Inglehart, R. (1993) *World Values Survey 1990–1991*. Ann Arbor: Institute for Social Research, University of Michigan [computer file].

Inkeles, A. (1981) 'Convergence and divergence in industrial societies', in M.O. Attir, B. Holzner and Z. Suda (eds), *Directions of Change: Modernization Theory, Research, and Realities*. Boulder, CO: Westview Press. pp. 3–38.

Inkeles, A. (1983) *Exploring Individual Modernity*. New York: Columbia University Press.

Internet: Political Sciences Resources by Richard Kimber at the University of Keele: http// www.keele.ac.uk/depts/po/psr.htm.

Ishiyama, J.T. (1995) 'Communist parties in transition: Structures, leaders, and processes of democratization in Eastern Europe', *Comparative Politics*, 27, 147–66.

Jachtenfuchs, M. and Kohler-Koch, B. (eds) (1996) *Europäische Integration*. Opladen: Leske and Budrich.

Jackman, R.W. and Miller, R.A. (1995) 'Voter turnout in the industrial democracies during the 1980s', *Comparative Political Studies*, 27, 467–92.

Jaggers, K. and Gurr, T.R. (1995) 'Tracking democracy's third wave with the Polity III data', *Journal of Peace Research*, 32, 469–82.

Janda, K. (1980) *Political Parties: A Cross-National Survey*. New York: Free Press.

Janda, K. (1993) 'Comparative political parties: research and theory', in A.W. Finifter (ed.), *Political Science: The State of the Discipline II*. Washington, DC: APSA. pp. 163–91.

Janos, A.C. (1994) 'Continuity and change in Eastern Europe: Strategies of post-communist politics', *Eastern European Politics and Societies*, 8, 1–31.

Janova, M. and Sineau, M. (1992) 'Women's participation in political power in Europe: An essay in East–West comparison', *Women's Studies International Forum*, 15, 115–28.

Jasiewicz, K. (1992) 'Poland', in R. Koole and P. Mair (eds), *Political Data Yearbook, 1992*. *European Journal of Political Research*, 22, 489–504.

Jasiewicz, K. (1994) 'Poland', in R. Koole and P. Mair (eds), *Political Data Yearbook, 1994*. *European Journal of Political Research*, 26, 397–408.

Jovic, D. (1995) 'Formation of the Croatian party system from the 1992 elections to the parliamentary crisis 1994', *Budapest Papers on Democratic Transition*, no. 134.

Kaase, M. and Newton, K. (eds) (1995) *Beliefs in Government*. Oxford: Oxford University Press.

Kaelberer, M. (1993) 'The emergence of Green parties in Western Europe', *Comparative Politics*, 25, 229–43.

Kaelble, H. (1987) *Auf dem Weg zu einer europäischen Gesellschaft: eine Sozialgeschichte Westeuropas 1880–1980*. Munich: Beck.

Kalberg, S. (1993) 'Convergence thesis', in J. Krieger (ed.), *The Oxford Companion to Politics*. New York: Oxford University Press. pp. 193–4.

Kaplan, K. (1981) *Der kurze March: kommunitische Machtübernahme in der Tschechoslowakei 1945–1948*. Munich: Oldenburg.

Karasimeonov, G. (1995) 'Parliamentary elections of 1994 and the development of the Bulgarian party system', *Party Politics*, 1, 579–87.

Karpinski, J. (1995) 'The constitutional mosaic' [Poland], *Transition*, 1, 14, 4–9.

Karvonen, L. (1993a) *Fragmentation and Consensus: Political Organization and the Interwar Crisis in Europe*. Boulder, CO: Social Science Monographs.

Karvonen, L. (1993b) 'In from the cold?: Christian parties in Scandinavia', *Scandinavian Political Studies*, 16, 25–48.

Karvonen, L. and Sundberg, J. (eds) (1991) *Social Democracy in Transition: Northern, Southern and Eastern Europe*. Aldershot: Dartmouth.

Katz, R.S. and Mair, P. (1995) 'Changing models of party organization and party democracy: The emergence of the cartel party', *Party Politics*, 1, 5–28.

Keating, M. (1993) *The Politics of Modern Europe: The State and Political Authority in the Major Democracies*. Aldershot: Edward Elgar.

Keating, M. and Jones, B. (eds) (1985) *Regions in the European Community*. Oxford: Clarendon.

Keating, M. and Hooghe, L. (1996) 'By-passing the nation state? Regions in the EU policy process', in J.J. Richardson (ed.), *Policy Making in the European Union*. London: Routledge.

Keating, M. and Loughlin, J. (eds) (1996) *The Political Economy of Regionalism*. London: Frank Cass.

Keesing's Record of World Events (1990–5) Cambridge: Catermill.

Keman, H. (1994) 'The search for the centre: Pivot parties in West European party systems', *West European Politics*, 17, 4, 124–48.

Keman, H. and Pennings, P. (1995) 'Managing political and societal conflict in democracies: Do consensus and corporatism matter?', *British Journal of Political Science*, 25, 271–81.

Kerr, C. (1983) *The Future of Industrial Societies: Convergence or Continuing Diversity?*, Cambridge, MA: Harvard University Press.

Kettle, S. (1995) 'The rise of the Social Democrats' [The Czech Republic], *Transition*, 1, 13, 70–4.

Kirchner, E.J. (ed.) (1988) *Liberal Parties in Western Europe*. Cambridge: Cambridge University Press.

Kirk, D. (1946) *Europe's Population in the Interwar Years*. Geneva: League of Nations.

Kirch, A., Kirch, M. and Tuisk, T. (1993) 'Russians in the Baltic states: To be or not to be?', *Journal of Baltic Studies*, 24, 173–88.

Kitchen, M. (1988) *Europe between the Wars: A Political History*. London: Longman.

Kitschelt, H. (1992) 'The formation of party systems in East Central Europe', *Politics and Society*, 20, 7–50.

Kitschelt, H. (1994) *The Transformation of European Social Democracy*. Cambridge: Cambridge University Press.

Kitschelt, H. (1995a) 'Formation of party cleavages in post-communist democracies: Theoretical propositions', *Party Politics*, 1, 447–72.

Kitschelt, H. (1995b) *The Radical Right in Western Europe: A Comparative Analysis*. Ann Arbor: University of Michigan Press.

Klingemann, H.-D. and Fuchs, D. (eds) (1995) *Citizens and the State*. Oxford: Oxford University Press.

Knutsen, O. (1995a) 'The impact of old parties and new politics values orientation on party choice: A comparative study', *Journal of Public Policy*, 15, 1–63.

Knutsen, O. (1995b) 'Left–right materialist value orientations', in J.W. Van Deth and E. Scarbrough (eds), *The Impact of Values*. Oxford: Oxford University Press. pp. 160–96.

Kobach, K.W. (1994) 'Switzerland', in D. Butler and A. Ranney (eds), *Referendums around the World: The Growing Use of Direct Democracy*. Basingstoke: Macmillan. pp. 98–153.

Korinman, M. and Caracciolo, L. (eds) (1995) *A Quoi Sert L'Italie*. Paris: La Découverte.

Kostova, D. (1992) 'Parliamentary elections in Bulgaria, October 1991', *The Journal of Communist Studies*, 8, 1, 196–203.

Kriesi, H., Koopmans, R., Duyvendak, J.W. and Giugni, M.G. (1992) 'New social movements and political opportunities in Western Europe', *European Journal of Political Research*, 22, 219–44.

Kriesi, H., Koopmans, R., Duyvendak, J.W. and Giugni, M.G. (1995) *New Social Movements in Western Europe: A Comparative Analysis*. Minneapolis: University of Minneapolis Press.

Kurth, J. and Petras, J. (eds) (1993) *Mediterranean Paradoxes: Politics and Social Structure in Southern Europe*. Providence, RI: Berg.

Laakso, M. and Taagepera, R. (1979) ' "Effective" number of parties: A measure with applications to West Europe', *Comparative Political Studies*, 12, 2–27.

Ladner, A. (1992) 'Switzerland', in R. Koole and P. Mair (eds), *Political Data Yearbook, 1992. European Journal of Political Research*, 22, 527–36.

Lancieri, E. (1993) 'Dollar GNP estimates for Central and Eastern Europe 1970–1990: A survey and a comparison with Western countries', *World Development*, 21, 161–75.

Lane, J.-E. (ed.) (1991) 'Understanding the Swedish Model', *West European Politics*, 14, 3.

Langlois, S., Caplan, T., Mendzas, H. and Glatzer, W. (1994) *Convergence or Divergence: Recent Social Trends in Industrial Societies*. Frankfurt: Campus Verlag.

Lash, S. (1990) *The Sociology of Postmodernism*. London: Sage.

Laundy, P. (1989) *Parliaments in the Modern World*. Aldershot: Dartmouth.

Lavaux, P. (1994) 'L'évolution des fonctions exécutives en Europe', *Cahiers Francais*, 268, 30–43.

Laver, M.J. and Budge, I. (eds) (1992) *Party Policy and Government Coalitions*. Basingstoke: Macmillan.

Laver, M. and Schofield, N. (1990) *Multiparty Government: The Politics of Coalition in Europe*. Oxford: Oxford University Press.

Layton-Henry, Z. (ed.) (1982) *Conservative Politics in Western Europe*. London: Macmillan.

Lee, S.J. (1987) *The European Dictatorships 1918–1945*. London: Routledge.

Leff, C.S. (1988) *National Conflict in Czechoslovakia: The Making and Remaking of a State, 1918–1987*. Princeton: Princeton University Press.

Lehmbruch, G. (1992) 'Konkordanzdemokratie', in M. Schmidt (ed.), *Lexikon der Politik*. Munich: Piper. Band 3, pp. 206–11.

Lehmbruch, G. and Schmitter, P.C. (eds) (1982) *Patterns of Corporatist Policy-Making*. London: Sage.

Léonard, Y. (1994) *Le Portugal: Vingt ans aprés la Révolution des oeillets*. Paris: La documentation Française.

Levy, M. (1952) *The Structure of Society*. Princeton, NJ: Princeton University Press.

Lewis-Beck, M.S. and Lockerbie, B. (1989) 'Economics, votes, protests', *Comparative Poltical Studies*, 22, 155–77.

Lijphart, A. (1971) 'Comparative politics and the comparative method', *American Political Science Review*, 65, 682–93.

Lijphart, A. (1975) 'The comparable-cases strategy in comparative research', *Comparative Political Studies*, 8, 158–77.

Lijphart, A. (1977) *Democracy in Plural Societies: A Comparative Exploration*. New Haven, CT: Yale University Press.

Lijphart, A. (1984) *Democracies: Patterns of Majoritarian and Consensus Government in Twenty-One Countries*. New Haven, CT: Yale University Press.

Lijphart, A. (1992) 'Democratization and constitutional choices in Czecho-Slovakia, Hungary and Poland, 1989–91', *Journal of Theoretical Politics*, 4, 207–23.

Lijphart, A. (1994a) *Electoral Systems and Party Systems: A Study of Twenty-Seven Democracies, 1945–1990*. Oxford: Oxford University Press.

Lijphart, A. (1994b) 'Democracies: Forms, performance, and constitutional engineering', *European Journal of Political Research*, 25, 1–17.

Lijphart, A. and Crepatz, M. (1991) 'Corporatism and consensus democracy in eighteen countries', *British Journal of Political Science*, 21, 235–46.

Lijphart, A., Bruneau, T.C., Diamandouros, P.N. and Gunther, R. (1988) 'A Mediterranean model of democracy?: The Southern European democracies in comparative perspective', *West European Politics*, 11, 1, 7–25.

Lijphart, A. and Grofman, B. (eds) (1984) *Choosing an Electoral System: Issues and Alternatives*. New York: Praeger.

Lindström, U. (1991) 'East European social democracy: Reborn to be rejected', in L. Karvonen and J. Sundberg (eds), *Social Democracy in Transition: Northern, Southern and Eastern Europe*. Aldershot: Dartmouth. pp. 269–301.

Linz, J.J. (1990) 'The perils of presidentialism', *Journal of Democracy*, 1, 51–70.

Linz, J.J. (1994) 'Presidential or parliamentary democracy: Does it make a difference?', in J.J. Linz and A. Valenzuela (eds), *The Failure of Presidential Democracy*. Vol. 1. Baltimore: Johns Hopkins University Press, pp. 3–87.

Linz, J.J. and Valenzuela, A. (eds) (1994) *The Failure of Presidential Democracy. Volume 1: Comparative Perspectives*. Baltimore: Johns Hopkins University Press.

Lipset, S.M. (1994) 'The social requisites of democracy revisited', *American Sociological Review*, 59, 1–22.

Lipset, S.M. and Rokkan, S. (eds) (1967) *Party Systems and Voter Alignments: Cross-National Perspectives*. New York: Free Press.

Lipset, S.M., Seong, K.-R. and Torres, J.C. (1993) 'A comparative analysis of the social requisites of democracy', *International Social Science Journal*, 136, May, 155–75.

Little, A. and Silber, L. (1995) *The Death of Yugoslavia*. London: Penguin.

Lo Verso, L. and McLean, I. (1995) 'The Italian general election of 1994', *Electoral Studies*, 14, 81–6.

Lovenduski, J. and Woodall, J. (1987) *Politics and Society in Eastern Europe*. Basingstoke: Macmillan.

Luebbert, G.M. (1991) *Liberalism, Fascism or Social Democracy: Social Classes and the Political Origins of Regimes in Interwar Europe*. New York: Oxford University Press.

Luther, K.R. and Müller, W.C. (eds) (1992) 'Politics in Austria: Still a Case of Consociationalism?', *West European Politics*, 15, 1.

McGregor, J. (1993) 'How electoral laws shape Eastern Europe's parliaments', *RFE/RL Research Report*, 2, 4, 11–18.

McGregor, J. (1994) 'The presidency in East Central Europe', *RFE/RL Research Report*, 3, 2, 23–31.

McIntosh, M.E and Mac Iver, M.A. (1992) 'Coping with freedom and uncertainty: Public opinion in Hungary, Poland, and Czechoslovakia 1989–1992', *International Journal of Public Opinion Research*, 4, 375–91.

Mackie, T.T. (1992) 'General elections in Western nations during 1990', *European Journal of Political Research*, 21, 317–32.

Mackie, T.T. (1993) 'United Kingdom', in R. Koole and P. Mair (eds), *Political Data Yearbook, 1993. European Journal of Political Research*, 24, 555–62.

Maddison, A. (1995) *Monitoring the World Economy 1820–1992*. Paris: OECD.

Madeley, J. (1982) 'Politics and the pulpit: The case of the protestant Europe', *West European Politics*, 5, 2, 149–71.

Mahr, A. and Nagle, J. (1995) 'Resurrection of the successor parties and democratization in East-Central Europe', *Communist and Post-Communist Studies*, 28, 393–409.

Mair, P. (1993) 'Myths of electoral change and the survival of traditional parties', *European Journal of Political Research*, 24, 121–33.

Mair, P. (1994) 'The correlates of consensus democracy and the puzzle of Dutch politics', *West European Politics*, 17, 4, 97–123.

Mair, P. and Smith, G. (eds) (1989) 'Understanding party system change in Western Europe', *West European Politics*, 12, 4.

Malmström, C. (1995) *Stor i Orden men Liten på Jorden?: Regionala Partier i Västeuropa*. Göteborg: Statsvetenskapliga Institutionen.

Marer, P., Arvay, J., O'Connor, J., Schrenk, M. and Swanson, D. (1992) *Historically Planned Economies: A Guide to the Data*. Washington, DC: The World Bank.

Marer, P., Arvay, J., O'Connor, J., Schrenk, M. and Swanson, D. (1993) *Historically Planned Economies: A Guide to the Data*. Washington, DC: The World Bank.

Marsh, M. (1993) 'Ireland', in R. Koole and P. Mair (eds), *Political Data Yearbook, 1993. European Journal of Political Research*, 24, 455–66.

Mavrogordatos, G.T. (1994) 'Greece', in R. Koole and P. Mair (eds), *Political Data Yearbook, 1994. European Journal of Political Research*, 26, 313–18.

Mény, Y. (1993) *Government and Politics in Western Europe: Britain, France, Italy, Germany*. Oxford: Oxford University Press.

Mény, Y. (1994) 'L'évolution des fonctions des parlements', *Cahiers Français*, 268, 44–52.

Mezey, M.L. (1995) 'Parliament in the new Europe', in J. Hayward and E.C. Page (eds), *Governing the New Europe*. Cambridge: Polity Press. pp. 196–223.

Mink, G. (1993) 'Les partis politiques de l'Europe central postcommuniste: état des lieux et essai de typologie', in E. Lhomel and T. Schreiber (eds), *L'Europe centrale et orientale*. Paris: La Documentation Française. pp. 13–23.

Minority Rights Group (1993) *Minorites in Central and Eastern Europe*. Report 1993: 1.

Moe, T.M. and Caldwell, M. (1994) 'The institutional foundations of democratic government: A comparison of presidential and parliamentary systems', *Journal of Institutional and Theoretical Economics*, 150, 171–95.

Morgan, R. and Silvestri, S. (eds) (1982) *Moderates and Conservatives in Western Europe*. London: Heinemann.

Moore, W.E. (1945) *Economic Demography of Eastern and Southern Europe*. Geneva: League of Nations.

Müller-Rommel, F. (ed.) (1991) *New Politics in Western Europe: The Rise and Success of Green Parties*. Boulder, CO: Westview Press.

Myant, M. (1981) *Socialism and Democracy in Czechoslovakia 1945–1948*. Cambridge: Cambridge University Press.

Neven, D. and Gouyette, C. (1994) 'Regional convergence in the European Community', *Journal of Common Market Studies*, 33, 47–65.

Niedermayer, O. and Sinnott, R. (eds) (1995) *Public Opinion and International Governance*. Oxford: Oxford University Press.

Nohlen, D. (1978) *Wahlsysteme der Welt: Daten und Analysen: ein Handbuch*. Munich: Piper.

Norton, A. (1994) *International Handbook of Local and Regional Government: A Comparative Analysis of Advanced Democracies*. Aldershot: Edward Elgar.

Norton, P. (ed.) (1990) 'Parliaments in Western Europe', *West European Politics*, 13, 3.

Nugent, N. (1994) *Government and Politics of the European Community*. 3rd edn. Basingstoke: Macmillan.

O'Brien, J. and Palmer, M. (1993) *The State of Religion Atlas*. New York: Simon and Schuster.

O'Connor, J.S. (1988) 'Convergence or divergence?: Change in welfare effort in OECD countries 1960–1980', *European Journal of Political Research*, 16, 277–99.

O'Neil, P. (1993) 'Presidential power in post-communist Europe: The Hungarian case in comparative perspective', *The Journal of Communist Studies*, 9, 3, 177–201.

OECD (1983) *Historical Statistics 1960–1981*. Paris: OECD.

OECD (1992) *Labour Force Statistics 1970–1990*. Paris: OECD.

OECD (1994a) *Employment Outlook: July 1994*. Paris: OECD.

OECD (1994b) *Labour Force Statistics 1972–1992*. Paris: OECD.

OECD (1994c) *National Accounts: Main Aggregates. Volume I 1960–1992*. Paris: OECD.

OECD (1994d) *National Accounts: Detailed Tables. Volume II 1980–1992*. Paris: OECD.

OECD (1994e) *OECD Economic Outlook 55: June 1994*. Paris: OECD.

OECD (1995a) *Historical Statistics 1960–1993*. Paris: OECD.

OECD (1995b) *Main Economic Indicators*. Paris: OECD.

OECD (1995c) *OECD Economic Outlook 57: June 1995*. Paris: OECD.

OECD (1995d) *OECD Economic Outlook 58: December 1995*. Paris: OECD.

Olson, D.M. (1994) *Democratic Legislative Institutions: A Comparative View*. Armonk, NY: M.E. Sharpe.

Ost, D. (1993) 'The politics of interest in post-communist East Europe', *Theory and Society*, 22, 453–86.

Ostrom, V. (1991) *The Meaning of American Federalism: Constituting a Self-governing Society*. San Francisco: ICS Press.

Overbye, E. (1994) 'Convergence in policy outcomes: Social security systems in perspective', *Journal of Public Policy*, 14, 147–74.

Page, E.C. and Goldsmith, M.J. (eds) (1987) *Central and Local Government Relations: A Comparative Analysis of West European Unitary States*. London: Sage.

Pappi, F.U., König, T. and Knohe, D. (1995) *Entscheidungsprozesse in der Arbeits- und Sozialpolitik*. Frankfurt: Campus.

Peters, B.G. (1991) *European Politics Reconsidered*. New York: Holmes and Meier.

Pelassy, D. (1992) *Qui gouverne en Europe?* Paris: Fayard.

Philips, A.L. (1995) 'An island of stability?: The German political party system and the elections of 1994', *West European Politics*, 18, 3, 219–29.

Pierre, J. and Widfeldt, A. (1992) 'Sweden', in R. Koole and P. Mair (eds), *Political Data Yearbook, 1992. European Journal of Political Research*, 22, 519–26.

Poulton, H. (1991) *The Balkans: Minorities and States in Conflict*. London: Minority Rights Publications.

Powell, G.B. (1986) 'American voter turnout in comparative perspective', *American Political Science Review*, 80, 17–43.

Przeworski, A. (1991) *Democracy and the Market*. Cambridge: Cambridge University Press.

Przeworski, A. and Teune, H. (1970) *The Logic of Comparative Social Inquiry*. New York: Wiley.

Pridham, G. (ed.) (1986) *Coalitional Behaviour in Theory and Practice*. Cambridge: Cambridge University Press.

Pridham, G. (1995) 'Party systems, factionalism and patterns of democratization: Cross-national comparisons in Southern Europe', *Democratization*, 2, 8–30.

Pridham, G. and Vanhanen, T. (eds) (1994) *Democratization in Eastern Europe*. London: Routledge.

Pridham, G., Sanford, G. and Herring, E. (eds) (1994) *Building Democracy?: The International Dimension of Democratisation in Eastern Europe*. London: Leicester University Press.

Pulzer, P. (1995) 'The Austrian 1994 national election', *West European Politics*, 18, 2, 429–37.

Putnam, R. (1993) *Making Democracy Work: Civic Traditions in Modern Italy*. Princeton: Princeton University Press.

Quah, D. (1993) 'Galton's fallacy and tests of the convergence hypothesis', *Scandinavian Journal of Economics*, 95, 427–43.

Rae, D.W. (1971) *The Political Consequences of Electoral Laws*. 2nd edn. New Haven, CT: Yale University Press.

Rae, D.W. and Taylor, M. (1970) *The Analysis of Political Cleavages*. New Haven, CT: Yale University Press.

Rageau, J-.P. (1981) *Prague 48: le rideau de fer s'est abattu*. Brussels: Editions Complexe.

Ramet, S.P. (1993) 'Slovenia's road to democracy', *Europe–Asia Studies*, 45, 869–86.

Reif, K. and Cunningham, G. (1992) *Central and Eastern Euro-Barometer 2*. Autumn 1991 [Computer File]. Cologne. Zentralarchiv für empirische Sozialforschung [producer].

Reif, K. and Cunningham, G. (1993) *Central and Eastern Euro-Barometer 3*. Autumn 1992 [Computer File]. Cologne. Zentralarchiv für empirische Sozialforschung [producer].

Reif, K. and Cunningham, G. (1994) *Central and Eastern Euro-Barometer 4*. Autumn 1993 [Computer File]. Cologne. Zentralarchiv für empirische Sozialforschung [producer].

Reif, K. and Cunningham, G. (1995) *Central and Eastern Euro-Barometer 5*. Autumn 1994 [Computer File]. Cologne. Zentralarchiv für empirische Sozialforschung [producer].

Reiter, H. (1989) 'Party decline in the West: A skeptic's view', *Journal of Theoretical Politics*, 1, 325–48.

Remington, T.F. (ed.) (1994) *Parliaments in Transition: The New Legislative Politics in the Former USSR and Eastern Europe*. Boulder, CO: Westview Press.

Reutter, W. (1994) 'Tripartism without corporatism: Trade unions in East Central Europe', *Budapest Papers on Democratic Transition*, no. 104.

Rhodes, R.A.W. (1992) *Beyond Westminster and Whitehall: The Sub-central Governments of Britain*. London: Routledge.

Riker, W.H. (1962) *A Theory of Political Coalitions*. New Haven, CT: Yale University Press.

Rivera, S.W. (1996) 'Historical cleavages or transition mode?: Influences on the emerging party systems in Poland, Hungary and Czechoslovakia', *Party Politics*, 2, 177–208.

Rohrschneider, R. (1993) 'Impact of social movements on European party systems', *Annals of the American Academy of Political and Social Science*, 528, July, 157–70.

Roper, S.D. (1995) 'The Romanian party system and the catch-all party phenomenon', *East European Quarterly*, 28, 519–32.

Rose, R. (1984) *Understanding Big Government: The Programme Approach*. London: Sage.

Rose, R. and Harpfer, C. (1994) 'Mass response to transformation in post-communist societies', *Europe–Asia Studies*, 46, 3–28.

Rose, R. and Mishler, W.T.E. (1994) 'Mass reaction to regime change in Eastern Europe: Polarization or leaders and laggards?', *British Journal of Political Science*, 24, 159–82.

Roskin, M.G. (1993) 'The emerging party systems of Central and Eastern Europe', *East European Quarterly*, 27, 47–63.

Roskin, M.G. (1994) *The Rebirth of East Europe*. Englewood Cliffs, NJ: Prentice Hall.

Rostow, W.W. (1960) *The Stages of Economic Growth: A Non-Communist Manifesto*. Cambridge: Cambridge University Press.

Rothschild, J. (1974) *East Central Europe between the Two World Wars*. Seattle: University of Washington Press.

Rothschild, J. (1993) *Return to Diversity: A Political History of East Central Europe since World War II*. New York: Oxford University Press.

Roussellier, N. (1991) *L'Europe des liberaux*. Brussels: Editions Complexe.

Rüdig, W. (1988) 'Peace and ecology movements in Western Europe', *West European Politics*, 11, 1, 26–39.

Rupnik, J. (1993) *L'autre Europe: crise et fin du communisme*. Paris: Editions Odile Jacob.

Russett, B., Singer, J.D. and Small, M. (1968) 'National political units in the twentieth century', *American Political Science Review*, 62, 930–51.

Rys, V. (1993) 'Social security reform in Central Europe: Issues and strategies', *Journal of European Social Policy*, 3, 163–75.

Sachs, J. (1990) 'What is to be done?', *The Economist*, 13 January, 19–24.

Sachs, J. (1993) *Poland's Jump to the Market Economy*. Cambridge, MA: MIT Press.

Salt, J., Singleton, A. and Hogarth, J. (1994) *Europe's International Migrants: Data Sources, Patterns and Trends*. London: HMSO.

Sanford, G. (1993) 'Delay and disappointment: The fully free Polish election of 27 October 1991', *The Journal of Communist Studies*, 9, 2, 107–18.

Sartori, G. (1976) *Parties and Party Systems: A Framework for Analysis*. Cambridge: Cambridge University Press.

Sartori, G. (1991) 'Comparing and miscomparing', *Journal of Theoretical Politics*, 3, 243–57.

Scharpf, F.W., Reissert, B. and Schnabel, F. (1976) *Politikverflechtung: Theorie und Empirie des koperativen Föderalismus in der Bundesrepublik*. Kronberg: Hain.

Schmidt, M.G. (1995) *Demokratietheorien: eine Einführung*. Opladen: Leske and Budrich.

Schmidt, S. (1989) 'Convergence theory, labour movements, and corporatism: The case of housing', *Scandinavian Housing and Planning Research*, 6, 83–101.

Schmiedling, H. (1993) 'From plan to market: On the nature of the transformation crisis', *Weltwirtschaftliches Archiv*, 129, 216–53.

Schmitt, H. and Holmberg, S. (1995) 'Political parties in decline?', in H.-D. Klingemann and D. Fuchs (eds), *Citizens and the State*. Oxford: Oxford University Press. pp. 95–133.

Schmitter, P.C. (1981) 'Interest intermediation and regime governability in contemporary Western Europe and North America', in S. Berger (ed.), *Organizing Interests in Western Europe*. Cambridge: Cambridge University Press. pp. 285–327.

Schumpeter, J.A. ([1918] 1954) 'The crisis of the tax state', *International Economic Papers*, 4, 5–38.

Schwartz, H. (1993) 'The new East European constitutional courts', in A.E.D. Howard (ed.), *Constitution Making in Eastern Europe*. Baltimore: Johns Hopkins University Press. pp. 163–207.

Seiler, D.L. (1992) *Les partis politiques en Europe*. Paris: PUF.

Seiler, D.L. (1994) *Les partis autonomistes*. Paris: PUF.

Sellier, A. and Sellier, J. (1991) *Atlas des peuples d'Europe Centrale*. Paris: Découverte.

Seton Watson, H. (1950) *The East European Revolution*. London: Methuen.

Shafir, M. (1992a) 'Romania's elections: Why the Democratic Convention lost', *RFE/RL Research Report*, 1, 43, 1–7.

Shafir, M. (1992b) 'Romania's elections: More change than meets the eye', *RFE/RL Research Report*, 1, 44, 1–8.

Shoup, P.S. (1981) *The East European and Soviet Data Handbook: Political, Social, and Developmental Indicators, 1945–1975*. New York: Columbia University Press.

Shugart, M.S. and Carey, J.M. (1992) *Presidents and Assemblies: Constitutional Design and Electoral Dynamics*. Cambridge: Cambridge University Press.

Sigelman, L. and Yough, S.N. (1978) 'Left–right polarization in national party systems: A cross-national analysis', *Comparative Political Studies*, 11, 355–79.

Smart, M. (1995) 'Luxembourg: European Parliament and national elections of 1994', *West European Politics*, 18, 1, 194–6.

Smith, G. (1979) 'Western European party systems: On the trail of a typology', *West European Politics*, 2, 128–43.

Smith, G. (1989a) 'A system perspective on party system change', *Journal of Theoretical Politics*, 1, 349–63.

Smith, G. (1989b) *Politics in Western Europe: A Comparative Analysis*. Aldershot: Gower.

Smith, Gr. (ed.) (1994) *The Baltic States: The National Self-Determination of Estonia, Latvia and Lithuania*. Basingstoke: Macmillan.

Statesman's Yearbook 1995. Basingstoke: Macmillan.

Steiner, J. (1994) *European Democracies*. New York: Longman.

Stephens, M. (1976) *Linguistic Minorities in Western Europe*. Llandysul: Gomer Press.

Sternberger, D. and Vogel, B. (eds) (1969) *Die Wahl der Parlamente und andere Staatsorgane: ein Handbuch*. Berlin: Walter de Gruyter.

Stevens, A. (1992) *The Government and Politics of France*. Basingstoke: Macmillan.

Stoetzel, J. (1983) *Les valeurs du temps présent: une enquête européenne*. Paris: Presses Universitaires de France.

Stock, M. (1992) 'Portugal', in R. Koole and P. Mair (eds), *Political Data Yearbook, 1992*. *European Journal of Political Research*, 22, 505–11.

Stone, A. (1995) 'Governing with judges: The new constitutionalism', in J. Hayward and E.C. Page (eds), *Governing the New Europe*. Cambridge: Polity Press. pp. 286–314.

Streeck, W. (1992) *Social Institutions and Economic Performance*. London: Sage.

Strom, K. (1990) *Minority Government and Majority Rule*. Cambridge: Cambridge University Press.

Summers, L., Gruber, J. and Vergara, R. (1993) 'Taxation and the structure of labor markets: The case of corporatism', *Quarterly Journal of Economics*, 108, 385–411.

Summers, R. and Heston, A. (1988) 'A new set of international comparisons of real product and price level estimates for 130 countries, 1950–1985', *Review of Income and Wealth*, 34, 1–25.

Sundberg, J. (1992) 'Finland', in R. Koole and P. Mair (eds), *Political Data Yearbook, 1992*. *European Journal of Political Research*, 22, 391–9.

Sutton, F.X. (1963) 'Social theory and comparative politics', in H. Eckstein and D.A. Apter (eds), *Comparative Politics: A Reader*. New York: Free Press. pp. 67–81.

Szajkowski, B. (1992a) 'The Albanian election of 1991', *Electoral Studies*, 11, 157–61.
Szajkowski, B. (1992b) 'The 1992 Albanian election', *The Journal of Communist Studies*, 8, 3, 119–28.
Szajkowski, B. (ed.) (1994) *Political Parties of Eastern Europe, Russia and the Successor States*. Harlow: Longman.
Sztompka, P. (1993) *The Sociology of Social Change*. Oxford: Blackwell.
Taagepera, R. (1993) *Estonia: Return to Independence*. Boulder, CO: Westview Press.
Taggart, P. (1995) 'New populist parties in Western Europe', *West European Politics*, 18, 1, 34–51.
Taras, R. (1995) *Consolidating Democracy in Poland*. Boulder, CO: Westview Press.
Tesnière, L. (1928) 'Statistiques des langues de l'Europe', in A. Meillet (ed.), *Les Langues dans l'Europe Nouvelle*. Paris: Payot. pp. 291–484.
Therborn, G. (1977) 'The rule of capital and the rise of democracy', *New Left Review*, 103, 3–41.
Therborn, G. (1995) *European Modernity and Beyond: The Trajectory of European Societies 1945–2000*. London: Sage.
Thompson, M., Ellis, R.J. and Wildavsky, A. (1990) *Cultural Theory*. Boulder, CO: Westview Press.
Tinbergen, J. (1961) 'Do communist and free economies show a convergent pattern?', *Soviet Studies*, 12, 333–41.
Tingsten, H. (1965) *The Problems of Democracy*. Totowa, NJ: Bedminster Press.
Todd, E. (1983) *La troisième planète: structures familiales et systèmes idéologiques*. Paris: Seuil.
Todd, E. (1990) *L'Invention de L'Europe*. Paris: Seuil.
Toth, A.G. (ed.) (1991) *The Oxford Encyclopedia of European Community Law*. Vol. 1. Oxford: Clarendon Press.
Topf, R. (1995) 'Electoral participation', in H.-D. Klingemann and D. Fuchs (eds), *Citizens and the State*. Oxford: Oxford University Press. pp. 27–51.
Towers, B. (1992) 'From AIDS to Altzheimer's: Policy and politics in setting new health agendas', in J. Bailey (ed.), *Social Europe*. London: Longman. pp. 190–215.
Trausch, G. (1992) *Historie du Luxembourg*. Paris: Hatier.
UN (United Nations) (1991) *The World's Women 1970–1990: Trends and Statistics*. New York: United Nations.
UN (United Nations) (1993a) *International Trade Statistics Yearbook: 1992*. New York: United Nations.
UN (United Nations) (1993b) *Statistical Yearbook 1990/91*. New York: United Nations.
UN (United Nations) (1994) *Demographic Yearbook 1992*. New York: United Nations.
UNDP (United Nations Development Programme) (1990) *Human Development Report 1990*. New York: Oxford University Press.
UNDP (United Nations Development Programme) (1991) *Human Development Report 1991*. New York: Oxford University Press.
UNDP (United Nations Development Programme) (1992) *Human Development Report 1992*. New York: Oxford University Press.
UNDP (United Nations Development Programme) (1994) *Human Development Report 1994*. New York: Oxford University Press.
UNDP (United Nations Development Programme) (1995) *Human Development Report 1995*. New York: Oxford University Press.
USCR (US Committee for Refugees) (1994) *World Refugee Survey: 1994*. Washington, DC: USCR.
Van Deth, J.W. (1995) 'A macro setting for micro politics', in J.W. Van Deth and E. Scarbrough (eds), *The Impact of Values*. Oxford: Oxford University Press. pp. 48–75.
Van Deth, J.W. and Scarbrough, E. (eds) (1995) *The Impact of Values*. Oxford: Oxford University Press.
Vienna (The Vienna Institute for Comparative Economic Studies) (1991) *COMECON Data 1990*. Basingstoke: Macmillan.

Vienna (The Vienna Institute for Comparative Economic Studies) (1995) *Countries in Transition 1995*. Vienna: WIIW.

Villiers, de B. (ed.) (1994) *Evaluating Federal Systems*. Dordrecht: Martinus Nijhoff.

Vincent, A. (1987) *Theories of the State*. Oxford: Blackwell.

Vinton, L. (1993) 'Poland goes left', *RFE/RL Research Report*, 2, 40, 21–3.

Visser, J. (1991) 'Trends in trade union membership', *OECD Employment Outlook*, 97–134.

Visser, J. (1993) 'Syndicalisme et désyndicalisation', *Le Mouvement Social*, 162, 17–39.

Waller, M. and Myant, M. (eds) (1993) 'Parties, trade unions and society in East-Central Europe', *Journal of Communist Studies*, 9, 4.

Waller, M., Coppieters, B. and Deschouwer, K. (eds) (1994) *Social Democracy in a Post-Communist Europe*. London: Frank Cass.

Waters, S. (1994) ' "Tangentopoli" and the emergence of a new political order in Italy', *West European Politics*, 17, 1, 169–82.

Weber, M. ([1922] 1978) *Economy and Society: An Outline of Interpretative Sociology*. 2 vols. Berkeley: University of California Press.

Wehrle, F. (1994) *Le Divorce Tchéco-Slovaque: Vie et mort de la Tchéchoslovaquie 1918–1992*. Paris: L'Harmattan.

Western, B. (1993) 'Postwar unionization in eighteen advanced capitalist countries', *American Sociological Review*, 58, 266–82.

Western, B. (1995) 'A comparative study of working-class disorganization: Union decline in eighteen advanced capitalist countries', *American Sociological Review*, 60, 179–201.

Wheaton, B. and Kavan, Z. (1992) *The Velvet Revolution: Czechoslovakia, 1988–1991*. Boulder, CO: Westview Press.

Whightman, G. (1995) (ed.) *Party Formation in East-Central Europe*. Aldershot: Edward Elgar.

White, S., Batt, J. and Lewis, P.G. (eds) (1993) *Developments in East European Politics*. Basingstoke: Macmillan.

Whitefeld, S. (ed.) (1993) *The New Institutional Architecture of Eastern Europe*. Basingstoke: Macmillan.

Widfeldt, A. (1995) 'Party membership and party representatives', in H.-D. Klingemann and D. Fuchs (eds), *Citizens and the State*. Oxford: Oxford University Press. pp. 134–82.

Wiesenthal, H. (1995) 'Organized interests and public policy: West European experience with joint decision-making and East-Central European perspectives', *Budapest Papers on Democratic Transition*, 135.

Wilensky, H. (1975) *The Welfare State and Equality*. Berkeley: University of California Press.

Winiecki, J. (1994) 'East-central Europe: A regional survey – The Czech republic, Hungary, Poland and Slovakia in 1993', *Europe–Asia Studies*, 46, 709–34.

Witte, E. (1992) 'Belgian federalism: Towards complexity and asymmetry', *West European Politics*, 15, 4, 95–117.

Wolchik, S.L. (1991) *Czechoslovakia in Transition: Politics, Economics and Society*. London: Pinter.

Wolchik, S.L. (1993) 'The repluralization of politics in Czechoslovakia', *Communist and Post-Communist Studies*, 26, 412–31.

Woldentorp, J., Keman, H. and Budge, I. (eds) (1993) 'Poltical data 1945–1990: Party governments in 20 democracies', *European Journal of Political Research*, 24, 1.

Wolinetz, S.B. (1995) 'The Dutch parliamentary elections of 1994', *West European Politics*, 18, 188–92.

World Bank (1980) *World Tables: The Second Edition*. Baltimore: Johns Hopkins University Press.

World Bank (1984) *World Tables: The Third Edition: Volume II: Social Data*. Baltimore: Johns Hopkins University Press.

World Bank (1987) *The World Bank Atlas 1987*. Washington, DC: The World Bank.

World Bank (1993) *World Development Report 1993*. New York: Oxford University Press.

World Bank (1994) *World Development Report 1994*. New York: Oxford University Press.

World Bank (1995a) *The World Bank Atlas 1995*. Washington, DC: The World Bank.

World Bank (1995b) *World Development Report 1995*. New York: Oxford University Press.

World Bank (1996) *The World Bank Atlas 1996*. Washington, DC: The World Bank.

Wright, L.M. (1982) 'A comparative survey of economic freedoms', in R.D. Gastil (ed.), *Freedom in the World: Political Rights and Civil Liberties, 1982*. Westport, CT: Greenwood Press. pp. 51–90.

Ysmal, C. (1994) 'France', in R. Koole and P. Mair (eds), *Political Data Yearbook, 1994. European Journal of Political Research*, 26, 293–304.

Zinner, P.E. (1963) *Communist Strategy and Tactics in Czechoslovakia, 1918–48*. London: Pall Mall Press.

Index

Groupings of countries have been indexed both under geographical terms (eg Eastern Europe, Northern Europe etc), and under the terms used in the text (Core East, Core EC, East Periphery, Other EC and Outside EC). Countries have also been indexed individually. The abbreviation EU has been used for European Union.